An Ethical Approach to Leading Change

An Ethical Approach to Leading Change

An Alternative and Sustainable Application

Mervyn Conroy
Senior Fellow, University of Birmingham

First published 2010 by
PALGRAVE MACMILLAN

Palgrave Macmillan in the UK is an imprint of Macmillan Publishers Limited, registered in England, company number 785998, of Houndmills, Basingstoke, Hampshire RG21 6XS.

Palgrave Macmillan in the US is a division of St Martin's Press LLC, 175 Fifth Avenue, New York, NY 10010.

Palgrave Macmillan is the global academic imprint of the above companies and has companies and representatives throughout the world.

Palgrave® and Macmillan® are registered trademarks in the United States, the United Kingdom, Europe and other countries.

ISBN: 978–0–230–23847–3 hardback

This book is printed on paper suitable for recycling and made from fully managed and sustained forest sources. Logging, pulping and manufacturing processes are expected to conform to the environmental regulations of the country of origin.

A catalogue record for this book is available from the British Library.

A catalog record for this book is available from the Library of Congress.

10 9 8 7 6 5 4 3 2 1
19 18 17 16 15 14 13 12 11 10

Printed and bound in Great Britain by
CPI Antony Rowe, Chippenham and Eastbourne

To my Family: Beth, Ben and Kiya

Contents

Acknowledgements

The writing of this book would not have been possible without the support and motivation provided by my family. I am most grateful to Professor Steve Fox, who saw this book in me and who also gave me inspiration to dig deeper. Professor Frank Blackler gave moral support and shared his knowledge of the NHS and organisational change, both of which were invaluable. My close friend and walking companion, Dr Tony Morton-Jones, gave personal support and extended philosophical debating time on the fells and in tea shops around the Lake District. Notable comments and contributions on draft versions were gratefully accepted from Dr Gill Helsby, Dr Steve Kempster, Dr Sheila Marsh and Nigel Saxton. Finally to the participants in my research and the senior managers from Omega I pass on a heartfelt thank you.

Foreword

All too often organisational change or improvement projects do not achieve their desired impact. Staff become more and more distanced and alienated from what managers and the board are trying to achieve. For instance, in the UK NHS, the second largest organisation in the world with one million employees, managers and staff are subject to the same pressure to deliver cost effective care. Management tend to get pulled towards goals, measures and targets and clinical staff are pulled towards the immediate care of patients and the vulnerable in our society. What often happens is a major gap in understanding develops and can widen as more external pressure and targets are applied to do more with less to a higher standard. Any medium and large and some small organisations can experience this phenomenon.

The CE and the Board often feel they are missing something in their understanding of the culture of the organisation as they steer a path through a political minefield with a crew who claim low morale but work until they drop. That goodwill can sometimes run out. Ironically people at all levels usually want to meet the principles of improvement projects and develop service and product excellence that will benefit others in an ethical and equitable way.

This book aims to offer an understanding of why the failing change programme phenomenon is so prevalent by looking at change from the perspective of the ethics involved. It meets the needs of leaders and others who want to understand what they are missing in their efforts to improve economic, social or environmental outcomes. Increased funding, new resources and changes in structure have often been seen as the solution. Massive resources are often spent on public sector IT projects without taking this ethical dimension into consideration. When the ethical dimension is considered then an alternative approach presents itself which does not involve funding, resources and structural change. In this respect it meets the needs of policy makers, the board and senior and middle managers who are invariably trying to find ways of saving money whilst improving the quality of their services and products.

What makes this book distinctive?

Ethics is back in literary studies, philosophy, politics and organisation theory. This book breaks new ground as part of an emerging 'ethical turn' in organisational studies (Moore and Beadle 2006). It is the first study to apply the virtue ethics of MacIntyre to the subject of leading organisational change and probably the first to apply an ethical analysis to in an in depth case study to the politically charged sector of healthcare provision. The complexity of factors involved in the health sector means it provides a case study that has within it most of the issues experienced by any medium or large organisation in the world, public or private.

In his seminal thesis on virtue ethics MacIntyre (1981) provided us with a diagnosis on the modern condition and made us aware of what we have lost as a society. That loss is our connection to our social and historical roots and along with that a vital binding of what we want from work lives (the goods of our labour), the practices that we engage in and the virtues that enable us to achieve the goods we desire. For MacIntyre that loss means that modern working practices are highly susceptible to being corrupted especially when an institution places money, status or power above the goods of excellence. This book includes empirical material that supports what he and now others are saying in theory and as such has the potential to catch a very powerful wave of questioning not just the changes to the public sector but the lifestyle and financial crisis that we have all brought into being. The radical cultural metaphor of 'Reality TV' captures, with wider social resonance, what we as a society have unwittingly sanctioned and socially constructed under the guise of effectiveness, efficiency and unbridled innovation. The credit crunch and crisis in the financial markets in 2009 is arguably one of the symptoms of this way of working and living.

MacIntyre's narrative based virtue ethics have for the first time in this book been applied to an organisation undergoing change driven by market forces and a society that wants more for less with scant regard for the means by which that is achieved. The considerable practical potential of these insights is explored in the case study that runs through the book. The final chapter contains a detailed application of the findings to a leadership education programme along with a very positive evaluation. People who have read the book say it is refreshing because of the new take on the leadership of organisational change. They also find the synthesised narrative methodology very exciting because it breaks new ground in the domain of management and organisational enquiry. Academics, practitioners and policy makers will find the book of interest because it meets their needs for rigour, practical usefulness and policy guidance respectively. The book will be particularly relevant to people with responsibility for researching into or leading change in their organisation.

The names of all organisations and individuals have been changed to preserve confidentiality.

1
Introduction

It feels like I am on the edge of a vortex, and that if I step forward
I will be sucked into a downward spiralling confusion.

Senior manager after four weeks in a post and
in the midst of a major change programme

Significant investments in time, resources and energy (both physical and
emotional) are being made in organisational change programmes across
the world. However, little is known about what implementing change
means to people responsible for leading the translation of change policies
into practice. The purpose of this book is threefold: first, to understand
better, through their narratives, what it means to a group of managers to lead and implement change; second, to appreciate what they say
they need to support them in that process; and third, to demonstrate
an approach to meeting those needs by viewing them in the context
of a moral philosophical framework. The health sector is the primary
case study for the study. The 'modernising' narrative introduced into the
sector involved economic notions of efficiency and effectiveness, social
elements in the transfer of care in hospital wards to care in the community, organisational factors in the increased level of multi-agency working and performance aspects with an emphasis on targets, ratings and
standards. The narratives that run this book convey a sample of managers' social reality over a period of 12 months. Raw accounts of how they
handle situations where personal integrity, patient needs, government
policy and public interests are at odds with each other form the core
of the book. The finding that many of their narratives convey an ethical conflict or dilemma led to MacIntyre's narrative-based virtue ethics
(1985) and concepts that proved to be a powerful way of conversing
with the data. By viewing the virtue conflicts[1] in the managers' storied

scenes as reflections of wider ideological battles further understanding of the difficulties and complexities are exposed. In opening an ethical dimension to the cynicism, resistance and low morale that has been found to pervade change management in the health sector (Greener & Powell 2003), new understandings of what change means to managers are revealed. Existing conceptualisations of resistance to change within organisational change management theory are extended to include a form of 'ethical resistance'. Rather than viewing resistance as something to be weakened, managed or resolved this study understands resistance to be narrative constructed and a healthy response to reform virtues which threaten the virtues that, for them, enable excellence in health-care practice, equity of care and improved access for all. In developing this dimension this book adds to the voices that challenge the under-lying assumption of a 'ubiquitous' (Sturdy & Grey 2003) mechanical model of organisational change framed within an 'epochal' discourse of change being inevitable, desirable and something that can be managed (du Gay 2003). The study reported in this book then takes this further by applying the findings to a leading change programme for manag-ers and includes an evaluation of the programme. The book in essence offers an alternative ethical approach to the leadership of change in any organisation underpinned with a synopsis of the research that led to the approach.

Governments have, over the last two decades, experimented with var-ious management fads and fashions. This is true of the UK government according to Hunter (2000: 69) and is an attempt to achieve what they has been rhetorically depicted as 'a movement from a "failed" bureau-cratic model to a system of entrepreneurial governance that would help it survive' (Currie & Brown 2003: 568). In the case of the UK healthcare sector, since 1999 the pace of change has been driven by the govern-ment's NHS *Plan* (2000a), that in turn is part of a larger project of 'mod-ernisation' across all public sector service provision. The healthcare context, therefore, has the capacity to expand our understanding of the dynamics of public-sector organisational change. Particular emphasis has been given to the notion that 'key people' such as managers are pivotal to the success or otherwise of change (Hunter 1996: 799). This study contributes by drawing on narrative and on moral philosophy to increase understanding both of the complexity and challenge faced by healthcare managers in translating policy into service changes 'on the ground' and also of the needs they express in the midst of change. Hunter (2000) argued that reform of healthcare based on a welter of centrally imposed targets and performance measures is unlikely to succeed. Hunter's view is that they will be resisted by staff if they run counter to professional values. Lasting reform may be better achieved if local initiatives are allowed to develop that respect the culture of professional groups such as doctors, nurses and managers. This study finds a very strong construction of resistance in the narrative enactments of reform implementation and a call for respect of people and their cultures. It also backs up Hunter's conclusion with empirical data and an analysis that specifically focuses on the virtue ethics of practice-based health service communities.

The focus of the study is a group of managers from Omega Healthcare Trust who were in the process of radically overhauling mental health services for a population of approximately 330,000 in one region of the UK. It seeks to understand their social reality through their narratives over a period of 12 months. It offers methodological, empirical and theoretical contributions to enrich public-sector change theory from a localised study of reform. In particular, it aims to offer a better understanding of what is behind the increasing levels of staff cynicism that seem to accompany recent government led change initiatives (Greener & Powell 2003). Findings from my study, which convey the often tumultuous lived reality of managers, have resonated strongly with managers from public sector organisations across the UK.

This research also aims to demonstrate the usefulness of narrative in organisational change research. Czarniawska's advocacy of narrative as a useful 'device' to study organisational change (1997) builds on, amongst others, Ricoeur (1991) and MacIntyre (1985). She summarises her viewpoint as follows.

> Narrative can provide a different and valuable form of knowledge that enables researchers to engage with the lived realities of organisational life – the 'truth' that people at work live through every day. This is not a knowledge that aspires to certainty and control but rather emerges from a reflection on the messy realities of organisational practice It is this embodied and lived knowledge that narrative methods enable researchers to access and engage with while embracing scholarly values. (Czarniawska 2004: 16)

This study therefore explores the nature of organisational change through narratives elicited from a group of 37 managers working in the healthcare sector. A better understanding of their narratives and the social reality they construct in relation to the implementation of change has been largely ignored until now. The research builds on other public-sector reform studies to offer further understanding of what leading the implementation of change means to managers. It also explores the phenomenon of public-sector change initiatives that rarely meet their objectives, are often abandoned and then replaced with another initiative (Jessop 2000). Chapman's (2000) notion that top down reform approaches actually work against achieving aims is also examined through managers' narratives. Further, the study offers a better understanding of the nature of support that managers are calling for in order to help them cope with challenges they experience in the midst of reform. This has the potential to contribute to the enhancement of current approaches to public-sector management education[2]. More broadly, this study could contribute to understandings of how organisational change in public and private sector contexts can be better conceived and designed by policymakers.

In seeking to understand the nature of organisational change, stories and narratives from the participants are explored in terms of the morality they unfold into the organisation. By drawing on MacIntyre's *After Virtue* (1985) and recent interpretations of his work (Moore & Beadle 2006) a multitude of ethical clashes derived from opposing social and moral traditions and standpoints are revealed, most notably public service versus market ethos (Dyck & Weber 2006). Feeling under extreme pressure to meet government targets, managers enact a variety of options in their narratives in response to their ethical conundrums. Their narratives offer a window into their social reality in situations where there is apparently no solution and where their personal values, patient needs, government policy and public interests are at odds with each other.

This book offers an insight into what organisational change, driven in the main by government reform policy, means to healthcare managers. In summary, what the accounts convey is their feeling of being under siege from a barrage of 'must dos', which require them to do more despite having fewer resources. These requirements can appear contradictory, impossible to meet and even detrimental to patient welfare. Through many of the narratives runs the theme of chaos, stress and inner turmoil as they attempt to implement the new directives whilst maintaining the public service ethos which brought them into the job. Accounts of the way they handle the challenge vary. There are epic and heroic stories of leaders facilitating the change process, enabled in some cases by leadership and management training. But running against the success stories are tragic ones of people suffering loss and feeling overwhelmed. There are also many accounts of how managers cope with the saga of change and what meaning they make out of it.

To broaden the analysis, narratives of change are conceptualised as reflections of different ideological horizons in conflict and the drama as hotspots in movements of history (MacIntyre 1985). Various poetic modes are employed by the managers to enact the 'battle' scenes of change. This latter phenomenon has been previously observed by Downing (1997: 27) who argues that the enactments develop 'emotional momentum'. In my study managers' narratives have been analysed in three different ways: first as stories, second as a serial of episodes and third as a set of themes. Together they reflect the level of wellbeing of the organisation (and of the individuals) in the midst of change.

By drawing on MacIntyre's *After Virtue* (1985) and the notion of organisational change as a set of evolving narratives (Ford 1999) this book contributes to the organisational change literature. It does so by adding to the understanding of what it means to managers to be leading the implementation of government-driven reform and what needs they construct for support in that role. This book also contributes to the generic organisational change literature by viewing the implementation of change through narratives. Stories, serials and themes offer insight into the complexity and nature of the challenge associated with changes. The approach also reveals accounts of the suffering of people in organisations where the virtues of the change processes are socially constructed as disputed, confused or absent. This finding puts into question the morality of the change approaches currently being employed at all levels from government downwards. One example given is the serial of restructuring associated with the implementation of community mental health teams that managers claim have left staff depressed and patients worse off. The moral disunity seems to emerge unscathed by the restructuring 'solution', highlighting the importance of having the moral debate prior to deciding on the solution.

The strong link between leading change, virtues and narrative is highlighted in this research. Within public sector institutions, virtues are revealed and co-constructed by the narratives that describe what it means to managers to be leading change. MacIntyre (1985) also argues that narrative plays a central role in the formation and re-formation of the virtues of the institution. The role of managers at all levels in constructing those virtues (or vices) is explored in this book. MacIntyre emphasises the significance to the wellbeing of the institution of there being a set of virtues negotiated through a communal narrative that informs practice improvement. In this study the managers' narratives of what it means to be leading change and their expressed needs in the midst of change support MacIntyre's viewpoint. An examination of the managers' narratives offers an opportunity to explore the concept of narrative unity both in terms of a personal unity (their own story meshing with the change story) and of a communal unity, (personal stories meshing to secure purpose and morality) for people in the midst of change. This examination reveals virtues from well established moral traditions battling for the moral high ground at the grass roots of healthcare provision. The struggle to maintain personal narrative unity or even any kind of collective unity is explored with a view to understanding the cynicism and anger towards any reform programme (Greener & Powell 2003).

The discourse of organisational change has been broadly identified as residing in two camps: structural functional and social constructionist. Outcomes from the former are generally a set of qualitative factors, or a theory, that contributes to managing change successfully or unsuccessfully (Pettigrew 1992; Dawson 1999). A common theme in this literature is the notion of 'key people' or 'change agents' playing a significant role in the successful organisational change. Social constructionist-based studies have offered descriptions and understandings of the life of 'key people' such as managers and clinicians in the midst of implementing public-sector reform and raised issues such as 'tensions', 'disempowerment' (Blackler et al. 1999; Blackler 2006 respectively), 'frictions', 'paradoxes' (Czarniawska 1997). What it means to managers to be 'leading change' (Cameron et al. 2001), what support they need (Blackler et al. 1999; Blackler 2006) and the significance of values or virtues (Moore & Beadle 2006) are aspects of public-sector institutional change hitherto reported as under researched. This study explores the extent to which enacted narratives of morality conflicts and confusion over purpose play a role in the social construction of cynicism, anger and mistrust towards government-driven reform programmes in the public sector. It argues that studying change through narrative offers a window into the virtues at stake and illuminates the difficulty in reconciling them when they are rooted in different moral traditions (MacIntyre 1985). I argue that when the social reality of organisational change is conceptualised as an evolving set of narratives, those narratives can be viewed as constructing the virtues of the organisation. Viewed in this light it is argued that when actors enact tragic, comic and romantic narrative enactments of change they construct resistance and cynicism towards any kind of change agenda, a moral fragmentation occurs and practice is corrupted. MacIntyre argues that in this situation the 'internal goods'[3] of practice, those goods that offer wellbeing to the members of the institution are lost. In my study participants claim they are suffering stress, depression and sickness, meaning time off work. We will see managers enacting narratives of defending, fighting for and losing what they believe to be of worth in the way they practice healthcare. Managers ('key people' or 'change agents') acting as virtual soldiers on the front line of much wider ideological power battles, in some cases unaware of the deep rooted antecedents with which they are contending. Blackler (2006) argues that the rhetoric of 'leadership' is in reality empty for chief Executives of healthcare organisations and that they are mere conduits of policy from the centre. Blacker finds that some CEOs were not surprised when their jobs lost meaning. Greener and Powell (2003), based on their survey of healthcare managers, argue that cynicism towards reform pervades the healthcare sector. This book develops both those arguments and enhances understanding of the narrative-based social constructions of reform that can generate cynicism, demotivate and reduce morale.

Sturdy and Grey (2003) raise concerns about the dominance of the view that organisational change is inevitable, desirable and or manageable and they argue a case for research that provides 'alternative (additional) voices and therefore choices' (ibid.: 659). They suggest that MacIntyre, amongst others, challenges theories that underpin organisational change management.

> ...MacIntyre's (1981) contention [is] that the social sciences have completely failed to develop predictive generalities, and moreover, that they will never do so. OCM has no such inhibitions. For example, in Pettigrew et al. although there is a familiar recognition of a 'complex, dynamic and internationally conscious world', a 'search for general patterns of change' remains (2001: 697). If OCM is, as we have suggested, both managerialist and universalist, what might be done to articulate a different kind of understanding of change? (Sturdy & Grey 2003: 657)

Through a MacIntyre-inspired analysis of managers' narratives in the midst of change this book adds to the voices that challenge the way changes to health services are being managed. This has potentially profound organisational and political implications.

Finally, reality TV is proposed as a development of Czarniawska's serial metaphor (1997) as a new cultural metaphor for what public sector reform means to the participants in this study.

Hope is offered in this book with a suggested approach for management education which is to build on the notion that it is through conflict and sometimes only through conflict that we learn what our ends and purposes are, with the question 'Of what (wider) conflicts is (my conflict) the scene?' (adapted from MacIntyre 1985: 163, who draws on Passmore 1962). The book concludes with a report back on a pilot programme with a group of senior healthcare managers, in response to their expressed needs, to follow this line of enquiry. The programme attempts to discover options that, in the midst of massive reform, still offer them 'internal goods' in their management practice and that are faithful to a collective purpose (telos) of improving the quality of health care offered by the services they manage. Some of the programme participants claim they have rediscovered the virtue of courage to 'break the rules' and enable them 'to do the right thing' in the midst of competing and conflicting reform pressures. This book argues that doing 'the right thing' means leading the implementation of ethical and sustainable quality improvements to healthcare provision which by their nature will be affordable. Red Adair, the highly respected firefighter, explains this principle in an erudite comment when he justified his fee for extinguishing oil well fires after the first Gulf war by saying: "If you think it's expensive to hire a professional to do the job, wait until you hire an amateur." This book offers the justification in the form of research for an alternative or additional approach to forming a community of professionals who can lead affordable excellence in practice improvements.

1.1 Aim of the research

The initial aims of this research were focussed on understanding what it means to a group of senior and middle managers from one primary (health) care trust (PCT) and partnering local authority (LA) social services to be leading the implementation of mental health service 'modernisation' in one region in the UK. This was in response to calls to understand what managing change means in practice for healthcare managers in the midst of reform. For example, in an award-winning literature review on organisational change written specifically for healthcare managers Cameron et al. (2001: 5) states:

> Substantial numbers of managers and clinical professionals argue that much of the evidence about effective change management is located in the heads of practitioners and has yet to find its way into the scholarly journals.

Further to the above was a call to understand how best to support managers with the task of translating policy into practice. (Blackler et al. 1999). It was recognised that as the research progressed these aims would be refined and possibly refocussed, influenced by undertaking the literature review and research in the field. In order to respond to these calls the research commenced with the specific aims of increasing understanding of:

- What it means to managers to be implementing organisational change aimed at improving the quality of healthcare
- What the similarities are in the participants' accounts of change
- What managers' accounts say about whether reform is working
- What managers need in terms of support in the midst of leading reform

These aims were refined as the study progressed and significant themes emerged. Early analysis of the data and my exposure to writers such as MacIntyre (1985), Bruner (1986) and Polkinghorne (1988), all of whom made contributions to the narrative turn in social sciences, resulted in the emergence of a number of key themes that were incorporated into the initial research aims:

- To explore the power of narrative approach in organisational change research and in maintaining a dialogue with participants
- To understand the nature of the conflicts and dilemmas enacted in the narratives and what kind of social reality they construct
- To examine the narratives using the lens of MacIntyre's virtues-goods-practices-institution schema (Moore and Beadle &2006 – see Appendix 1) in order to add an ethical dimension to organisational change management theory and in doing so add to the voices that challenge the manageability of change

1.2   Structure of the book

The book has five main sections. The first is the Introduction; the second consists of Chapters 2 to 4 which contain the literature review. Chapter 5, the methodology and research design, forms the third section; the fourth section comprises Chapters 6 to 9 which report on the empirical data and analysis. Finally Chapter 10, the fifth section, contains the discussion and conclusions. The chapters are summarised below.

Chapter 2: Healthcare and the Modernisation Agenda provides contextual information ranging from a broad public sector perspective through to the National Health Service and the local situation for Omega. I begin by briefly discussing the UK government modernisation agenda, healthcare modernisation agenda, and more specifically the National Service Frameworks (NSFs), which are the core of modernisation that the participants in this study are implementing. More specifically, I introduce the mental health NSF which is the single NSF with which this study was originally concerned. The participants in the study, all managers, discussed a whole range of other changes. These were 'must dos' that they were attempting to implement in parallel with the NSF. These other changes are still, in the main, part of the modernisation plan. I outline some of these other changes so that as they arise in the text the reader will have some background. The appeal of the 'modernising' discourse along with criticisms of it are reviewed. This will enable the reader to gain an understanding of the controversy of healthcare change as a lead-in to the next chapter. The structure of healthcare provision in the UK and where the managers in the study fit in is also explained in this chapter.

Chapter 3: Organisational Change and the Healthcare Sector provides a literature review of the debates associated with organisational change as it relates to healthcare. This review pieces together a story that begins in the structural functionalist (SF) paradigm and moves to the context of healthcare and social constructionist (SC) theorised research, highlighting the current gap in literature. The notion of key people 'leading change' is examined from both SF and SC perspectives. Much of the SF genre and healthcare literature on change highlights this notion as a strong contributing factor in the achievement of change (Pettigrew 1992; Dawson 1999). Chapman (2004) suggests a top–down, target-driven approach can actually be very wasteful of resources. 'Tensions' (Blackler et al. 1999), 'frictions' (Czarniawska 1997), and 'identity fragmentation' (Humphreys & Brown 2002) have already been highlighted by SC studies as issues for those leading change in the public sector. However, a deeper understanding of what change means to managers and of their support needs in the midst of change are called for by researchers. According to Cameron et al. (2001) despite the amount of significant reform going on in the healthcare sector and many other public and private sector organisations, the body of literature offered to date does not seem to resonate with many practitioners who are interested in understanding and learning more about change.

The chapter examines the difficulties in eliciting the type of knowledge being signalled as needed both by practitioners and researchers and proposes a narrative approach as capable of offering an alternative voice and choice (Sturdy & Grey 2003).

Chapter 4: Turning to Narrative (to study organisational change) positions the narrative approach in management studies as standing within a long tradition of respect for narrative in literary and cultural studies and, in this case, as an important tool for developing a deeper understanding of the social reality of organisational participants in the midst of organisational change. The chapter reviews the linguistic turn in philosophy and moves to the period in which the narrative turn emerged. The strong link between narrative, storytelling and the life of the organisation is traced to the point where it has now become a valuable instrument in management research. It explains how the focus of management studies on understanding meanings opens an important role for narrative. Organisational change studies that have employed narrative are highlighted and their relevance to this study discussed. One particular writer of significance to the narrative turn, MacIntyre, a moral philosopher, is profiled in the chapter for two reasons: first because his seminal thesis (1985) connects narrative, virtues, practices and institutions and second because it is contended that his concepts offer the potential to enrich understanding of the nature of some of the 'tensions' and 'frictions' inherent in public-sector organisational change. The chapter concludes by framing and positioning a contribution to organisational change theory within the emerging body of literature that uses narrative approaches to study organisational change.

Chapter 5: Research Methodology, develops the case for a narrative approach to address the central question of what it means to managers to be implementing government-driven reform. The case is initially built by considering two main theoretical options: structural functionalist and social constructionist. The chapter then proceeds to develop the rationale for a narrative form of social constructionism as an appropriate means to answer the research questions. Examination of other narrative-based studies help to elicit criticisms of the approach and the strategies to address those criticisms in my study. Recent narrative studies that focus on organisational change are also reviewed in order to frame the methodological contribution in context. The strategies amount to a synthesis of narrative approaches that are turned into specific methods in the second part of the chapter which describes the detailed research design. The research design and process is described in terms of the methods employed during the study to answer the research questions. Data gathering took place in a longitudinal 12-month fieldwork phase with several interview phases or 'dips' using in-depth semi-structured interviews and a 'social poetic' (Cunliffe 2002) style of enquiry. Initial analysis of the data draws on Czarniawska (1997) and narratives are categorised in three different ways: stories, themes and a serial. By including other narrative 'technologies' elicited from Gabriel (2000) and Boje (2001) the chapter shows how the research design provides the basis for addressing the research aims outlined in the first section. To ensure I had represented meaning to the managers across Omega and regionally, I explain methods of feeding back the narratives to the participants individually and in focus groups. Finally, the chapter expands on the way I later mediate conversations between the data and MacIntyre and other writers to arrive at the contributions.

Chapters 6, 7 and 8: Stories, Themes and Serial, are the core data chapters and demonstrate how empirical material relating to leading organisational change in the public sector can be analysed using a synthesis of narrative approaches. The analysis is in three stages. First, localised *stories* of change, narrative *themes* and a *serial* of change episodes are extracted from the interview transcripts and the question of what leading change means to the managers is examined. This approach follows the precedent set by Czarniawska in her extensive study of public-sector organisational change (1997). Each chapter explains how the different treatments contribute to addressing the aims described above. Second, 'poetic story modes', following the example of Gabriel (2000), are used to categorise the stories into different types of plot (epic, tragic, comic and romantic) as originally discerned in Aristotle's *Poetics*. Third, conversations are mediated between key narrative theorists mentioned in the preceding chapters to suggest what the participants' narratives are doing or constructing as well as what they are saying. The final part of the analysis majors on MacIntyre's virtues-goods-practices-institution schema (Moore & Beadle 2006). This enables a closer examination of the nature of the conflicts described in the stories, themes and serial and the constructing influence of their narrative enactments on the social reality of the managers across the service. The analyses are presented as a triad. This reveals the range of meanings and shows the importance of having all three present to support the developing arguments and contributions. In this way the three chapters could be viewed as a three-legged stool to support the argument that virtue conflict and the ensuing social constructions have been largely neglected in theories of public-sector change and yet they feature so strongly in this in-depth case study. The moral history and philosophy embedded in MacIntyre's thesis, it is argued, offers a wider perspective on those conflicts experienced by managers and in doing so begins to identify ways in which they might be supported in the midst of reform. The next chapter, in addition to arguing that I have fairly attributed meaning to managers[4] in the narratives selected, also reports on their expressed needs and compares that to what the analysis suggests in terms of support.

Chapter 9: Feedback and Focus Groups, provides a fourth data chapter and an account of what happened when the stories, themes and serial were fed back in five main stages:

1. Director of mental health
2. Mental health managers meeting
3. Third round of interviews with a wider group of managers
4. Workshop and focus groups with 70 Omega managers
5. Workshop and focus groups with 50 senior managers from other healthcare organisations in the region

The chapter outlines the response from each group to the findings. The responses are then exposed to MacIntyre's concepts, to promote understanding of what 'leading change' means in a wider context. The first response from the managers was one of strong resonance with the findings and that their social reality had been articulated in a way that covered the full spectrum of what it means to be implementing healthcare reform initiatives. The second was the question, 'Given that this is how it is for us, what does it mean for our particular service area?' The dialogue, on their initiation, then moved to narratives of expressed needs and practical ways to meet those needs. A thematic analysis of the needs is contained in this chapter using their definitions in the form of quotes to support each need identified. Further data is obtained from the regional focus group where the themed needs were presented back to a wider group of healthcare managers from across one region of the UK. That there is low morale currently across the healthcare sector is not in dispute by most commentators and that is evidenced in the comments made by these managers. Through MacIntyre's lens we see at a grass-roots regional management level the constructed cynicism and demotivation that, it is argued, contributes strongly to low morale. This book argues in concert with MacIntyre that when two (or more) incompatible moral traditions (for example, market and equality of care) are brought together then managers are effectively being asked to carry out mission impossible. The final chapter discusses the contributions made and implications for theory and practice.

Chapter 10: Discussion and conclusions, draws the contributions of the study together summarising each chapter and reflecting on the findings in relation to the key aims outlined above. Discrete methodological and empirical contributions are outlined as a precursor to the substantive theoretical contributions. New research agendas are discussed both with regard to methodological and theoretical options. The contributions are then reviewed with regard to their implications for policy, theory and management education. The major contribution is framed within organisational change theory and an alternative understanding of resistance to change based on social constructionist theorising and the virtue ethics of MacIntyre. Resistance is conceptualised as a polyphony of narrative constructions of protection against virtues that practitioners perceive as damaging to their practice. The chapter describes how this insight was enabled with a synthesis of narrative approaches. That synthesis also offers a discrete methodological contribution. The chapter argues that the empirical contributions gain their uniqueness from the MacIntyre-inspired analysis and by offering an ethical dimension to public-sector reform. This theorising adds to other voices that question the underlying assumptions of the dominant structural functional conceptions of change that currently inform modernisation policy implementation. Finally it suggests that the kind of change that improves practice in any sustainable way needs to come from the centre of that practice, from the practitioners and be grown in a meshing of their personal narrative unities.

The next chapter explains the public-sector reform context for the study, from a UK government perspective to the local situation for the managers who took part.

2
The Healthcare Sector and the Modernising Agenda

The aim of this chapter are threefold: first, to provide contextual information about the UK National Health Service (NHS) including some history of change; second, to describe the policy changes that the participants are attempting to translate into practice; and third, to position this study with respect to the debates and critiques relating to the modernisation agenda.

I begin by briefly discussing the UK Government modernisation agenda and healthcare reform agenda (DoH 2000a) and I introduce the mental health (MH) National Service Framework (NSF) (DoH 1999) which is the main NSF that most of the study participants were concerned with. The participants in the study, mainly managers from a single PCT, discussed a whole range of other changes[1] that they were attempting to implement in parallel with the NSF. I outline some of these other changes so that as they arise in the text the reader will have some basic background. I then outline the organisations involved in the implementation of the MH NSF, and the way in which the local implementation plan has been structured and resourced. The current and evolving structure of healthcare and local authority social services are also outlined in this chapter and in particular as they relate to mental health services. Following this context chapter I discuss my research approach and the methods I have chosen to answer the research questions.

2.1 UK government modernisation agenda

Following its election in 1997 the Labour government brought in a programme of radical changes to the public sector. The essence of the programme was a reshaping of the ways in which public services were conceptualised, designed and delivered, for instance through a customer-driven model or in the case of the healthcare sector with a 'focus on creating a step change in the way services are commissioned by front line staff to reflect patient choices' (DoH 2005a: 1).

The heart of the programme is delivering better results, and more responsive and high-quality public services that match what people need. There is a focus on users rather than organisational structures and on applying new technology to make government simpler and more accessible. It covers not just the civil service but the whole five million people working in the public sector, with a new drive on working together to deliver outcomes.

In December 1999, Sir Richard Wilson presented to the prime minister a programme for modernising the Civil Service based on the work of groups within the Civil Service management committee. On the cabinet office website (HMG 1999b), the government claims that:

> *The modernising government agenda builds on the administrative reforms of the UK over the last 15 years. But there are some crucial differences. There is a change in focus from a managerial agenda to the user's agenda. The programme mobilises the whole resources of the public sector to work together across organisational boundaries to deliver real results on the ground, not just interim activity. It is based on a continuing drive for efficiency and effectiveness, but in a pragmatic rather than dogmatic way.*

It is significant that Tony Blair rather than the then Health Secretary, Alan Milburn, launched the NHS Plan (DoH 2000a). It signifies the importance that Blair placed on the healthcare sector to his government. The healthcare sector modernisation agenda contained in the plan was drawn up by the Department of Health following Labour's election to government in 1997, and was published as *The NHS Plan* in 2000. This document set out the case for modernising the healthcare sector and outlined the areas where patients and the public could expect to see change and improvement at service level. The targets contained in the Plan were ambitious in comparison to anything which had gone before, and public expectation was correspondingly raised. A pressing task for the government, therefore, was to make the Plan a reality on the ground. A new healthcare service (DoH 1998a) and modernised social services (DoH 1998b) were part the programme of improvements to achieve the above. To this end the National Service Frameworks were produced and the next section explicates in general terms then focuses on the mental health NSF.

2.2 The national service frameworks

A number of medical conditions were selected by the government for early modernisation, and the NSFs were the vehicles designed to achieve this. The conditions chosen were either those with a high morbidity/ mortality rate, such as cancer (DoH 2000b) or coronary heart disease (DoH 2000c), or those which consume significant amounts of health care funding such as mental health (DoH 1999). Later the NSFs were based on care groups such as children or older people. An NSF represents an attempt to standardise the management of a medical condition, so that wherever patients live they receive broadly the same type and level of treatment. This involves specifying evidence-based standards for treatment and setting targets for patient outcomes. In the case of the NSF for mental health, which I am following, there are seven standards set in five areas covering:

Titled Area	Standard	Description
1.	1.	Mental health promotion
2.	2. and 3.	Primary care and access to services
3.	4. and 5.	Effective services for people with severe mental illness
4.	6.	Caring about carers
5.	7.	Preventing suicide

We shall see most of these areas mentioned in excerpts from the transcripts which are analysed in Chapters 69. The NSFs were gradually introduced from 2000 onwards, and new ones are still being added. Each NSF is accompanied by a Policy Implementation Guideline (PIG) and a delivery strategy that details what should be delivered 'on the ground', for example, the make-up of community mental health teams (CMHTs) and the roles and responsibilities each individual in the team should have. Targets for achievement are set and these targets are monitored for compliance, and deviance is picked up and performance managed from 'The Centre', as the DoH is often referred to by the participants. Local implementation teams (LITs) made up of representatives from the healthcare organisations, social services, user and carer groups and voluntary provider groups are part of the requirement for the development and delivery of local implementation plans. The concept is that by involving all these groups in the local instantiation of the NSFs the change process will be easier. In practice the interface for partnerships is complex and problematic with local authority social services, voluntary services and public-service healthcare all bringing different approaches to care, institutional cultures, boundaries, finances, procedures, and so forth. What it means to bring these different interests together to implement change and what the participants say they need to make it work will be addressed in this book.

This, then, is the backdrop against which my research is set. I began my fieldwork in January 2004, when the service had been implementing the guidance contained in MH PIGs (DoH 2001a) for the previous 12 months and still had much to do to raise standards to the level described therein.

In addition to the service reforms described above the healthcare sector has an ever-changing structure. The next section describes the structure and some of the major changes that occurred during the period in which the fieldwork took place.

2.3   Structure of the public healthcare sector

When the fieldwork began in 2004, 28 Strategic Health Authorities (SHAs) existed. By 2007 that number had been reduced to 10. Each SHA is directly accountable to the DoH and is charged with ensuring the delivery of healthcare services and with meeting targets in its locality – effectively a performance management role. Within an SHA area there are a number of healthcare organisations bearing different responsibilities – the number varies according to the size of the SHA. The two types of organisation that are relevant to my research are acute trusts and primary care trusts (PCTs). Broadly, acute trusts are general hospitals providing the usual range of hospital services (A&E, surgery, maternity, orthopaedics, and so forth). PCTs are community-based organisations which are responsible for a) providing community health services (such as GPs, community nursing, health visiting, school nurses) and b) commissioning health care on behalf of their local population. In other words, PCTs hold the resources for purchasing the full range of care needed to keep a population alive and well, and there are performance indicators in place to measure their success in doing this.

Some PCTs also have a provider role as well as a commissioner role; the PCT concerned in this study was one of those. It provides mental health services in partnership with local authority social services. Since at the time of writing the PCT covered two counties it had two social services departments to work with in order to deliver mental health services. Towards the end of my fieldwork, in summer 2005, a new plan from the DoH was proposed to split the PCT and join the halves to other PCTs in order to make the PCT boundaries concomitant with the local authority boundaries. A further change was to divest the PCT of its mental health provider status and create a separate provider or transfer the services to an existing provider in one of the two counties covered by the PCT. This was typical of the constant restructuring of the healthcare sector that managers have to implement and patients have to endure. At the start of 2007 the aforementioned split had come into effect and Omega no longer existed.

Groups of healthcare organisations in a given locality are collectively known as a 'local health economy', a term introduced to encourage 'joined-up thinking' regarding healthcare provision. Increasingly organisations are expected to collaborate and co-operate in providing services across an entire area, not just to focus on their own geographical locality or their own specialty. For example, a city and its environs (which would come under one of the regional SHA) would constitute a local health economy comprising a PCT, an acute hospital, mental health and learning disability services plus an ambulance service. There are also a number of collaboratives and networks in place to co-ordinate, say, cancer, critical care and young people services across the economy. Therefore, in relation to my research, although I focussed initially on mental health services in a PCT, I was in effect researching within a local health economy, it being impossible to study one part of the system in isolation. For this reason, once the initial findings from mental health services were produced, they were fed back to managers from other service areas within the health economy and then eventually across the region.

2.4   Local situation

Two main organisations were involved in implementing the mental health services NSF. The first is a primary care trust mental health service and the second is the local authority social services. Together these will be known as Omega Mental Health Services. These two core organisations along with a number of partnering organisations in the independent sector are responsible for delivering the service in the region. They also rent services from the acute trusts such as wards and the supporting infrastructure to run the ward. All the initial participants came from the core organisations, however, later as described above the study expanded through focus groups to include managers from some of the partnering organisations as well.

Collectively these partners are in the process of introducing a radically new service model with the aim of improving patient outcomes. According to a local mental health service review, produced prior to my involvement, users experience 'good intentions and commitment but also a fragmented and unresponsive service that overlooks ordinary but important needs and one that appears overstretched and impoverished in ways that convey a lack of value and humanity' (Omega 2003). In addition to this challenge was severe overspending to the tune of £100m per annum. Therefore, in addition to improving quality of services in line with users needs and government service reform policy there was a need to do this with reducing resource in order to bring the service out of the red. The change to the new service model includes a number of discrete change projects such as the closure of certain units, new approaches to community mental health care provision and asking all practitioners to think from a more holistic paradigm, that is, one using collaborative and preventative approaches that adhere to the principles of the NSF. Active involvement of users and carers also forms a fundamental part of the shift to social models of care.

This organisational change study illuminates what it means to the managers concerned to implement the changes described above. The objective is to convey their accounts in narrative form over a period of one year to gain insight into what it means to them and for the service they construct. The research study aims to offer a deeper understanding of organisational change partly in order to help the organisation appreciate how best to support managers within a changing healthcare sector and in this way contribute to the overall improvement of the service for its vulnerable users.

2.5   Positioning in the literature on healthcare reform

Despite the highly seductive rhetoric of modernisation and its appeals on many fronts to improve public services (du Gay 2003) it has been heavily criticised. Peter Hyman, after a career change from senior government advisor to a teacher in a London comprehensive, reported that the approach he had been part of creating was 'entirely wrong' for ensuring 'effective delivery' (Hyman 2005). More specific criticism has been levelled at the regime of targets and the move to central performance management (O'Neill 2002; Pidd 2005; Wanless 2004; Chapman 2004; Seddon 2003). Some of these writers argue that the system of targets can be improved; others suggest that command and control by targets should be abandoned. The latter suggest that targets distract people from the core purposes of their work and the possibility of ongoing performance improvement. My view is that human interaction and behaviour is infinitely subtler than setting targets can allow for. Alternative solutions range from continuous learning (Chapman 2004) to the involvement of front line workers in the analysis and improvement of service delivery (Seddon 2003). In the view of Calman et al. (2002) only the frontline management can undertake detailed redesign of services, but instead of improving frontline services; senior management time is taken up with demands from government. The result, according to Hunter 2000, is 'the climate surrounding the government style of managing is one of fear and mistrust'. In Greener and Powell's study of healthcare reform programmes, they find a salient theme of 'cynicism': 'this element is the most striking and consistently expressed theme' (2003: 38). This book supports both Hunter's and Greener and Powell's findings and adds further understanding of the nature of the cynicism through an in-depth study of the narratives of managers in the midst of reform. A deeper understanding of the day to day social reality and how narrative enactments of change enforce the construction of cynicism, fear and mistrust is revealed. However, the suggested solutions of more sophisticated targets, improved performance management and support to managers as such learning and involvement are all challenged both by participants expressed needs and by my analysis of their accounts of change. That challenge extends to the mechanical based conceptions of change that pervade the field of organisational change management in general and to the view that change can be managed.

A further focus of criticisms of relevance to this study has been the changing ethics, public to private, of public service (for example, Brereton & Temple 1999; Pollock 2004). Wendy Savage, a former senior adviser to the government's Department of Health, argues that reform programmes encourage privatisation and undermine the values and efficiency of healthcare provision (Severn 2006). The government dropped her from its advisory body because of her stance. She expresses a wide variety of concerns and one that is of relevance to this study is that the healthcare sector 'is being subjected to market-driven policies, the aim of which is to convert services into commodities and to have a workforce that is orientated towards profit, whilst getting the government to underwrite the risk'. The ultimate result, she claims, is 'a commercial driven health service resembling the American system, which despite its costs is unable to provide equity of care'. Her views, according to Severn (2006), coincide with the British Medical Association (BMA) 2006 Annual Representative meeting resolution. The BMA resolution restates its belief in the core values of the NHS, which it declares 'cannot be maintained' if it is broken up and tendered to private corporations. With such a strong centre, managers increasingly look to the DoH rather than their local communities for guidance, which according to Hunter (2000) is in danger of creating a 'managerial infantilism' that cannot deliver the modernisation agenda. This research does support the notion of 'managerial infantilism' and arguably this now exists. It also develops further understanding of how this forms through weak and conflicting ethics embedded within a blunderbuss of policies. Further that the strength of the centre is not in terms of cohesive and binding narrative carrying a communal purpose and ethics, that may help to form solid ethical management outwards from the centre but is wielded, with a 'your jobs are on the line' bullying approach (Blackler 2006) that is driven with a regime of targets and measures. This study therefore exposes further critical weaknesses in delivering the modernisation agenda.

2.5.1   CMS, NPM and the modernisation agenda

A further body of literature takes a critical stance, not just towards the practice of management that modernisation engenders but towards the practice of researching management in general. Following Alvesson and Wilmott (1992) it is now known as Critical Management Studies (CMS). This literature has turned its gaze on the healthcare sector and the modernisation agenda taking for example poststructuralist, feminist and deconstructionist lenses to critically examine management. The 'managing change better' approach, according to Hearn and Parkin (1995: 4), leaves significant areas like exploitation, manipulation, and subordination in a 'booming silence'. My study is open in its aspiration to allow a voice to all, including those who may have been previously muted in the drive to perform better.

The UK's public sector has seen fundamental reform over an extended period. According to Blackler (2006: 10) central to such developments was the development in the 1990s of the New Public Management (NPM) (Hood 1991) which involved the introduction of private sector style competition and incentives to the sector. Blackler observes that 'in recent years general discussions about NPM have shaded into discussions of New Labour's modernisation agenda'. In this study I refer mainly to the modernisation agenda and the reforms to mental health services since 1999 when the NSF for mental health was issued. In a notable and detailed review of a significant body of healthcare contextualised CMS literature Learmonth (2003) acknowledges writers that have focussed on NPM and points to studies that have voiced unease, powerless, a sense of contradiction and anger (Traynor 1999: 156) about

NPM. My study still finds strong resonance in the accounts of participants with these feelings and offers an ethical dimension to understand more about the continued construction of this social reality for managers on the front line of change.

Learmonth (2003: 106) suggests that critical management studies are sympathetic to 'understanding managers' worlds' type studies, however, he says they 'rarely invite us to reflect upon whether or not management practices may be complicit with wider sociological structures'. This study is enabled in two respects to extend reflection into wider society: first, by drawing on and developing Czarniawska's 'serial' cultural metaphor into the modern cultural metaphor of reality TV which encompasses the researcher in the complicity; and second, by drawing on MacIntyre to highlight the ideological horizons reflected in the virtue conflict enacted narratives of the participants. In a particularly relevant excerpt Learmonth also raises concerns about a priori assumptions about what managers do derived from standard texts rather from empirical material and therefore could also be taken as a particularly loaded view of what managers do. Learmonth's conclusion is that 'managerial values (and arguably virtues) remain more or less in the background and, whilst they still influence the work, the assumptions themselves are not subject to rigorous theoretical and empirical consideration'. I agree with Learmonth and this study attempts to bring managerial virtues to the foreground and in doing so open up a hidden dimension to scrutiny that it is hoped will offer some very interesting and worthwhile contributions to CMS and to the substantive area of public-sector reform policy and practice that continues to spawn from the modernisation agenda.

2.5.2 Summing up

Although the context is the education sector, Frank Coffield's summing up of the situation in his inaugural lecture for the Institute for Education would resonate with the health sector.

> The sector is now weighed down by layer upon layer of policy, some well thought out, others ill-considered; some still in place, others abandoned; most create new responsibilities but responsibilities are never shed; some contain not only inconsistent, but irreconcilable, strategies to be run simultaneously; and some move power to the centre, some to the region and some to the locality. The upshot is a curious mixture of advances (e.g. a new, more appropriate shape for the LSC) and of regressions (e.g. the growing number of schools outwith local democratic accountability). We are witnessing the main tensions within the sector being played out in the professional lives

of staff i.e. those between competition and collaboration, between standardisation and innovation, between centralisation and local flexibility, between enabling and controlling strategies, and between long-term sustainability and short-term goals and targets.

   The challenges of creating radical and enduring reform have been seriously underestimated by government; the language of 'transformation' is inappropriate for a long, slow process which may take more than a decade to complete; the battery of mechanisms selected to 'deliver' such change has proved too mechanical; and the climate of fear which permeates the sector must give way to a climate of mutual trust. (Coffield 2006: 24)

   Both the government's rhetorical narrative arguments for their change policies and the critical narratives arguments are apparent in the participants' narratives. Many of the above critical themes are exposed and supported by the analysis of the narratives of managers who are implementing the reform agenda and at the same time trying to hold on to the core values which brought them into the service. It is argued that public-sector change studies to date, in addition to neglecting the narrative accounts of managers and in particular their poetic form and constructing effects, have also underplayed the importance of considering individual and collective construction of the ethics of practice in the reform process. This research demonstrates that these issues are crucial to the understanding of what it means for managers to be implementing organisational change, important to consider when creating reform policy and a vital part of public-sector management education, especially those who are expected to take a lead in change implementation. This study represents the first attempt to analyse public-sector reform using MacIntyre's virtue ethics perspective (1985). This is surprising since much of the criticism levelled at the reform programme refers to competing ideologies and the ethics of change practice. MacIntyre suggests that in order for virtuous and excellent practice to flourish institutions are required to provide for their sustenance. Through developing a deeper understanding of their social reality this study asks what form that sustenance to managers, in the midst of implementing reform, would take.

2.6   Management and organisational change in healthcare

This section offers a potted history of management and organisational changes leading up to my study and what was current during the research period. The purpose is to gain a sense of what many of the managers in this study have already been through and the other changes they were fielding in addition to the service changes.

Management in the public healthcare system has a very short history. Blackler (2006: 3) summarises the salient events from 1983, when managers were introduced, up to when the Labour government came to power in 1997. He states that up to 1983 the NHS had 'officials' who worked to find compromises between the various parties (Harrison 1988) but little in the way of management. Following the Griffiths enquiry (1983), managers were introduced to the service. Later their role was to be reinforced when the Conservative government under Thatcher introduced a 'purchaser-provider split' (DoH 1989). According to the Office for Public Management (OPM) (2003) at the start of the 1990s there were two main developments intended to improve choice and quality of services: first, the publication of the Patient's Charter and second the structural reforms contained in the *NHS and Community Care Act* (HMG 1990). The latter introduced the internal or quasi market to the healthcare sector influenced by thinkers such as Alain Einthoven and the belief that competition would benefit users by offering greater choice and raising the quality of standards. Widespread reforms in financial management ensued across the service. Contractual relationships were arranged with health authorities and general practitioners commissioning healthcare services from provider organisations. Provider organisations were allowed some freedoms from central policy restraints, for example, newly constituted hospital trusts were given some freedoms from national pay scales and were allowed to accumulate financial surpluses. Eventually by 1994 nearly all acute services had achieved trust status.

Did all these changes work? Evidence suggests that choice did not improve matters, even though many GPs took up the fund-holding option. Patients did not shop around so there was little pressure on providers to compete for patients. Instead of shopping around the health authorities increasingly moved towards negotiating long-term agreements. The freedom of trusts was also severely constrained by the Department of Health. Trusts were not permitted to behave as true profit-seeking firms but were required to break even and prices were strongly regulated. As one commentator put it *'the incentives were too weak and the constraints were too strong'*. In a very short time the government began to soften its rhetoric and improving the health of the population came to the foreground with new supporting policies and the 'market' faded into the background. OPM (2003) conclude that

'*Fundamentally, then, government was caught between its faith in the power of the market to deliver choice and raise quality, and fear that a true market would lead to strong health inequalities and fractured planning*'.

In 1997, following a general election in which the performance and future of healthcare provision had been a major issue, the incoming Labour government partially dismantled the market mechanism with *The New* NHS: *Modern, Dependable* (DoH 1997) which stressed the importance of partnership arrangements in place of both hierarchies and markets. The constitution of healthcare trusts was retained however and extended to primary care and mental health and moves were begun to make chief executives (CEs) of trusts responsible for the clinical as well as the financial performance of their organisations with *A first class service: Quality in the new* NHS (DoH 1998a).

Some key events largely drawn from Rivett (1998/ 2007) that impact on the managers interviewed after 1997 and up to the present time are highlighted in the table below.

Year	Event
1998	Green Paper – *A First Class Service* *Information for health* strategy NHS Direct launched (a one-stop shop for healthcare) Independent Inquiry into inequalities in health
1999	Nurse shortage; substantial pay award Royal Commission on Long-Term Care of the Elderly White Paper *Saving Lives: Our Healthier Nation* (HMG) Abolition of fundholding Establishment of primary care groups/trusts clinical performance data on English hospitals Alan Milburn appointed secretary of state
2000	Substantial increase in healthcare funding White Paper –*The NHS Plan: A plan for investment; a plan for reform* (DoH) sets targets for cutting waiting lists and improving care Abolition of NHS Executive, with incorporation of its functions in Department of Health White Paper – *Reforming the Mental Health Act* (HMG) NHS/private sector concordat
2001	Health and Social Care Act (HMG) White Paper – *Shifting the Balance of Power* (DoH) and introduction of legislation Hospital 'star' system of league tables begins Wanless (2001) preliminary report on NHS finance

Continued

Continued

Year	Event
2002	*National Health Service Reform and Health Care Professions Act* (HMG) Devolution day: new structure with four regional directorates of health and social care, 28 SHAs replace health authorities and PCTs established PCTs take over commissioning April budget announces major funding increase/Wanless Review NHS foundation trusts proposed
2003	Resignation of Alan Milburn; John Reid appointed Secretary of State for Health GPs and consultants accept new contract *Health and Social Care (Community Standards) Act* (HMG) *Agenda for Change* pay system and *Key Skills Framework* launched incurring massive HR and management project (DoH) *Building on the Best* (patient choice) (DoH)
2004	Financial flows – payment by Results First wave foundation trusts *NHS Improvement Plan* (DoH) *Choosing Health* – public health White paper Healthcare Commission established
2005	*Commissioning a Patient-led NHS* (DoH) *Payment by Results* (DoH) introduces a new funding system Proposed further expansion of nurse and pharmacist prescribing
2006	Hospital star/league tables abolished *Our Health, Our Care, Our Say – Community Care* (DoH) Ban on smoking in public places Commissioning a Patient-Led NHS: SHAs reduced to 10, PCTs reduced to 152 PM speaks on personal responsibility for health Plans for 'super-unit' A & E Omega's NHS trust dismantled following implementation of CPL
2007	All research participants working in four different organisations

Many of the above changes along with the long and fraught attempts to update the mental health act are mentioned by the participants in their interviews. In the next section I describe the approach that Omega took to meet the change requirements placed on them.

2.7 Omega's local implementation plan

The trust employs 2500 staff and provides a range of health services, including mental health, to a population of 330,000. In February 2003, a new director was appointed at Omega Mental Health[2] (OMH). He focussed on the delivery of a new kind of mental health service with a local implementation plan that sat within a strategic framework of clinical and corporate governance and a national context. Bringing all the current and previous changes together into one plan for the development of mental health services is what the local implementation plan was intended to do for Omega's mental health services. Briefly, it encompassed:

- *Modernisation*: the reshaping of the style of public service, shaping it around service users; transcending boundaries of profession and organisation and working in partnership.
- NHS *Plan* (DoH 2000a)*:* This relates to the wider modernisation, establishes a primary care lead and sets some specific targets.
- *National Service Frameworks* (for example, DoH 1999): The standards are non-negotiable as are the functions and outcomes of the Policy Implementation Guidance (for example, DoH 2001a) but the models are capable of being locally shaped.
- *Finance:* The new service model must achieve their objective for not more than the current budgeted resources.
- *Evidence:* The tasks confronting OMH only differ in detail from elsewhere across the country.
- *Integration:* The emerging plans must be such that the service users experience the service as an integrated system of care.

Requirements that cut across some of the above are:

Clinical governance
- Patient-centred vision
- Shared values
- Commitment to continuous quality improvement
- System of accountability and responsibility

Developing the workforce
- Improving recruitment to increase capacity in undergraduate and postgraduate education
- Developing existing clinical staff to deliver services in new ways
- Enhancing clinical and managerial leadership
- Innovative approaches to lifelong learning
- Developing multidisciplinary teams
- Capacity and skills to become a learning organisation

Service

- Partnership with social services, primary care and third sector
- User involvement
- Public consultation

In addition to these government health service modernisation requirements there are also local requirements for improvement. The following builds a picture of what these amount to.

2.7.1   Local input to the plan

According to the Director there is a history of poorly provided for and managed finances within Omega and a culture that does not like change. There is no additional money and there is a need to cut back on the current service provision which may mean closing down some of the current units. The following is an extract from a paper produced by the director describing a new service model for adult mental health:

> *The current mental health service in this region does not meet national targets. By general agreement and in spite of the best efforts of the staff nor does it adequately and consistently meet local need. There is little additional money to invest and therefore the deficiencies cannot be resolved simply by adding new components.* (Omega 2003)

The service users and carers have described how they experience the service now. They find good intentions and commitment but a fragmented and unresponsive service that overlooks ordinary but important needs. The services appear to be overstretched and impoverished in ways that convey a lack of value and humanity.

The PCT concerned is provider of both primary care and specialist mental health services and there are commitments to partnership working between agencies and to engagement with service users. Currently within the UK health sector, the response to 90 per cent of people with mental health problems is in primary care.

Having carried out consultations with the local communities, the users and carers described how they want the mental health Service to be. This includes:

- Ordinary and available
- Help when I need it – especially outside office hours
- Not waiting for the crisis but helping stop it

- Help that comes to me or that is easy to get
- Listening to me
- Taking notice when I say I am not coping/ taking notice when we say he is not well
- Having time
- Bringing me the best treatment that is available
- Not requiring me to tell my story over and over
- Recognising my abilities and perhaps using them even though I need some help

Staff also voiced similar frustrations to the users and reflected similar needs. This conveyed a need for a softer, more humane service that is closer to people's lives.

2.7.2   Perceived implementation challenges

The leadership team at OMH say they are well aware of the difficulty in implementing such a radical and challenging change programme in the context of the public sector in the region. They view the area as characterised to some extent by local cultures that fight passionately to maintain their existing ways and therefore are against change. Another significant factor they point to is low staff turnover in public services in the area. They claim that their approach to implementing the model is a participative process to build on the strong foundation of local knowledge and experience whilst trying to overcome some of the constraints and limitations of traditional assumptions. It is recognised that the leaders of change will need special qualities, expertise and all the support and feedback they can obtain to create the new service model. Especially so given that for many of the leaders this 'developmental' role will be additional to their existing full-time clinical or operational role/s and with a user group that places infinite demands on personal coping strategies.

In addition to the service model change a reorganisation is currently underway that could mean the closure of certain units and the redistribution of services to other units. So in effect the participants are being asked to make quality improvements whilst at the same time cutting back on the resources and facilities available to them.

Given the situation described above this case offers the opportunity to study organisational change from the perspective of managers who are being asked to lead the implementation of changes in line with national policy, that meet local needs and to do that whilst recovering a large overspend. Whilst recognising that every situation has a unique context and dynamics (Pettigrew et al. 2001) this kind of challenge is fairly typical in other parts of the healthcare sector, and in other public-sector services and has parallels with large private sector organisational change programmes.

This chapter has explained the context of the study starting with the modernisation agenda in terms of the government rhetoric and critiques. Other healthcare organisational changes that were contemporaneous with the study have been catalogued so that the reader can gain an insight into the range of changes that were impacting on the managers. It has described the local situation and implementation plan and the views of some of the senior managers in the service at the time and what they wanted from the study.

It has shown how this study contributes a deeper understanding of the growing cynicism towards change and the nature of support managers in the midst of change are calling for. Through a review of the healthcare reform literature its empirical contribution is highlighted as the first study to take a narrative-based virtue ethics perspective on public-sector reform.

So far we have looked at a whole range of interests in the form of narratives from different parties: Government, patients, carers, funders and senior managers. In Chapter 3 I review some of the relevant organisational change literature and position the book and its contribution in that literature.

3
Organisational Change and Healthcare

There are many ways of conceiving of organisational change. Two broad conceptions emerge: the structural functionalist approach (Burrell & Morgan 1979) and the social constructionist approach (Berger & Luckmann 1967). This brief review attempts to piece together a story that begins in the generic structural functionalist paradigm and moves to the context of healthcare and alternative conceptions of narratives and social constructionist theory, highlighting a gap in research literature.

3.1   Structural conceptions of change

Many of the structural functionalist conceptions of change can be traced back to Lewin's force field theory (1952), which incorporates the idea that change is a three-stage process: unfreezing, change and then refreezing. In addition to its links with the Gestalt movement (Perls 1972) and the concept of emerging socialised identities, field theory also includes an undercurrent of impersonal forces in the environment or person which supposedly help to shape motivation and behaviour.

> To instigate changes ... a situation has to be created for a certain period where the leader is sufficiently in control to rule out influences he does not want and to manipulate the situation to a sufficient degree. (Lewin 1948: 39)

Most accounts of organisational change and learning derived from this perspective describe or employ a mixture of cognitive and political strategies and follow a model of successive phases of unfreezing, change and refreezing.

A further development of the structural functionalist approach can be attributed to Schein (1985). Schein developed the idea of organisational 'cultures' that called for a whole range of change strategies including analytical, educational/learning and political process. Tushman et al. (1986) add more radical approaches which include sacking and replacing the CEO and/or introduction of new staff into existing structures in order to channel behaviour in new directions. Subtle ideas of legitimising certain meanings through the construction of political agendas, narratives, and role models also feature in this era (Pettigrew 1987). Behind all of these strategies is the belief that resistance to change can be managed either educationally or politically depending on how the resistance is defined (Kotter & Schlesinger 1979). Much of this echoes Lewin's theory that it is better to weaken restraining forces against change than to increase pressure for change: for example, remove people or adopt an educational approach. Interestingly the heavily subscribed approach of creating shared values (Peters & Waterman 1982; Senge 1992) and imposing them top-down to create/educate the company person flies in the face of Lewin's counsel and has been shown in some cases to have little impact, set up opposing or subversive currents (Kunda 1992) and have 'strongly negative effects on communication channels' (Turnbull 2000: 315).

A critique of the top-down nature of change literature is contained in an award-winning literature review on managing change and organisational change that was produced specifically for healthcare managers (Iles & Sutherland 2001). In this review Iles and Sutherland highlight the prescriptive nature of most generic change management literature. They find that empirically based publications that study organisational change are relatively rare and lacking in rigour. They find the same lack of published research in health services organisational change research and point to Pettigrew et al.'s (1992) in-depth study of strategic change as the most comprehensive study of health service change to date. Pettigrew uses a conceptual framework of *content, process* and *context* to identify eight factors that differentiate the higher from the lower 'change performers' in his study. These are:

- Quality and coherence of local policy
- Key people leading change
- Co-operative interorganisational networks
- Supportive organisational culture, including the managerial subculture
- Environmental pressure, moderate, predictable and long term

- Simplicity and clarity of goals and priorities
- Positive pattern of managerial and clinical relations
- Fit between the change agenda and the locale

A key finding is that there is a pattern of association between the eight factors but there are no simple cause-and-effect relationships between them. Pettigrew's significant contribution is rooted in the qualitative factor analysis approach, producing 'factors having a bearing on change' as a set of guidelines for practitioners and prompts for researchers.

One of these factors is a consistent theme in the generic and health-care literature: 'key people' playing a significant role in 'leading' organisational learning and change (Argyris & Schon 1978; Daft & Weick 1984; Pettigrew 1992; Senge 1990; Stocking 1985, 1992). In a more recent study by Dawson et al. (1998), this theme is taken up with the aim of understanding the role of management in securing organisational change in clinical practice. Dawson et al. suggests that it is important to recognise how 'Individuals in roles as leaders, mentors, change agents and consolidators can make a real difference to the way in which local managerial and organisational systems are created and sustained' (1998: 21). Dawson et al. also found that in talking about their practice, doctors and managers speak in terms of their own autobiography – in other words, they account for their lived experiences. This resonates with Shotter and Cunliffe's (2002) view of 'managers as practical authors' and Czarniawska's (1998) narrative approach to understanding organisations. So although Dawson et al.'s study hints at the importance of personal narrative, the perspective is not taken up by their study. Instead the approach taken is to formulate a set of seven 'conclusions' that can be viewed as building on Pettigrew et al. (1992) eight factors from a perspective of the manager as change leader:

- The first step in being able to achieve change is for those involved to realise that change is possible.
- Healthcare managers and practitioners are likely to stress that they learn best from doing and through direct experience, that is, from patients, from colleagues and from seniors to whom they consider themselves to be or have been apprenticed.
- Work in health cannot be subject to mass standardisation or detailed hierarchical control.
- Health provision needs to be customised to the context in which it is undertaken.

- Local ownership and commitment are needed to solve inevitable problems as they arise.
- Grand policies must be translated into meaningful action and meaningful lives at the local level.
- The role of leadership is critical in this translation.

The finding that the leadership role is a 'translation role' again offers a link to narration, interpretation and storytelling. 'Meaningful action and meaningful lives' offers a further connection in that people and organisations develop meaning and some would argue identity (Ricoeur 1991) through recounting their stories of lived experience. Dawson complements and builds on Pettigrew but remains rooted in qualitative factor analysis within the structural functionalist domain. Dawson concludes:

> We need to understand the practitioners' world, to see it through their eyes. Only then can we hope to be able to develop a dialogue in which the findings of the research can enlighten practice. (Dawson 1999: 23)

This suggests that, despite Pettigrew et al.'s extensive study and many others, the 'practitioners' world' still remains elusive to researchers. This point is emphasised by Cameron et al.:

> Substantial numbers of managers and clinical professionals argue that much of the evidence about effective change management is located in the heads of practitioners and has yet to find its way into the scholarly journals. (Cameron et al. 2001: 5)

Much of the structural functional literature presents all change as desirable, inevitable, and manageable; however, as will be elaborated in Chapter 4, that universalising assumption has been challenged (Sturdy & Grey 2003). In some of the accounts collected in my study change appears to make the situation worse and people claim they know it will. Organisational change management theory utilised in public administration has already been criticised as managerialist (for example, Smith et al. 2001) and as a discursive arena of 'epochalism' that has 'silenced other discursive possibilities' (du Gay 2003: 658). In the wake of these criticisms this study responds to calls for new conceptions of change. Social constructionist and discursive approaches in particular, according to (Sturdy & Grey 2003: 659), have the potential to 'provide alternative (additional) voices and therefore choices'. So in the next section we look at social constructionist studies of change and what has been written about the social reality of change in the context of healthcare.

3.2   Practitioners and change

Some insight into the healthcare practitioner's world can be gained from Blackler et al. (1999). They identify tensions such as professional identity and collaborative team identity, demand and resource, technological capacity and meaningfulness and life and quality of life. They illustrate this through case studies where they apply activity theory[1] (Engestrom et al. 1987) to the situation in order to offer practitioners a way to understand the complexities involved. They emphasise that activity systems are tension producing and make the point that these tensions 'are the driving forces for collective learning'. Blackler et al. 1999 claim that the activity theory approach offers a way of 'understanding processes central to ongoing collaboration in systems that are characterised by tensions and paradoxes' and draws parallels between the healthcare and business organisations competing in a fast-moving global market. Using the lens of Activity Theory Blackler et al. add further understanding from a healthcare leadership perspective of what is experienced during the change process. In a similar study of change to that in focus here, involving cross-disciplinary collaboration, Blackler et al. (1999: 238) describe the following.

At the beginning:

- Difficulty in building an activity system that bridges between different professional groups
- The emergent sense of identity reflecting the dilemmas of its activity and characterised by its sense of struggle
- Tension between doctors and other professionals relating to evolutions in divisions of labour and knowledge
- Certain members experiencing proposed changes as encroachments into their domains
- Change as the harbinger of dangerous downstream changes in quality

Later:

- The view that practitioners could reinterpret over time and so realise what each could bring

- Recontextualisation of their objective and beginning to develop a collaborative approach
- Resource allocation starting when the specifics of their problem were reinterpreted in the broader context of wide scale social changes
- Tensions around what is technologically possible and what is socially possible
- As the processes were supported by informed debate it became more tolerable to discuss overlapping roles and contributions.

Their study admits limitations in applying a theory, in this case activity theory, to a situation to understand what is happening. The analysis is that activity system theory breaks down when applied across different professional groupings. They conclude that '…despite the difficulties staff cope exceptionally well and demonstrate sophisticated understanding of the complexity of their situations and powerful response to paradox[2] and dilemma'. Their call is to understand these abilities better and to actively support and develop them. My study responds, in part, to this call in that it hopes to illuminate what it means to managers to be implementing change and what they say they need to support them in the process of making improvements to the quality of patient care and access to that care. I also draw on theory but rather than applying a theory to a situation and trying to understand in a deductive way, I start with an inductive approach: seeing what emerges from the empirical data and then finding an existing theory that has affinity with the emergent. The existing theory is that presented in MacIntyre's *After Virtue* (1985), which enables the exploration of the relatively uncharted territory of the ethical conflicts narrated by managers who are leading the implementation of public-sector organisational change.

Watson (2003); MacIntyre (1999b) notes that ethical considerations have been examined in a very limited way to date. He explores the ethical dimension from a managerial perspective including issues associated with change or imperatives placed on the organisation from external sources. His interest is in moral agency and he finds that managers can influence the morality of the organisation as long as they can establish 'business grounds'. According to MacIntyre (1985) managers, whether they intend it or not, business grounds or not, influence the morality of the organisation (and society) through their enacted stories and narratives. Watson's call is to examine the extent to which managers take into account the ethical pressures when exchanging with sources on which they rely for resources and vice versa. The healthcare sector has many of these – the DoH and the public are probably the most prominent – and managers under reform are often caught in ethical clashes between the two. My study has aspirations to respond to these calls and contribute to the organisational change literature by offering an ethical perspective, not from an agency perspective but by viewing 'resistance to change' with the ethical lens provided by MacIntyre. The term 'ethical resistance' is now used retrospectively to refer to the approach taken by abolitionists like Gandhi and Steve Biko: they are referred to as 'ethical resisters' but didn't apply the term to themselves. It now seems to be particularly involved with whistleblowing in the business ethics literature (De Maria 2006) referring to the outing of corporate malpractice. However the term seems to be absent from the organisational change literature, as is the notion of resisting the corruption of virtues of practice excellence with which MacIntyre concerns himself. This is one of the gaps into which this book hopes to contribute new understandings by opening an ethical dimension to organisational change.

Burgoyne et al. (1997) in their investigation of issues associated with 'contracting' in health service reforms found the pivotal issues to be around the nature and management of information and the process of contracting about *meaning* as a precursor to contracting about *activities*. Blackler et al.'s (1999) findings expand on this idea and emphasise that it is only through informed debate on what the changes mean in the broader context of wider scale social changes that the actors can move on to discussing collaborative activity. This study strongly supports Blackler et al.'s argument since the empirical data contains traces of much wider social conflicts in the managers' narratives. Understanding the different and competing wider scale social changes was also one of the expressed needs of our participants. They wanted to understand *why* they were being asked to make the changes. The study findings did translate into a management education follow-up programme to meet that need; more will be said about that in the conclusions.

The importance of understanding meaning to participants in situations of leadership and/or organisational change is illustrated by Burgoyne et al. (1997) and Blackler et al. (1999) and they both suggest that without that understanding, agreement on what activities to engage in is difficult to achieve. In both these studies we get fragments of understanding of what it means to be in the midst of healthcare change but much is left unsaid especially in the areas of resistance to and the ethics of change. Therefore, this study begins with an interest in what it means to managers to be in the midst of change and attempts to convey, through managers' narratives, a broader landscape of meaning that includes these two aspects.

In conclusion, despite the amount of significant reform going on in the healthcare sector and many other public and private sector organisations, the body of structural functionalist literature offered to date does not 'hit the mark' especially for many practitioners (Cameron et al. 2001). The difficulty in hitting the mark is not so surprising, partly because of the dominance of mechanical conceptions of change but also because the knowledge requested seems to be of the tacit kind (Polyani 1966) and is therefore inherently difficult to collate and convey. What seems to be missing is case study material that takes a discursive approach, offering accounts from practitioners' perspectives and one that draws out what is normally concealed. Two related aspects, resistance and ethics, have been given limited attention to date. To understand more about what change means to practitioners in these areas would therefore offer a contribution to knowledge on organisational change, to the trusts concerned that are keen to support their staff in the midst of change, and finally to the practitioners themselves who are calling for candid accounts of change rather than theoretical prescriptions or guidelines. Finally, from a methodological perspective, exploring the power of discursive approaches such as narrative in order to add to understanding of organisational change would also be of value. In the next section I review some of the studies of relevance to this book that have used such an approach.

3.3 Narrative and organisational change

Following social construction theory (Berger & Luckmann 1967; Weick 1979) and Ricoeur's[3] trilogy on time and narrative (1983–5) organisational studies have become increasingly sensitive to narrative and stories (White 1981; Wilkins 1983; Boje 1995; Czarniawska 1997; Gabriel 2000). A subset of that genre contends that narrative approaches are an appropriate means to study organisational change (Skoldberg 1994; Czarniawska 1997; O'Connor 2000; Currie & Brown 2003). Skoldberg (1994) takes up the concept of trope to show that during periods of change different story modes combine to produce certain organisational effects. For instance, he suggests that comic and tragic stories combine to produce 'satirical disengagement' of the workforce. Czarniawska (1997) explores the literary forms of serial, stories and themes to disclose the paradoxical nature of organisational change, for example we follow routines in order to change. In the 'Drama of Institutional Identity' she suggests that by confronting such paradoxes we bring crisis to institutions which enable them to change. According to O'Connor (2000) 'embedded narrative' offers a way of linking particular texts to the larger text in which it is embedded. Currie and Brown (2003), researching in a healthcare context, argues that narratives are significant vehicles for the expression of political activity and one means by which ideas and practices are legitimised, especially during change.

In their search for an organisational behaviour, effect, interpretation, explanation, theory or cultural metaphor, what seems to be missing is a focus on the multiplicity of stories that are told by organisational participants and what that multiplicity constructs in terms of meanings of organisation change to the actors. Additionally, what managers construct as needs to support them in the midst of change is also missing. More recent narrative studies of organisations and organisational change (Anderson 2003; Brown et al. 2005; Bryant & Cox 2004; Collins & Rainwater 2005) do consider multiplicity. These studies show that organisational change in a narrative perspective is polyphonic and organisations are flooded with dialogues (Boje 1991a; Hazen 1993; Jabri 2004; Oswick et al. 2005; Tsoukas 2005). Pedersen (2006) suggests that to learn more about the consequences of these interactions, new studies of stories about change must elucidate the contextual interaction of these many voices. She goes on to analyse employees stories of change in a hospital ward, first in order to understand change from their perspective and second is to understand how this results in new organisational stories. Her conclusion is that for example epic stories of change do not always construct further epic stories. They are more likely to construct tragic stories of change.

One perspective on change from a narrative perspective requires that change be seen as story-driven. Collins and Rainwater argue that stories create organisational meaning and organisational realities (Collins & Rainwater 2005: 20). To take this argument further, stories create change in the social reality to participants and therefore to the organisation. Downing (1997) analyses organisational change based on the stories of managers and employees about it. He analyses the plots of the stories and how these function as guidelines for the characters when making sense of change (Downing 1997: 230). Downing argues that the typologies of plots enable the organisational members to make sense of change via social dramas. He draws inspiration from Turner (1957) who describes how radical organisational change results in social dramas that can be characterised in terms of the emotional and interpretational conflicts that they arouse. In relation to change, the task of management is, according to Downing, to manage and solve the conflicts caused by change stories. So we return to managers playing a crucial role in managing conflict and resistance but as yet the nature of those 'emotional and interpretational' conflicts are yet to be elucidated and it could be argued that until they are the conflicts will persist despite best efforts by managers to resolve. This study suggests a different approach, which is to understand the conflicts in terms of the virtues conveyed in the narrative enactments rather than 'solve' them. MacIntyre suggests that some of the conflicts are irresolvable since the 'sides' are rooted in different moral traditions, built on different premises, presenting perfectly reasonable but incompatible rational arguments. For MacIntyre, unless the virtue conflicts carried in the narratives are built on the same moral premise then they will be irresolvable. Does this offer insight as to why change programmes rarely achieve their intended outcomes? This suggestion will be examined further from the perspective of resistance and ethics as the story of this book unfolds.

In conclusion this chapter argues that two dominant perspectives on organisational change exist. First is the Lewin-based (1952) concept of moving the organisation from one phase to another at varying speeds by managing and influencing a set of qualitative factors. In this view change is a result of strategic behaviour, the outcome of which is stable structures, routines and rationality. Second is the view that change is socially constructed and that meanings are negotiated, intertextual, multivoiced and alternative. Within this perspective a narrative approach to change requires that change be seen as an evolving set of stories and that stories carry meaning, constructing and describing the social reality to participants. It is argued that change viewed from this latter perspective can offer fresh insights into change related issues and in this case to what it means to managers to implementing government-driven healthcare reform. This is manifestly very different to the structural functional assumptions. Studies on healthcare organisations have used both these perspectives. The structural perspective has highlighted a strong theme associated with the importance of key people leading change. Social constructionist approaches have highlighted tensions, frictions and conflicts in that role. A narrative-based study, it is argued, provides the opportunity to gain a deeper understanding of those conflicts and to draw out fresh insights.

Chapter 4 explores the 'narrative turn' in social sciences. The chapter reviews the work of many writers who contributed to the narrative turn, developed the narrative approach and features one writer in particular, Alasdair MacIntyre (1985), who in writing from a moral philosophical perspective has influenced recent thinking on narrative and organisational studies (for example, Moore & Beadle 2006). MacIntyre's virtues-goods-practices-institution schema is explained in terms of how it has the potential to illuminate the ethical dimension of change, develop further understanding of the cynicism and resistance associated with the style of implementing change and questions appropriateness particularly to the public sector. It also describes how this perspective can illustrates the needs of practitioners in the midst of change.

4
Turning to Narrative

The purpose of this chapter is twofold. First, it will examine the period leading up to the 'narrative turn'[1] and the debates which have emerged in the context of organisational change following the uptake of narrative as a device for studying organisations. Second, through an examination of the narrative-based virtue ethics concepts of MacIntyre it will identify areas where this study can make a contribution. In Chapter 3, we saw how there has been some exploration of organisational change using narrative and that this methodology has revealed that narrative and stories construct meaning and social reality to participants. There is also an acceptance that a multiplicity of stories, polyphony, is observed when narrative approaches are employed. When change is happening further stories are enacted which offer insight into what change means to organisational actors. The nature of those stories with regard to what they construct into the unfolding and changing social reality has been viewed from dramatic (Czarniawska 1997) and emotional and interpretational (Downing 1997) perspectives but as yet the moral perspective of narrative-organisational change has received little if any attention. Even a recent upsurge of interest in studying the morality of the management of organisations from Weberian (e.g. Watson 2003; Dyck & Weber 2006) and MacIntyrian (e.g. Moore & Beadle 2006) perspectives has only made passing reference to organisational change. What this upsurge has done, however, is to highlight the opportunity of illuminating narratives of an institution in change with MacIntyre's brand of virtue ethics and to ask what kind of morality is socially constructed in the reform of the healthcare sector. Is it the morality intended by the reform of public services? As we saw in Chapter 3, writers have referred to conflict, tensions, identity fragmentation and old versus new in narratives from managers in the midst of public-sector changes. I argue that uncharted territory lies in understanding the ethical nature of these conflicts as enacted narratives and what they in their multiplicity unfold into the morality of the institution.

This chapter follows the growing argument for narrative being an important device for developing a deeper understanding of the social reality to organisational actors and makes the case for it being a suitable approach to expand theory of public-sector organisational change. The chapter describes the work of many writers who contributed to the 'narrative turn' and features one writer in particular, Alasdair MacIntyre (1985), who in writing from a moral philosophical perspective has influenced recent thinking on narrative approaches and organisational studies in general (Czarniawska 2004; Moore & Beadle 2006). MacIntyre came to prominence in my study during the analysis of the data. I noticed the prevalence of something I have called 'virtue conflict' enacted in the narratives from practitioners in this study. What MacIntyre's virtues-goods-practices-institution conceptual schema provides is a way to converse with the data from a narrative perspective and at the same time illuminate ethical dilemmas contained within enacted narratives of conflict. This important aspect of organisations and organisational change in the public sector in particular has received little attention to date – Bryman (2006) suggests that understanding the ethical issues is 'critical work' for leaders. MacIntyre's analytical framework takes on more importance as the implications of what MacIntyre argues are understood in the context of the healthcare reform and its aims of equitable, high quality care to a growing number of people in the UK suffering from mental illness.

MacIntyre's virtues-goods-practices-institution schema is explained in terms of how it has the potential to illuminate ethical confusion, and the subsequent construction of cynicism towards change. This enables further understanding of the difficulties in implementing change, particularly in the public sector and contributes a potential avenue of management education.

This review is in three main sections. The first section starts well before the 'narrative turn' begins to address the 'linguistic turn'[2]. The reason for tracing back to this earlier turn is that some of the key concepts in this earlier movement are relevant to recent organisational studies from which this study draws inspiration. In the second section I cover the 'narrative turn' and some of the subsequent narrative studies that have focussed on organisational change that are relevant to my book. In the third section I describe MacIntyre's contribution in some detail and the key concepts that are important to this book.

4.1 'Literary studies' turn

Considering that narratives have been recorded and analysed in print for millennia – for example, the Bible, Talmud, Koran – and before that were orally handed down through countless generations it is surprising to find that interest in the narrative in the social sciences has a very recent history. The 'narrative turn' in social sciences is generally recognised as occurring around the late 1970s and early 1980s (Czarniawska 1997, 2004; Rhodes & Brown 2005). Earlier recognition of a 'literary studies turn' goes to the Russian Formalists who were constructing their ideas from the 1910s to the 1930s. One of the later formalists, Vladimir Propp, produced *The Morphology of the Folktale* (1928) providing one of the defining studies of the genre. Propp searches for the underlying structure of Russian folktales. Propp argued on the side of Marxism that folklore is fundamentally the genre of the working classes. For Propp folklore (stories, songs, ballads, stories, jokes, and so forth) expresses underlying feelings of discontent against oppression, exploitation and social injustice. Since then Western folklorists have contested this with the view that any group even the so-called dominant social classes may express protest and it does not necessarily have to be about counter-culture (Dundes 1980). It may, according to Dundes, be about conscious or unconscious (in the Freudian sense) shared fantasies. Gabriel (2000) develops Dundes' ideas to make a case for *fantasy* being the 'chief force' of the *unmanaged organisation*. Gabriel's idea is that fantasy offers a symbolic refashioning of official organisational practices in the interests of pleasure rather than oppression. In my study we see a group of managers creating a pantomime that was performed at Omega's social club and others choosing a comic form of narrative both for pleasure and in order to poke fun at new organisational practices that they feel run against their sense of what is right.

Summarising the contribution of the Russian formalists highlights their interest in the text as opposed to what the text was saying or the content (O'Toole & Shukman 1978). These contributions include:

- Placing the study of the actual work at the centre of literary scholarship, rather than looking for authorial biographical links or sociological influences
- Problematising the idea of 'literariness', and addressing the 'form' versus 'content' issue
- Viewing literary history and the evolution of literary genres as an internal dynamic process

- Contributing a wealth of analytical techniques to stylistic analysis, including sound patterns, metres and verse forms
- Providing analytical techniques for characterising a range of discursive styles and different modes of storytelling

What all of the above have in common and contrary to traditional hermeneutics[3] is an interest in text as such, not in the author's intentions or the circumstances of production. These contributions are especially relevant to the first stage and second stage in my analysis. The first stage was inspired by Czarniawska (1997) and the second by Gabriel (2000) who both refer to Propp (1928). The first stage was to categorise the narratives in terms of the literary genres of story, serial and theme and the second was to categorise the stories into different modes of storytelling.

Mikhail Bakhtin was influenced by if not directly linked with the Russian Formalists. He developed the concepts of polyphony and dialogism as alternatives to the univocality of literary texts and they represent part of his challenge to traditional monological relations between author and heroes in novelistic writing. When viewed as dialogic, narrative becomes an intersection of different accents and voices, which are fundamentally ambivalent in taking on meaning in relation to each other rather than to some absolute point of reference. The polyphonic principle keeps those voices as valued and authoritative as that of the writer. Bakhtin's ideas on novels in particular and language in general call for a world that is inhabited by different voices, differing vocabularies, and disparate dialects, which produce multiple stories of that world. What is important then is not single voices, but the relations between them. His contributions to the notion of dialogism and the notion of *voice* in literary discourse emerged contemporaneously with considerations of sound and rhythmic elements in Formalist analyses. Bakhtin and Medvedev proposed a sociology of poetics that asks the following questions:

> What is the literary work? What is its structure? What are the elements of the structure and what are their artistic functions? What is genre, style, plot, theme motif, hero, meter, rhythm, melody, etc.? All these questions and, in particular, the question of the reflection of the ideological horizon in the content of the work and of the functions of this reflection in the whole structure are within the sphere of sociological poetics. (Bakhtin & Medvedev 1928/1978: 30)

Bakhtin builds on the Russian formalists with multivocality, interest in the ideological horizons reflected within the narrative and the sociology of the storytelling. All these contributions are relevant to this study. First, the many voices of the managers and their different stories are included and form a valuable part of the analysis. Second, like Blackler et al. (1999), the study recognises the importance of discussing what implementing changes means in the broader context of wider scale social changes. According to Passmore (1962) John Anderson, the Australian philosopher, urges us not to ask of a social institution 'What end or purpose does it serve?' but rather 'Of what conflicts is it the scene?' The individual and the meaning of individual action are framed by the wider culture in which the action takes place (Benton & Craib 2001: 106). In this research access to the ideologies driving wider social change is through the virtue conflict narratives in a similar way to that demonstrated by Meyer (1995) who accessed values[4] through stories and narrative of organisations. His finding was that narrative provides an ideal medium for understanding the values at stake. The emerging narratives from the participants are questioned in a similar way to that proposed by Bakhtin. The ideological horizons reflected in the scenes depicted in the narratives of our managers are of particular interest. As we shall see in the analysis, many of the managers construct a moral battle, clash or disjuncture in their narratives of change which, it is argued, reflect much wider ideological battles. In many cases, what they say is worthy of defending is pitted against what 'modernisation' says is worthy of defending. The outcome as exhibited, rather than explained, in the narrative ordering of the scenes varies and ranges from heroic success to tragic failure. Finally, to help further the understanding of what change means to managers this study uses an enquiry style appreciative of Bakhtin's sociological poetics and is particularly inspired by the more recent work of Cunliffe (2002) who calls her approach 'social poetics[5]'.

According to Bakhtin (1986), *carnival* is the concept in which distinct individual voices are heard, flourish, and interact together. The carnival was Bakhtin's way of describing Dostoevsky's[6] polyphonic novel style: each individual character is strongly defined, and at the same time the reader witnesses the critical influence of each character upon the other. That is, the voices of others are heard by each individual, and each inescapably shapes the character of the other. In this study the polyphonic nature of the managers' voices is explored in Chapters 6 to 9 and their shaping of each other and the constructing effects on the social reality as a whole is examined.

Having painted some of the backdrop of Russian formalism and the work of Bakhtin I now travel forward to the 20-year period before the 'narrative turn' in social sciences began (around the early 1980s) and introduce some of the influential writers that according to Czarniawska (2004) shaped the turn to narrative. I also identify where they influence my study and where this study can make a contribution.

4.2   The narrative turn

The main purpose of this section is twofold: first, to review the work of key contributors to the narrative turn; and second, to provide a lead into the work of MacIntyre, a writer dedicated to issues of moral philosophy. According to Czarniawska (1997: 11) MacIntyre offered 'One of the important attempts to extend the use of the notion of narrative beyond literature'. She explains her view on the relationship between the narrative-based moral philosophy of MacIntyre and organisational studies of the public sector.

> A moral philosophy, as MacIntyre is the first to point out assumes a sociology, or theory of social life (and vice versa). Any contemporary sociology, on the other hand, must take organisations into account (Perrow 1991). Consequently, business management and public administration play an important role in MacIntyre's reasoning, which in turn makes his theory highly relevant to organisational theory.

MacIntyre, who wrote his mid-career thesis, *After Virtue*, in the late 1970s, brings together views on narrative, practice, unity, meaning and purpose and offers a 'virtue ethics' perspective to social life. For MacIntyre, 'practice is the arena in which virtues are exhibited and receive their primary definition' (1985: 187). His view of humans as storytelling animals leads him to argue that narrative is the 'basic and essential genre for the characterisation of human action'. Actions are only understandable when considered within their intentional and contextualised setting. Intentions when contextually and temporally ordered create narrative. MacIntyre provides the example of a man gardening who might be digging, taking exercise or pleasing his wife. Each narrative is situated in a particular context such as the narrative of his health or his marriage. Thus there is a *telos* or a sense of future goals or ends within particular narratives.

Narrative is also relevant to MacIntyre's ideas about 'internal goods'. For him there are two types of internal goods: goods of excellence and goods of a certain type of life. According to MacIntyre only by the exercise of virtues are internal goods of practice available to us. An internal good in general is an intrinsic good, something that is valued for itself without respect to other ends. MacIntyre sets internal goods in opposition to external goods which he describes as money, status or power. For MacIntyre a communal narrative in the form of a moral tradition exists where individual narratives mesh with each other to describe the virtues of practice that contribute to the overall *telos* of the institution. In that meshing we can make sense of our lives or nonsense.

For Barthes what runs through all life, 'caring for nothing', is narrative and in one of the most quoted excerpts from his 'Introduction to the Structural Analysis of the Narrative' (1977) he states:

> Narrative is present in every age, in every society; it begins with the history of mankind and there nowhere is or nor has been people without narrative. All classes, all human groups, have their narratives…Caring for nothing for the division between good and bad literature, narrative is international, transhistorical, transcultural; it is simply there, like life itself. (Barthes 1977: 79)

Another French philosopher concerned with identity and narrative is Paul Ricoeur. His *Time and Narrative* trilogy (1983–5) marked a further turn towards the recognition of the importance of narrative. Ricoeur called the mediating between time and narrative the threefold moments of mimesis: mimesis 1, mimesis 2 and mimesis 3. Mimesis 2 is a mediating function between mimesis 1 and mimesis 3 (1984 1:53). Briefly, mimesis 1 is the raw story prior to emplotment, similar to antenarrative (Boje 2001), mimesis 2 is the emplotment of the narrative, and mimesis 3 is characterised as the restoration of narrative to the time of action and of suffering Ricoeur (1984: Vol 1, 70). In other words, mimesis 3 is the movement to action, based on what was heard or read by the listener. Ricoeur's startling conclusion that we entrust human time to narrative and in doing so we entrust our identity over time to narrative was challenging to the notion of identity. Ricoeur's position on self-identity is that narrative mediates between the two poles of *ipse* (selfhood) and *idem* (character) and is a means for us to define a position between the two poles that asserts 'Here I am'. From that place, we have a model for action that allows other people to count on us and therefore identify us. For those who do not settle on a narrative that describes their position and offers a sense of an ending (Kermode 1967) then low self-esteem or self-hatred could, according to Ricoeur be the outcome. Such is the importance of narrative in our lives for Ricoeur. This book does not explore the notion of narrative identity but some of the managers' narratives, referring as they do to numerous dilemmas about what is the right course of action given competing virtues, do have some resonance with this theory and I have explored that resonance in a separate paper (Conroy 2005).

The two powerful voices of Ricoeur (1983–1985) and MacIntyre (1985) came just after Lyotard's report (1979) to the Conseil des Universities of the government of Quebec on the irony and paradox of scientific knowledge. His argument was that science relies on narrative for its claims yet does not recognise the importance of narrative knowledge. According to Czarniawska (2004: 7) after this report 'the grand narratives of science lost their privileged status and both science and narrative came back into the light of scrutiny'.

Bruner (1986) takes up the scrutiny and compared the narrative mode of knowing with the logo-scientific mode of knowing. According to Bruner, the narrative mode consists of organising experience with the help of a scheme, a plot, that assumes the intentionality of human action.

Polkinghorne (1988) followed Bruner in exploring narrative and argued:

> Human beings exist in three realms – the material realm, the organic realm and the realm of meaning. The realm of meaning is structured according to linguistic forms, and one of the most important forms for creating meaning in human existence is the narrative. The narrative attends to the temporal dimension of human existence and configures events into a unity. The events become meaningful in relation to the theme or point of the narrative. Narratives organise events into wholes that have beginnings, middles and ends.

Also (ibid.: 150):

> We achieve our personal identities and self-concept through use of the narrative configuration and make our existence into a whole by understanding it as a single unfolding and developing story. We are in the middle of our stories and cannot be sure how they will end; we are constantly having to revise the plot as new events are added to our lives. Self then is not a static thing or substance, but a configuring of personal events into a historical unit which includes not only what has been but also anticipation of what one will be

A little later, Bruner (1991) credited Polkinghorne with capturing the current state of play and pointed out that that the strength of narrative lies in its indifference to extralinguistic reality (ibid.: 44). In narrative, the sequence (temporal ordering of events rather than whether the story is true or false) determines the plot and thus the power of the narrative as a story. For me, this is the power of the social reality constructing influence of the narrative and just as MacIntyre argues that virtues are carried in the communal set of narratives that flow in that society then so can a society or an institution be filled with non-virtuous constructions. For this study I am primarily interested in narrative's role in the context of a healthcare institution in change but I also recognise the crucible of society and history. The central intention of this book is to understand through their narratives what it means to managers to be implementing organisational change. Czarniawska (1997: 14) suggests that

> By observing how conversations are repeated and how they change we can classify them according to their genre, as in literary critique. In order to do this we have to see participants as actors in their dramatised stories. They are authors, directors and producers. In other words, conversations in particular and human action in general are enacted narratives.
>
> ... it is most important to note that a common way of understanding human action is by placing it in a narrative, that is a narrative of an individual history which in turn must be placed in a narrative of social history or in a history of the narrative.

She goes on to argue that in order to understand our own lives and the lives of other people we put them into a narrative form and therefore every action acquires *meaning* by acquiring a place in a narrative of life narrative – a narrative of identity. One criticism of this type of constructivism is that it conceives of the world as a collection of subjectively concocted stories. In every conversation including participant-researcher there is a positioning (Davies & Harre 1991). It is recognised here that we are rarely the sole authors of our narratives and that a positioning takes place in any conversation or meeting between groups of people that may alter the narrative.

Czarniawska suggests that in addition to positioning altering narrative, we sometimes live within a narrative that someone else has concocted for us, without including us in any conversation. Jobs, where we live, our identities, can all be decided by those with power to do so. This has recently become true for the managers in this study who were told that their organisation, Omega, would no longer exist in its present form but that it would be split into four and the four parts would be joined with other organisations. As Czarniawska points out this is what power is about.

4.2.1 Narrative genres

For Czarniawska it makes sense for interpretive purposes to speak of a dominant narrative genre at any one time. She suggests that the novel is regarded as the most characteristic genre of modern times and new genres such as biographies and autobiographies are a consequence of the 'modern institution' of personal identity. Bruss (1976: 5) argues that 'a literary institution must reflect and give focus to some consistent need for and sense of possibility in the community it serves, but at the same time, a genre helps to define what is possible and the appropriate means for meeting that expressive need'.

The genre of the soap opera is used by Czarniawska to meet the 'expressive need' of conveying meaning in terms of what it feels like to be part of the never-ending serial of changes in the Swedish public sector she investigates. Czarniawska adds instrumental (to make something happen) needs to the expressive needs and says that organisational theory and practice can be seen as special genres of narratives situated within other narratives. In this study the managers' expressed needs are both expressive and instrumental in terms of the narratives they author in the study. The expressive and instrumental needs arose from a continued dialogue with the managers at Omega. That continued dialogue was made possible by not making any interpretation until much later in the study. According to Czarniawska by not restricting itself to one interpretation or prediction the study can continue the dialogue with the organisation without labelling it or its current condition. Czarniawska (1998: 17) states:

> By relinquishing some aspirations to power through the claim of factuality and one-to-one correspondence of theory and the world, organisation studies can open their texts for negotiation and thus enter in a dialogical relationship with organisational practice.

Negotiation with practice before theorising is a feature of this study and the stories in particular proved to be conducive for that negotiation. The negotiation in this case was about meaning and needs. By creating a dialogical relationship with focus groups the meaning to the cohort of managers at Omega along with their needs increased its credibility. By not interpreting it gave me the opportunity to continue the dialogue and allow the managers to interpret and decide on the course of action or more accurately their instrumental expressed needs.

Having discussed the conversation between the findings and wider groups of managers I now discuss the notion of conversing between the findings and theories such as MacIntyre's.

4.2.2 Conversing with theory

According to Czarniawska (1997) when a human event is said to not make sense, it is usually not because a person is unable to place it in the proper category. The difficulty instead comes from a person's inability to integrate the event into a plot whereby it becomes understandable in the context of what has happened. So in the conclusions I can talk about *exhibited* explanations from the narrators, and follow that explanation to what they say they need, but in the narrative mode I cannot talk about predictability or laws or demonstration of theories What can be done, however, is to mediate a conversation between the data and theories such as MacIntyre's that are based on a narrative understanding of the world.

Czarniawska goes so far as to claim

> The main fount of organisational knowledge is the narrative.... In all their different versions, organisational stories capture organisational life in a way that no compilation of facts ever can; this is because they are carriers of life itself, not just reports on it. (ibid.: 21)

Following up on this claim, the questions for me are: What is the nature of the life they are carrying? What does it mean to managers to be implementing government-driven reform? What are the narratives doing? What social reality are the managers' narratives constructing? The way I bring the narratives together in Chapters 69 offers a sample of the social reality (Czarniawska 2004: 49) for managers in the organisation under study. The analysis contained therein addresses these questions.

Before moving on to elaborate further on MacIntyre and my methodology I include now some of the critiques of the narrative view of social life.

4.2.3 Critiques of the narrative turn

I introduce here some of the broad-based critiques of the narrative turn – that is, a turn to using narrative as a way to understand the social world – and then in Chapter 5, I explore some of the methodological implications along with the counter strategies I employ to increase the robustness of the research design.

Rhodes and Brown (2005: 181) suggest that one of the strongest critiques comes from Habermas (1992). He warns about the consequences of 'turning science and philosophy into literature'. Rhodes and Brown explain that 'In response to what he sees as post-structuralism's concerted effort to blur, or even obliterate genre boundaries, Habermas maintains that the traditional demarcation between science and narrative/literature is still important'. The implication of Habermas' argument for this book comes down to a consideration of how we might understand the nature of that which I have investigated. The status of the narratives in this study is that they are 'poetic elaborations on the truth' (Gabriel 2000) and they bring the social reality or inter-subjective reality alive, rather than any kind of 'scientific reality'.

Rhodes and Brown (2005) also mention the broadside from critical realist philosophy which emerged out of the work of Bhaskar (1978, 1989). They state that 'Critical realism offers a critique of positivism that is quite different from that of the narrative mode. Critical realism believes in the fallibility of realist explanations about the world and is critical of positivist theories that lay claim to coincidence with the real world'. Critical realism does believe in 'causal powers' that have an effect in the social world and that those powers can be defined.

There is insufficient capacity in this book to explore the tensions between narrative, realism and critical realism in any depth. A considerable amount of academic capital has been invested in all these positions and I include some mention to acknowledge that the contestation continues. However, there is now a growing body of literature that has established narrative as a powerful and useful interpretive lens. My position is that narrative offers valuable insights to organisational change that can add to those already established through positivist, realist or critical realist perspectives. Like Rhodes and Brown (2005) I recognise that narrative has its limitations and this book acknowledges those whilst emphasising its strengths. What are those strengths? According to Czarniawska and Gagliardi (2003: 20)

> Narrative can provide a different, and valuable, form of knowledge that enables researchers to engage with the lived realities of organisational life – the 'truth' that people at work live through every day. This is not a knowledge that aspires to certainty and control but rather emerges from a reflection on the messy realities of organisational practice. It is this embodied and lived knowledge

that narrative methods enable researchers to access and engage with while embracing scholarly values.

Czarniawska (1997) argues that as organisational theorists we cannot lay claim to coincidence with theory but we can mediate a conversation between our texts from the field and other texts that lay a claim to be saying something about the world and in doing so create a new and helpful text about the social world. This is the way I see it and like Czarniawska I believe that we can contribute, through narrative, to the ongoing conversation about the world that started in the primal forests.

This research is not trying to predict or control but to gain a deeper understanding of the messy, lived social realities of what it means to the participants to be implementing organisational change. In this respect the study responds to Rhodes and Brown (2005) when they argue that:

> The issue for organisation theory is that, while the value and productivity of narrative knowledge has been demonstrated time and time again, this has been accomplished despite the dominance of positivistic (natural scientific) schema. If we who study organisations are to take the lives of others seriously and sympathetically – as a means to understand rather than to control, to accept ambiguity rather than demand certainty, and to engage with lived experience rather than to abstract from it – then the turn to narrative needs to be continued.

Having covered some of the history of the narrative approach, current debates and the positioning of this study in those debates I will now discuss some of the narrative-based organisational studies, focus on those that theorise organisational change and show where this study, with the help of MacIntyre's concepts, can make a contribution.

4.3   Narrative-based organisational studies

In this section I introduce organisational studies that have used narrative approaches and then I focus on organisational change studies in particular that have a bearing on this book. I start with early examples such as Mitroff and Kilmann's (1975) landmark study and work through to emergent research such as Pedersen (2006) and show how my study relates theoretically to theirs. Much of the recent narrative literature is reviewed by Rhodes and Brown (2005). Their aim is to evaluate the

contribution of narrative literature to the understanding of organisations and processes of organizing. Their detailed and thorough evaluation indicates the importance of the narrative mode to organisational
studies. Their assessment in the area of organisation change/ learning
is of particular interest to this study and the following draws heavily on
their insights.

Early examples of the use of narrative approaches to inform research
methodology in management and organisation studies can be found
in higher education (Clark 1972; Mitroff & Kilmann 1975). The latter
pair argue that narrative is under-utilised for organisational research
and broke with traditional research methods to gather short stories written by managers. As in this study, Mitroff and Kilmann were
interested in meaning to managers and in particular what the organisation means to them. Their analysis was based on a Jungian personality typology and according to them gave access to unconscious/
projective images of what the organisation meant to them. My study
claims that stories do convey meaning to the participants but does not
attempt a psychological/ personality analysis. Instead it is interested
in what the stories unfold into the social reality of the organisation
in change. That there are a multitude of stories that can be told about
any event presents a challenge to narrative research and one that I will
now briefly address before moving to discuss narrative-based studies of
organisational change.

The notion of polyphony (Bakhtin 1986) was raised in Chapter 3.
For my study polyphony presents the challenge of including different
stories told in organisations in a way that respects their multiplicity
but that does not combine into a single account or story from the field
that is really about the researcher rather than the researched. Rhodes
and Brown (2005: 180) highlight this issue and encourage researchers
to acknowledge that 'they too are telling a story and selecting which
stories are told'. I am selecting certain stories and narratives to build
as full a picture as possible of the social reality of healthcare reform
to managers. Even prior to this I as the interviewer respond with all
my history to the interviewees and recognise there will be an element
of me influencing their meaning-making despite all my attempts to
remain as neutral as possible. To ensure that I do not stray too far from
their meanings I arranged for the narratives I selected to be fed back to
focus groups of 70 local and 50 regional managers respectively to check
resonance with their social reality. According to Rhodes and Brown
(2005: 179) by being explicit about narrative in this way 'enables the
localities of practice to be examined in terms of their complexity,

contradictions and multivocity'. Further they suggest that 'it is in these ways that narrative offers the possibility of retreating from abstraction in a way that engages with the experiences of work, management and organizing'.

The next section privileges organisational change studies that have built on the groundwork of some of the people mentioned above who at the time were making a radical departure from scientific approaches.

4.4 Narrative studies of organisational change

Themes of interest to this study that have emerged from narrative-based studies of organisational change are examined in this section. They broadly fall into two categories: managing change and understanding change. It is the latter that is of interest to my study. Within the category of understanding change I briefly review literature that addresses meanings, learning and practice and multiple meanings as a lead in to framing the gap in theorising narratives of change from a moral perspective. Much of the following has been drawn and adapted from Rhodes and Brown (2005) and Pedersen (2006) who together cover much of the recent literature on narrative approaches to studying organisational change.

4.4.1 Managing change

As in the generic literature of organisational change we see a subset of the literature focussed on supporting practitioners using narrative and stories to manage change in culture. According to Rhodes and Brown (2005: 173) 'the major focus of this literature is focussed on how stories are a way of managing change in organisational culture'. However, they note that some theorists have argued the reverse – that is, organisational changes are often constituted by changes in the narratives that participants author (Ford 1999; Brown & Humphreys 2003). The application of narrative as a device to manage cultural change is not an interest of this study but I wish to acknowledge that it exists and draw out one particular aspect that relates to my study. That aspect is the notion that organisational values are encapsulated and entrenched in stories of change. Meyer (1995) suggests that stories achieve change by encapsulating and entrenching organisational values. I build on the notion of value encapsulated in stories with the view that virtue, the ethical cousin of value, can also be encapsulated and transmitted in stories and narrative in the way described by MacIntyre (1985). However I side with and maintain an interest in the notion that changes are constituted by changes in the narratives that participants author rather than stories as a viable means to manage change.

The notion that narratives can, like other structurally theorised mechanisms, support the management of change has been criticised. For example, Watson (1982) criticises this notion as part of the limited conceptualisation of organisation as a system and part of a politics that serves managerial ideology[7]. My view accords with Donald Anderson (2005): many ideologies embedded within multiple narratives intersect and compete in the organisation in change. Capturing the complexity and detail of change that lead to greater understanding of change is of interest to this book. By doing this the intention is to seed the development of additions to theories of organisational change. Meaning to participants in the midst of change was the starting point for my enquiry; I examine some of the debates associated with this aspect in the next section.

4.5   Understanding change

4.5.1   Meaning of change

A key interest of this book is to understand which particular meanings ascribed to organisational change become dominant in the intersubjective reality of the participants. Rhodes and Brown (2005: 173) claim that narrative approaches have contributed to understanding how particular meanings become dominant (Rhodes 2001). Some have suggested that stories encourage people to reformulate meanings (, McConkie & Boss 1994; Kaye 1995). Rhodes and Brown (2005) further note that 'stories that circulate culturally across organisations have been seen to provide accepted scripts through which to understand the dynamics of different organisational cultures (Martin et al. 1983). During change efforts, these collective stories can act as a means of social control that prescribe or reinforce managerially preferred behaviours and values (McConkie & Wayne 1986).

In order to appreciate more of the meanings that exist within organisations Boje (2001) makes a case for researchers to include antenarrative as a way to 'resituate and rebalance the great divide and marginalisation between narrative and story'. Boje encourages the researcher to think not just about narrative in its multiplicity but antenarrative, the story that comes before narrative, before plot and coherence are added. In his view narrative is post story. I agree with Boje and my study does respond to the call for multiple narrative perspectives and is inclusive of antenarrative as well as 'post storied' narratives. It does so by applying a triad of narrative analyses on the data to form a collection of catego-rised stories of change, a serial of change and a set of change themes. These are then put into a dialogue with narrative-based theories to pro-duce a new understanding of public-sector organisational change. More will be said on this 'synthesised' narrative approach in the methodol-ogy section.

Rhodes and Brown (2005) say that multiple narratives have been shown to stand in opposition to managerial monologues, Aaltio-Marjosola, I. (1994). For example, subversive and reactive narratives that emerge in response to unitary value narratives have been docu-mented by Kunda (1992) and Turnbull (2000). Their findings have reso-nance with the tactics of Svejk, the fictional good soldier created by Hasek (1973), who resists the discipline of the Austro-Hungarian Army through subtle forms of subversion that were invariably invisible to his superiors. Fleming and Sewell (2002) suggest Svejkian tactics in the workplace might help to 'undermine or dissolve power relationships in practical ways that also help to "unmask" the ideological absurdities that shore them up.' My research builds on this notion of opposition or resistance by understanding more about the nature and variety of opposition, the ideologies at stake and what the narrative enactments contribute to the social construction of reality for participants.

Introducing voices of those who were previously unheard in organisa-tional dialogues has also been a feature of some studies (Boje 1991; Humphreys & Brown 2002). I also take an interest in these types of narratives and indeed voices are revealed that were hidden from the normal channels of communication at Omega. Some of them in nar-rative form but others in their antenarrative form. Rhodes and Brown (2005: 173) note that people in organisations 'construct their own nar-ratives about change that are inconsistent with those storylines cen-trally promulgated' (Rhodes 2000; Vaara 2002). They go on to suggest that the meanings attached to change are not fixed or determined, but rather that people are reflexively engaged in developing their own interpretations of, and reactions to, change. This research supports their view and through a longitudinal study attempts to convey the develop-ing interpretations and meanings of change to participants. What is of interest to this research is that given this phenomenon, what are the constructing effects of such widely differing stories, interpretations and meanings? My interest is to understand what the different stories say (e.g. change opposition, subversion or acquiescence) but further what do the widely differing and developing story versions unfold into the inter-subjective reality of the organisation in change?

I will now examine the notion of multiple and changing meanings in more detail through the existing literature.

4.5.2   Multiple meanings

Some research has been conducted in this area but it is argued that a gap in knowledge exists in the area of understanding what is constructed, other than confusion, when a whole range of change stories exist within an organisation. Brown and Humphreys (2003: 139) suggest that 'change occurs with alterations in the stories that people tell, and it is these stories that demand increased attention from scholars'. Oswick et al. (2005) argue that that organisational change is socially constructed, and that meanings are negotiated, intertextual, multidisciplinary and alternative. Pedersen (2006) suggests that explanation lies in research seeking multiple meanings, stories and perspective instead of focussing on one or two dominating discursive voices in society. Some studies have attempted this (Anderson 2005; Brown & Humphreys 2003; Bryant & Cox 2004; Collins & Rainwater 2005). Rhodes and Brown (2005) suggest that one of the lessons learned from these studies has been that organisational change in a narrative perspective is polyphonic – organisations are flooded with dialogues (Boje 1991; Hazen 1993; Jabri 2004; Oswick et al. 2005; Tsoukas 2005). According to Pedersen (2006) to learn more about the consequences of these interactions, new studies of stories about change must elucidate the contextual interaction of these many voices. My study does find many different stories and narratives and examines one particular context, a serial of change which looks at the interactions relating to the implementation of a multi-agency team formation, within the general context of mental health services reform. Pedersen implies that stories of heroic adventures do not generate new stories of heroes, but rather tragic stories from employees. Her story is about a new initiative in a Danish hospital ward. The initiative is a new type of training programme that had been reported as successful in another hospital and then introduced by a clinical nursing manager. She argues that stories of heroes are individual mythological stories and that this mythic condition explains the distance between management and employees and conflicts and oppression between employees. She illustrates how a good idea led to unintended despair and conflicts between the employees because, she claims, narrations of change must be understood both as individual stories and collective/relational stories. I agree with Pedersen's recommendation and this study does elucidate individual stories of change in Chapter 6 but then moves to collective and relational narrative in Chapters 79 that follow. (As an aside, if the government's 'modernisation' agenda is viewed as an individual mythical heroic story of change then the effect would be to construct conflict and oppression amongst healthcare staff. Some writers (e.g. Hunter 2000) have argued that this *is* the general state amongst staff.)

Downing (1997) analyses organisational change based on the stories of managers and employees about it. He argues that radical organisational change constitutes a social drama which is characterised by emotional and interpretative conflict. Major organisational change generates uncertainty and anxiety about future arrangements and the level of talk and gossip increases dramatically. Downing argues that the sense making activities of actors facing major organisational change are fundamentally no different to the sense making which has taken place in human communities for thousands of years, notably as found in the telling of stories known as myths. Downing's focus is on the framing of emotions and learning in the generic plots of romance, tragedy, melodrama and irony. He analyses the plots of the stories and how these function as guidelines for the characters when making sense of change (Downing 1997: 230). My research follows Downing's initial arguments about high levels of narrative exchange during periods of organisational change and the enactment of change as plots. The kernel of my contribution, however, is in understanding more about narrative as a constructor of the morality of the organisation in change with regard to the virtues at stake and those constructed in the unfolding storytelling milieu (Boje 1995). In relation to change, the task of management is, according to Downing, to manage and solve the conflicts caused by change stories. I agree with Downing (1997) and Brown and Humphreys (2003) that typologies are helpful to understand change and to enable actors to decide how their character will play it. Rather than managing narrative conflicts or elucidating identities, however, I aim to better understand the nature of the conflict within the change stories and what those change stories do. Czarniawska (1997) draws out paradoxes from narratives of change through literary and screenplay metaphors and suggests that by confronting such paradoxes a crisis ensues that enables institutions to change. However, despite drawing heavily on MacIntyre to build a case for narrative 'devices' she does not surface the ethical or virtue conflicts constructed within the narratives or look at what the stories might unfold into the social reality of an organisation in change.

My contribution, therefore, to a narrative-organisational change approach is to offer a new dimension, through a synthesis of narrative analyses, on the different types of ethical conflicts enacted in the narratives of change. Further to understand more about the constructing power of the enacted virtue conflict narratives and particularly the opposition they construct against reform and organisational change.

MacIntyre offers a set of concepts to explore the ethical dimension of narrative organisational change and I now move to an elaboration of his thesis in *After Virtue* so that the reader has a grasp of the central concepts before moving to Chapter 5.

4.6   MacIntyre, narrative and organisational change

This section explores the contribution made by MacIntyre to narrative and the relationship of his work to the moral dilemmas of organisational change enacted in the narratives of the healthcare managers in this study. The reason for profiling MacIntyre's work above other contributors to the 'narrative turn' is that during the analysis of the data I encountered strong resonance between his thesis (1985) and the data. I also believe that in viewing the data through the lens of his ideas, organisation change theory especially in the public-sector context can be enriched. Concepts from his thesis are summarised here and I begin to mediate a conversation between these concepts and the overall messages coming from the data. In the analysis I draw out these concepts further and grow and strengthen the argument that is seeded here.

MacIntyre points out that the chief means of moral education in pre-modern society was the telling of stories in a genre fitting the kind of story being told. In the process of education, or more generally socialisation, individuals were helped to attribute meaning to their lives by relating them to the legitimate narrative of the society to which they belong. Thus the main narrative in heroic states was epic/ saga and in the city genre was tragedy expressing the prevalent stance towards human fate and human community.

MacIntyre claims that medieval cultures first encountered the 'problem' of multiple narratives on a global scale with many ideals, many ways of life and many religions.This raises the question of whether it is possible to construct any shared constructs, whether it is possible to have a conversation without recourse to metanarratives (Czarniawska 1997). MacIntyre emphasises the unpredictability of an enacted dramatic narrative of life and history. Such construction is never finished and in the negotiation of meaning the results are forever uncertain.

Building on MacIntyre, Czarniawska (1997: 15) states:

> The old meta-narratives sinned in their ambition to try to predict the outcome of conversations. If a canon is known, there is nothing to talk about. Narrative structure requires unpredictability and is paradoxically why the alleged failure of human science to predict is in fact their greatest asset namely their failure to formulate laws and consequently to predict. The phenomena they purport to explain that is, human social life fits perfectly to their unpredictable nature.

MacIntyre (1985) argues this failure to predict should be treated as a triumph, as a virtue rather than a vice. As Czarniawska (1997: 15) states, 'unpredictability does not imply inexplicability'. She states that explanations are possible because of a certain kind of circular teleology in all lived narratives. A life is lived with a goal but the most important aspect is the formulation and reformulation of that goal. This circular teleology (goal-directed activity) is what MacIntyre calls a *narrative quest*. According to MacIntyre this is different to a narrative goal in that a goal is known – a quest creates its goal rather than discovering it. According to Czarniawska (1997) this kind of narrative view gets rid of the problem of rational fixed goals by reinstating the role of goals as both the results and the antecedents of organisational action.

MacIntyre was interested in the narrative unity of life from the perspective of it forming our character as moral individuals, part of a practice-based community whose *telos* (purpose) is the living out a set of virtues that bring the good life for all. MacIntyre highlights some 'current' societal debates from the United States of the 1970s and 1980s which have a remarkable resonance with current debates in UK society. One in particular refers to the provision of health care and is highly relevant to this study. MacIntyre use this as an example of a highly influential debate in our society. This is how he describes two sides (a and b) of the debate (1985: 7):

> a) Justice demands that every citizen should enjoy equal opportunities to develop his or her talents. But prerequisites for the provision of such equal opportunity include the provision of equal access to health care and to education. Therefore justice requires the governmental provision of health and education services financed out of taxation, and it also requires that no citizen should be able to buy an unfair share of such services. This in turn requires the abolition of private schools and hospitals.

b) Everybody has a right to incur such and such obligations as he or she wishes, to be free to make such and only such contracts as he or she desires and to determine his or her own free choices. Physicians must therefore be free to practice on such terms as they desire and patients must be free to choose among physicians; teachers must be free to teach on such terms as they choose and pupils and parents to go where they wish for education. Freedom thus requires not only the existence of private practice in medicine ... but also the abolition of those restraints on private practice.

MacIntyre observes that with this debate and others each argument is logically valid or can be easily expanded so as to be made so; the conclusions follow the premises. But the rival premises are such that we possess no rational way of weighing the claims of one against the other. For each premise employs some quite different normative or evaluative concept from the other. In the above example it is the claim of equality matched against liberty. MacIntyre argues that in our society it is because we have no established way of deciding between these claims that our moral argument appears to be endless. Invocation of one premise against another becomes a matter of pure assertion and counter assertion. Hence perhaps the slightly shrill tone of much moral debate he suggests. MacIntyre (1985: 11) moves from highlighting the shrillness of this type of type of debate to challenging us with the assertion that no moral disagreements of this kind in any age past or present can be resolved. MacIntyre offers some genealogy of the debates he presents. He traces T. H. Green and Rousseau competing with Adam Smith as the grandfathers of the above debate. In T. H. Green's case the development of his ideas has to be seen in the context of the historic circumstances given during his lifetime. These were highly unequal socio-economic consequences of the industrial revolution. The drastic economic development was accompanied by poor work and health conditions. Similarly for Rousseau and his famous start to his classic work on political theory *The Social Contract* (published in 1762): 'Man was born free, and he is everywhere in chains'. It is an expression of his belief that we are corrupted by society. The social contract he explores in the book involves people recognising a collective 'general will'. This general will is supposed to represent the common good or public interest – and it is something that each individual has a hand in making. All citizens should participate – and should be committed to the general good – even if it means acting against their private or personal interests. For example, we might support a political party that proposes to tax us heavily (as we have a large income) because we can see the benefit that this taxation can bring to all. To this extent, Rousseau believed that the good individual, or citizen, should not put their private ambitions first.

Adam Smith, in contrast, assumed that consumers choose for the lowest price, and that entrepreneurs choose for the highest rate of profit. He asserted that by thus making their excess or insufficient demand known through market prices, consumers 'directed' entrepreneurs' investment money to the most profitable industry. This is the industry producing the goods most highly valued by consumers, so in general economic wellbeing is increased. In his 1776 book *An Inquiry into the Nature and Causes of the Wealth of Nations* Adam Smith set out the mechanism by which he felt economic society operated. Each individual strives to become wealthy 'intending only his own gain' but to this end he must exchange what he owns or produces with others who sufficiently value what he has to offer; in this way, by division of labour and a free market, public interest is advanced. We see Adam's theory mirrored in the latest policy and change programme to be rolled out in the health sector, 'choice', where in theory people choose which consultant they go to and the money follows that choice. The same theory is being applied to education and the choosing of schools.

These 'grandfathers' have many offspring and I am arguing that in the data, scenes (Passmore 1962) from the ongoing battle involving the offspring are enacted in the narratives from this group of healthcare managers. The theories are expanded here to offer a sense of the different and competing ideologies that can be traced and offer a sense of the much larger political narratives that are reflected and focussed onto the frontline of healthcare in change. I am arguing that this is a neglected area of theorising in organisational change in the public and private sectors where these ideologies are entangled in healthcare delivery and practice. Some managers, as we shall see are able to enact narratives of them personally holding on to their values in the midst of the tangle, presenting an epic and heroic story, whilst others enact tragic, comic or romantic forms that invariably show virtue clashes or disjuncture that results in an unsatisfactory ending to their stories. The virtue clashes exhibit (rather than demonstrate) a link, for some managers, to helplessness and powerlessness. Even if they had the theory and knowledge to understand the battles reflected in their everyday scenarios of change then it could be argued that the managers are not in a position to resolve the clashes. This latter argument is one that MacIntyre puts forward and it has some credence in the data since even the epic, heroic success stories of change are essentially about managers holding on to what they believe is the right thing to do rather than resolving the clashes, for example, going with the flow (with people who come onboard with their ideas), being subversive – carving out their own channel down the river etc. In all the other story types we are left with a construction that is about inability to resolve the conflicts. So one interpretation would be that rather than trying to resolve different virtue sets, successful change is constructed as being clear about what you stand for, finding others that stand for the same thing and creating change that reflects our own personal ideology – that is, recreating ourselves. Or put another way, successful accounts of change construct the ideology of the leader of the change. This is remarkably similar to Nietzsche's conclusion which I will now elaborate on.

Nietzsche (1968) contended that morality in European society since the archaic age in Greece has become nothing but a series of disguises for the will to power. 'The great man' cannot enter into relationships mediated by an appeal to shared standards of virtue or goods: he is his own authority and his relationships to others have to be exercises of that authority. According to MacIntyre (1985: 256) the practice of morality in our society is in grave disorder. He challenges Nietzsche's analysis (ibid.: 258) and proposes that it is the isolation and self-absorption of the 'great man' which thrust upon him the burden of him being his own self-sufficient moral authority. His argument is that 'to cut oneself off from shared activity in which one has to initially learn obediently as an apprentice learns, to isolate oneself from the[8] communities which find their point and purpose in such activities will be to debar oneself from finding any good outside oneself'. MacIntyre highlights what for him is a gap in Western thinking created by a focus on modernity and liberal individualism at the expense of a culture that transmits, through narrative and stories, virtues of practice with a *telos* of the wellbeing for all in society. MacIntyre's interest lies in the narratives that transmit virtues of a single tradition, a restated form of the Aristotelian tradition, rather than all traditions as suggested in the work of Gadamer (1960/1993). MacIntyre's conclusion is that:

> We still, in spite of three centuries of moral philosophy and one of sociology, lack any coherent rationally defensible statement of a liberal individualist point of view, and that on the other hand, the Aristotelian tradition can be restated in a way that restores intelligibility and rationality to our moral and social attitudes and commitments. (1985: 259)

MacIntyre then goes on to restate the Aristotelian tradition and create a schema that relates internal goods, practices, virtues and institutions (see Appendix 1). *After Virtue* manages to connect narrative, virtue, goods (internal and external) and practice and his work is now finding a resurgence of interest in organisational studies (Neilson 2006). Having covered some of MacIntyre's key arguments I shall now introduce some of the key concepts that will be referred to and expanded on in Chapters 6–9.

The nature of man's unity is a narrative unity for MacIntyre and he rebuffs Western society for abandoning discourse about virtue ethics for the enlightenment discourse and therefore losing the continuum of a moral society and instead being left with liberal individualism. Like Weber (1958), MacIntyre was highly critical of 'liberal individualism[9]': he saw it as a corrupting influence, since the enlightenment, on the moral fabric of society. MacIntyre goes so far as to claim that it fragmented the communal narrative that carried the virtues of practices, and therefore societal morality, that contributes to the *telos* of the good life for all. Weber (1958) offers the concept of 'ethical irrationality' of modern society and the 'paradox of consequences' and emphasised the need of the moral individual to take a heroic stand in the face of plurality of values. Willmott (1998) has criticised this stance on the basis of Weber's own recognition that 'no set of values is intrinsically any better than any other' and instead there is an endless clashing of many competing and irreconcilable value orientations. Like MacIntyre, Weber states that scientific analysis of the human condition will not produce a system of morality that will make every value consistent with every other. MacIntyre agrees with Weber up to a point but rejects emotivism and subjective values (individual or collective) and offers an alternative to the individual heroic stand and the endless clashing of value orientations. MacIntyre's alternative is a neo-Aristotelian notion of shared virtues (rather than values) that are socially and historically contextualised, formed and transmitted through a meshing of personal narratives. This study draws on MacIntyre's and Weber's analysis of the current multiplicity of morality that results in irreconcilable interests and MacIntyre's narrative framed alternative: a virtues-goods-practices-institution schema as described in (Moore & Beadle 2006). This is especially relevant to the public sector in change which has a need to reconcile the interests of many different groups.

MacIntyre argues that the Enlightenment project failed to the extent that it displaced narratives of a universalising rational morality and superseded it with a liberal individualistic morality that has produced the fragmented morality of the modern institution that reflects and fosters that state of moral theory. For MacIntyre it failed because it encouraged the disconnection of people from their social and historical roots. I explored the data without this notion in mind initially and then as the analysis progressed what I discerned in the managers' stories of change was a considerable number of narratives about moral courage, ethical clashes and virtue conflicts. Rather than a narrative unity I was seeing massive disunity. I will now expand on what MacIntyre means by 'narrative unity'.

4.6.1   Narrative unity

MacIntyre's relationship to narrative is captured in his notion of the 'narrative unity' of life (1985: 226) and is important to his and this book in general. He suggests that the self detached from its social and historical roles and statuses is a self very much at home in either a Sartre or Goffman perspective, a self that can have no history. He continues,

> The contrast with the narrative view of the self is clear. For the story of my life is always embedded in the stories of those communities from which I derive my identity. I am born with a past and to try to cut myself off from that past in the individualistic mode is to deform my present relationships. The possession of an historical identity and the possession of a social identity coincide. (1985: 221)

For healthcare (as in many first, second and third sector change programmes) there is an attempt to break free from the past and create a new, modern kind of service or product. Many of the narratives I have collected construct deformation, clashes and disjuncture in the moral landscape of healthcare practice as it changes. In the managers' needs they strongly express the need for their dilemmas to be understood and account be taken of their 'communities of practice' and their history as they change. This leads me to argue that organisational change theory and practice as it relates to healthcare practice has paid insufficient attention to the kind of narrative unity that MacIntyre is describing. Further, it is argued that developing an understanding of organisational change based on MacIntyre's concept of narrative unity and his wider virtue ethics schema seeds new understandings of public-sector change. The idea of virtues that lead to excellence in practice is a common strand that weaves through government policy, the narratives of our managers and MacIntyre's thesis. This strand has had little research attention to date (Beadle 2007) and yet I believe it offers strong potential for a deeper understanding between (and of unifying) the interests of the competing elements in organisational change. I will now further elaborate on MacIntyre's notion of the interrelationship of virtues, goods and practice and their institutional coherence as maintained in a narrative unity.

4.6.2   Relationship between virtues, goods, practice and institutions

MacIntyre's belief is that humans are storytelling animals and one of the purposes of stories is to carry a set of moral virtues that when enacted in practice with others bring the good life for all those that are part of the *polis* (society). Healthcare organisations are a significant part of our society and taking the MacIntyre viewpoint would be the importance of individual and collective narratives as the carriers of a set of virtues that when lived out offer internal goods for all healthcare practitioners. This concept is important for the public sector and links to MacIntyre's views on the failure of the enlightenment, that is, the collective matters. 'Internal goods' are intrinsic to practice as opposed to 'external goods' which MacIntyre summarises as money, status and power. What is the relationship between practices, internal goods and virtues? Starting with MacIntyre's notion of practice and its relationship to internal goods, he offers this:

> Any coherent and complex form of socially established cooperative human activity through which goods internal to that form of activity are realized in the course of trying to achieve those standards of excellence which are appropriate to, and partially definitive of, that form of activity, with the result that human powers to achieve excellence, and human conceptions of the ends and goods involved, are systematically extended. (MacIntyre [1985] 1985: 187)

MacIntyre illustrates this relationship between virtues and practices by reference to examples including football, chess, architecture, seascape painting and cricket (MacIntyre [1985: 187, 191), and argues that, 'it is not difficult to show for a whole range of key virtues that without them the goods internal to practices are barred to us ...' (MacIntyre [1981] 1985: 191). Moving now to virtue and the relationship to internal goods, he says:

> A virtue is an acquired human quality the possession and exercise of which tends to enable us to achieve those goods which are internal

to practices and the lack of which effectively prevents us from achieving any such goods. (MacIntyre 1985: 191)

Finally the way MacIntyre envisages the collective relationship of practices, the narrative of the institution and their potential disruption is summarised by McCann and Brownsberger (1990):

> The normative character of MacIntyre's definition of a social practice ... is secured within a larger account of the moral life as a whole. There must be some *telos* to human life, a vision anticipating the moral unity of life, given in the form of a narrative history that has meaning within a particular community's traditions; otherwise the various internal goods generated by the range of social practices will remain disordered and potentially subversive of one another. Without a community's shared sense of *telos,* there will be no way of signifying 'the overriding good' by which various internal goods may be ranked and evaluated. (McCann & Brownsberger 1990: 227–228)

Moore and Beadle bring us back to the individual (2006: 332) and state that:

> It is only within the context of this continuing and communal narrative that (she) can make sense of herself and that she can begin to make some sense of her *telos.* Initially this *telos* is derived from experiences of early childhood, but gradually it becomes hers as she embarks on her own narrative quest.

This book is not advocating a single set of virtues held within a communal narrative for healthcare to resolve all the problems of organisational change, nor does it want to enter into MacIntyre's philosophical arguments, rather it intends a mediated conversation between MacIntyre's ideas and the managers narratives encountered to reach a richer understanding of the social reality of managers on the front line of change. To date, studies of healthcare practice change have identified and discussed tensions, paradoxes, change conflict narratives etc. What is added with this work is an alternative understanding of the nature of those tensions. It identifies many of them as virtue or value clashes and disjuncture, discusses the implications for organisational change in public healthcare organisations and the wider public sector and offers some suggestions for further research. An analysis of ethical conflict has been carried out in the context of the private sector by Watson

(2003). He offers a Weberian perspective on the moral dilemmas in the corporate world. Watson (2003: 182) elegantly summarises one of the gap in understanding in the ethical dimension:

> It would be significant to discover how far managers vary in the extent to which they 'go with the flow' of the pressures from internal and external constituencies or tend to bring together such pressures with their private moral concerns and act in a way which is both corporately expedient and satisfies personal moral concerns.

He concludes that we need to look at the extent to which personal ethical assertiveness is possible. This book does explore this interest but at the same time tells a wider story, through managers' narratives, that allies with MacIntyre's call which is for research stories to be told about

> human flourishing and failure to flourish, about virtues and vices, about the practices and institutions, about communal tradition and its erosion, about the destructive effects of the world market. And only if the story deals with all of these in their interrelationship will it tell us what we need to know. (Coe & Beadle 2007: 2)

4.7   Concluding comments

This chapter has argued that the emerging narrative research pedigree has gained a credible standing in terms of it offering valuable insight into the personal and collective social reality of organisational actors – further, that it has increasingly been used to illuminate themes associated with organisational change. Those themes have included managing change, learning and practice, meaning of change, and the polyphony associated with change. All these have some relevance to this study, the last two especially so. An ethical perspective on narrative organisational change, however, has received little attention to date. The virtue ethics perspective provided by MacIntyre offers an opportunity to use concepts which to date have not been developed in the narrative organisational change literature. By drawing on his connected conceptions of virtues, practices, goods and institution it is hoped that new understandings of what it means to managers to be implementing change will be revealed.

This book seeks to explore the moral pressures that managers construct in the context of mental health services through participants' narrative enactments of change and what those enactments unfold into the social reality and morality of the organisation under reform.

Recalling Chapter 3, the structural genre of change understanding highlighted a strong theme associated with the importance of key people leading change. Post-structural organisational change literature has highlighted tensions, frictions and conflicts in that role. Through narrative-based concepts of virtue ethics this study will contribute generally in the field of narrative organisational change as well as in the specific context of the public sector. It will explore ways in which ethical conflicts are revealed in the in the narratives of those participating in the implementation of the healthcare reform agenda. In so doing, it will aim to contribute theoretically and empirically to the fields of public-sector reform, narrative understanding of organisational change and the ethics of change.

Having built the narrative foundations for the book, and stated its intentions, I now draw on and expand on some of the studies mentioned above to frame the methodology and research design of the study.

5
Research Methodology

The purpose of this chapter is to provide an overview of the research methodology. The aim is twofold: first, to articulate the ontological and epistemological stance of the study, and second, to provide an understanding of the decisions taken in relation to various aspects of undertaking the research.

The first section of this chapter (5.1–5.5) outlines the methodological approach to the research. Here I discuss methodological options and how the narrative approach is appropriate given the research questions. The second part of the chapter (5.6) provides a detailed description of the research design and the research process itself.

5.1   Methodological approach – an introduction

Mainstream research in organisational change and healthcare contributes towards and reinforces a dominant discourse of change being something that can be managed (for example, Iles & Sutherland 2001). It has been argued that organisational theory has too readily succumbed to client preferences and has therefore conceptualised organisations as rational, structural, mechanistic and predictive (Watson 1982). The nature of this knowledge has an imprisoning power effect (Foucault 1984) which limits our understanding of the 'uncomfortable realities that managers' responsibilities perhaps should demand they confront' (Watson 1982: 261). I think I experienced that imprisoning power – it led me to this study – and I will now say a little about my personal journey and how it relates to the methodological decisions taken.

5.1.1   A short story of my quest

My quest was related to having lived through multinational corporate organisational change imprisoned with the belief that change could be managed or driven like a car from A to B. Disconcerting happenings in the organisation caused me to question this belief and left me searching for new understandings. I had a good grounding in the psychological impact of change but I observed that during change, stories, identity, social phenomena and other mysteries were at play. I found very little of inspiration to enlighten me until I read Watson's ethnography *In search of Management* (1994) and Kunda's *Engineering Culture* (1992) which did convey something closer to the messy lived reality and particularly with Kunda the reactions and subversions that I had experienced as a change agent in a large organisation. They inspired me to write something similar about organisational change: blow-by-blow accounts of what it means to a manager to be in the midst of implementing initiatives that had been dreamed up by the powers that be Van Maanen (1979, 1988).

Later whilst working in the public sector and formulating my research proposal I read Czarniawska's *Dramas of Institutional Identity* (1997) which, for me, added to Watson's insights with issues of organisational identity and illustrated the power of narrative, literary theory and cultural metaphor in deepening understanding of organisational change. Partly because it was apposite for my quest and partly because I had experienced the power of stories of change (true or false) at first hand I decided to start by adopting Czarniawska's methodological triad of stories, serials and themes to categorise the data.

Much later, whilst analysing the data and rereading Czarniawska, I realised that Czarniawska's methodology was strongly predicated on MacIntyre's narrative-based moral philosophy and so started to read *After Virtue* (1985). I then found considerable affinity between the data and MacIntyre's thesis especially with his notion of virtues and the route to internal goods derived from excellence in practice. It seemed to me that many of my participants' enacted narratives were about virtue conflict and their fight on the side of virtues that bring excellence in practice and internal goods.

Although highlighting moral conflict was a strong theme in her data, Czarniawska had surprisingly and for me, fortunately not followed this aspect of what it means to be in the midst of change. Since other researchers had also neglected this aspect, I decided that a virtue-ethics dimension on public sector reform driven organisational change could offer a fruitful seam of uncharted theorising. This seam is important to reveal because organisational change theorising and the public sector context especially are in need of greater understanding of the nature of the conflict that so many practitioners say they experience but so far has proved hard for both practitioners and theorists to articulate. Many participants report feeling 'under siege' from a 'barrage' of 'must dos' but just what they are defending and who or what is attacking has been unclear. When you are in the middle of a battle it is helpful to know what you are fighting for and against. So I have arrived at a study which seeks to contribute to understanding the ethical dimension of organisational change in healthcare, not only by adopting a moral philosophical framework but also by using a methodological approach, narrative, that I hope brings fresh insights to the debates associated with discursive notions of resistance to change (Fleming & Spicer 2003).

The main turning points in my methodological decisions are touched on in the above even though it is a highly compressed version. I now explore the main options for studying organisational change that feature in my quest in the light of the initial research questions and aims.

5.1.2 Questions and aims

The research questions were initially framed as:

- What does it mean to managers to be implementing organisational change aimed at improving the quality of health care?
- What meanings are shared between the participants in how they account for being in the midst of change?

The aim was to explore qualitative approaches to organisational change research in healthcare in a way that would illuminate a deeper understanding of the complexities. It was also putting the manager at the heart of the enquiry in the sense of seeking to study accounts from people who were expected to be leading the implementation of change rather than all members of the institution. Both these aspects were identified in the literature review as missing from current understandings of organisational change (Cameron et al. 2001; Blackler et al. 1999).

5.2   Structural functionalist and social constructionist

Iles & Sutherland (2001) suggest that when investigating the management of change, what is needed are research methods that allow for the processes of change to be explored and understood. Qualitative case study approaches are therefore recommended (ibid.: 77; Peck 1997). As Chia and Tsoukas (2002) and Ashburner (2001) observe, the change processes occurring for practitioners remain relatively under-researched, especially, as noted by Pettigrew et al. (2001), processes over an extended period of time and tied to a specific context. In the light of this, I consider the suitability of the two main approaches to qualitative organisational change research that pervade the literature: the structural functionalist view (Burrell & Morgan 1979) and the social constructionist (for example, Czarniawska 1997). I then focus on the narrative subgenre of social constructionist approaches and expand on this as the selected approach.

In the structural world-view, the job of change agents is to align, fit or adapt organisations, through interventions, to an objective reality that exists 'out there'. The social constructionist lens, however, views organisations as socially constructing a changing reality, one that is interpreted, constructed, enacted and maintained through discourse (Berger & Luckmann 1967). This viewpoint sees actors' accounts as not representing or reproducing some underlying 'true' reality. Instead their narrative and conversations fashion reality as an ongoing process of meaning and sense making (Weick 1995).

Skoldberg (1994), in his narrative study of public administration reform in Sweden, employs literary modes to make sense of the organisational stories: in his case those of tragedy, romance, comedy and satire. These he found formed the texture of the reforms and offered a new perspective on and understanding of organisational change. Skoldberg argues that these archetypal narrative conventions use our most deeply ingrained preconscious conceptions of the structuring of social processes. He theorises that organisations are liable to follow the dictates of narrative tradition rather than the 'objective structures of problems and power or demands of shared symbolisms'. He suggests that literary theory might be a better alternative because its categories are the ones most suited to studying the ongoing dramas of organisations. In the next section I expand on the narrative sub-genre of social construction and lead on to explain the specific style of narrative approach that was adopted and developed in response to some of the criticisms of the approach.

5.2.1   Narrative social construction

My preferred perspective is that like the organisation in which change occurs, change is viewed as a polyphonic phenomenon (Boje 2001), a story of stories (Skoldberg 1994) or a set of themes within which narratives are introduced, developed, maintained and stopped. This perspective is evident in Czarniawska's (1997) study of Swedish government agencies in which she observes change consisting of a series of conversational episodes organised around particular themes (for example, company-isation, decentralisation or computerisation) and directs the unfolding of sequential and concurrent conversations into a network of already existing conversations. The narrative approach builds on a growing body of studies (Czarniawska 1997; Gabriel 1995; Boje 2001; Shotter & Cunliffe 2002) – all of which emphasise the process of dialogical interaction as the never-ending construction of meaning and identity of the organisation and its participants.

Of interest to this study is the way in which Barbara Czarniawska (BC) (1997) serialises the company-isation of the various departments in one local municipal administration. She describes a set of stories in the form of 'episodes' to illuminate a case study of the transformation from public to private sector. Through the episodes the case is brought to life; to give an example, this is a short extract from the fourth episode (ibid.: 106) where a manager (M) is giving an account . The context is that staff expectations were raised that salaries would be dramatically increased in line with pay demands but then dashed because there was no money available.

M: The next day, the atmosphere here was something which I hope I never experience again. The girls had heard that nobody thought they were worth anything and they were very upset. I sat all day talking with them … .

BC: But why were the girls affected in particular?

M: It's more difficult to deal with girls, because they get so downhearted that they start crying. That is one of the worst things, in my opinion. The guys, the technicians that is, are not so sensitive. They were extremely angry in fact, and that made it much easier to talk to them.

BC: …The atmosphere got better and then it got worse again. The central authorities came on the scene, offering assistance and making demands. The municipality supported then obstructed the company's development. Customers and suppliers cooperated and then turned against the company. And for the most part, everything cost more than anybody had imagined.

In the above study we find a mix of the actors' stories and then the author knitting the extracts together to fill in the gaps to tell the 'whole' story. I draw inspiration from Czarniawska's study and draw on her approach in a way that offers more in the way of the participants' stories rather than my account of what was happening and therefore, I hope, comes closer to their social reality rather than mine. Czarniawska says that

> each story is a unique combination of random events, intentions, interests, intentions, and counter intentions and existing routines. The encounters described in the stories lead to a construction of meaning; actors interpret what is happening for themselves and for their audience. In other words, narratives are created and negotiated (1997: 79).

I now explore what this means in terms of organisational change and examine some of the studies that I drew on initially to formulate my methodology.

5.3   A narrative approach to the study of organisations

The narrative approach taken in this study is based on the notion that groups comprise individuals and as individuals come together to form organisations they construct their social reality in narrative form and through narrative come to construct a mixture of individual and shared meanings (Bruner 1991). In the healthcare context of this study an incentivised and centralised government reform agenda is prompting the participants to implement changes to their organisation and practices. The National Service Framework for Mental Health (DoH 1999) along with the Policy Implementation Guidelines (2001a) state how the services should be structured and operate. I am interested in what it means to managers at all levels in Omega mental health services to be implementing change in line with the NSF and PIGs plus a whole host of other imperatives and what those meanings in the form of enacted stories and narratives unfold[1] into their social reality. According to Bakhtin (1986) working against unitary versions of what is and should be is a heteroglossia, a polyphonic discourse that opposes the centralising imposition of a single discourse such as the government's modernisation agenda out of which the NSFs were born. Ford's (1999) position is that the accumulation of sufficiently consistent narratives can objectify 'reality' for the people who author them within organisations. He suggests further that organisational change can be viewed as shifting conversations and that conversations set the stage for what will and will not be done. Currie and Brown (2003: 564) build on Ford (1999) when they claim that 'organisations literally are the narratives that people author in networks of conversations'. The resulting storytelling organisation for Boje (1995) is 'Tamara-like[2]', a polyphony of simultaneously and sequentially occurring stories and fragments of stories, some exposed, others hidden. It is this shifting 'polyphony of stories', revealing some of what change means to the participants, that I try to discover and describe in this study. To try to capture as much of the variance and texture of the polyphony as I could I brought together a synthesis of narrative approaches. The synthesis also created a more robust methodology that included strategies to address some of the critiques of narrative-based research. It is that synthesis that I now describe.

5.3.1 Organisational change as shifting narratives

With a narrative or conversational perspective, change is not being produced, rather it is an unfolding of narrative into already existing conversations where current narratives are shaped by both prior and anticipated conversations (for example, possible objections or questions). This perspective views organisational change therefore as shifting narratives and conversations (Ford 1999).

Given the perspective of change as shifting narratives, and therefore shifting meaning-making, it is contended that the most apposite method of enquiry into the meanings the leaders ascribe to the change programme is to collect their narratives on the change as it unfolds over a period of time. Humphreys and Brown (2002) take this approach in their study of a change programme in a British university. Their contention is that 'identity, both individual and collective are constituted in the shared narrative that managers author in their efforts to make sense of their world and read meaning into their lives'. Humphreys and Brown's (2002: 422) study illustrates how an organisation's 'identity narrative' evolves over time. They state, '... the stories that are authored through dialogue are one symbolic means by which meaning is variously negotiated, shared and contested'. The study illuminates the efforts of Westville Institute to manage a campaign to achieve university status. The campaign was unsuccessful and through the narratives they collect they find that the marker produced an identity crisis which led individuals and groups to question the purposes and strength of their connection to the organisation. The decision in Humphreys and Brown's case to represent the research in narrative genre reflects their belief (and mine) that stories most appropriately permit the exposition of the intersubjectivity of organisational life. They describe the whole process as a hegemonic struggle in a similar way to Boje et al. (1998).

Humphreys and Brown (2002) argue that identity is a central concern for participants because of the clash between self-authored and top-down imposed narratives, which can create dislocating, polarising identity dualities that complicate people's sense of who they are and what they stand for. My study builds on Humphreys and Brown's notion of change complicating and for me *challenging* people's sense of what they stand for. As we saw in the Chapter 4, Ricoeur (1983–1985) observes a very similar dilemma when people are faced with many different ways of authoring their narrative identity and are confused as to where to mediate between character (*ipse*) and selfhood (*idem*). Currie and Brown's narrative study of change in a UK hospital (2003) follows a similar line to Humphreys and Brown's and claims that workers authored a range of counter-narratives that placed limits on governments' attempts at hegemonic control. Amongst Currie and Brown's quotes from managers is this: 'A lot of people in the health service as a whole have felt that many of the changes are based on impractical ideology' (2003: 582). The 'ideology' cue is not followed by Currie and Brown; however, for MacIntyre(1985), ideology plays a fundamental role in understanding the difficulty in resolving ethical conflicts. This is a cue for my study and my interest is in where change ideology meets the individual and collective ideologies (Watson 1982) of the managers who are made responsible for implementing change and the resulting multiplicity of narratives that emerge from those meetings. Further interests are to understand more about the meaning constructions of the narratives, their relation to notions of 'resistance to change' and the morality they unfold on a personal, collective and institutional level.

Humphreys and Brown (2002) situate their study within broad debates in the social sciences centred on the dissolution of the unified subject (Foucault 1984) and its replacement by a 'contradictory' decentred subject displaced across the range of discourses in which he or she participates. Transposed into organisational analysis this leads, as the case illustrates, to a view of participants as a 'set of positional, relational, subjective and temporary ideas'. Viewing this conclusion from an ethical perspective we might conclude that participants were also constructing temporary moralities as suggested by MacIntyre (1985) in his description of the fragmented morality of the modern institution. The moral perspective is not explored by Humphreys and Brown, instead their study contributes to concepts of organisational identity. My interest is in demonstrating the power of a similar methodological approach to develop understanding of the ethical dimension of public-sector organisational change in three areas: first, to explore the multiplicity of narrative enactments of change, their meaning and what the enactments unfold into the social reality of the organisation in change; second, to understand what the enactments construct in terms of support needs; and finally, to illuminate the findings from MacIntyre's (1985) narrative-based virtues-goods-practices-institution schema to deepen understanding of the ethical dimensions of organisational change.

Czarniawska (1997) employs cultural metaphors to describe the kind of story enacted in the organisational narratives and how the dynamics of screenplay can illuminate the change processes. For instance, she develops two strong analogies: one (as described earlier) between public-sector organisations and TV serials; the other that the stories imitate reality by portraying women as the unintended victims of a course of events and that the public-sector campaign can be seen as the masculinisation of organisations with the emphasis on 'competition', 'autonomy' and 'free choice' and other elements from masculine drama. She notes (ibid.: 121) the 'reciprocal process by which life feeds materials to literature while literature returns the favour by conferring forms upon life'. If we replace literature with art, the picture, she suggests, will be complete.

These examples of narrative studies demonstrate two options for reading the stories that emerge. The first is to look at *thematic* or *categorical* content (Lieblich et al. 1998), reading across a number of stories as in the case of Humphreys and Brown (2002) who draw out different aspects of identity as themes. The second is the use of *whole content* reading as in the case of Czarniawska (1997) who uses cultural metaphors such as serial and screenplay to infer meaning.

For my study I include both thematic and whole content reading. I use the thematic approach because of the possibilities to express meanings that have affinity across different groups of participants in healthcare and the wider government sphere. Whole content reading allows the wider social environment to be included in the analysis and offers the potential for wider cultural resonance. This option is also used because the mental health service change is characterised by change serials and discrete change projects in a way that parallels the organisation Czarniawska studied.

5.4 Critiques and strategies

The foregoing demonstrates that the narrative approach can offer a way of illuminating the dynamic nature of practitioners' narratives, meanings and narrative identities as a change programme unfolds over time. The narrative approach (as with any approach) is not without its critics, as highlighted by Gabriel (2000: 151), and in the following table I address some of these criticisms along with my strategies for how they might be mitigated. I then move on to describing how I have drawn these strategies together to form a synthesised narrative approach and research design.

Critique	Mitigation strategies
A selective use of narratives can be used to amplify or reinforce the researcher's preconce ived ideas or assumptions.	Asking the open question 'What does it mean to be implementing change?' and not closing down to any particular story types or themes until they have emerged from the data Not just presenting themes but also stories and a serial (Czarniawska 1997) Feeding back the findings to groups of managers and asking if their meanings are represented in the findings.
There is a risk of regarding narratives as facts especially if the participant insists that the events described 'actually happened'.	Narratives can be viewed as poetic elaborations on actual events, as wish-fulfilling fantasies built on everyday experience and as expressions of deeper organisational and personal realities. 'The truth of a story lies not in its accuracy but in its meaning' (Gabriel 2000: 135). Stories can be masks, lies, distortions, inconsistent and illogical but also offer a path towards the deeper truth they contain. Narratives can be viewed as socially constructing the objective reality of change to participants and the unfolding moral landscape of the institution.
It favours good narrators and complete stories and might miss fragments of stories and hidden stories from those less adept at storytelling (Boje 2001).	Extending the narrative analysis to include 'antenarrative' analysis (Boje 2001). This involves tracing fragments of stories and those that conflict with the 'official' story, for example, Boje's (1995) analysis of Walt Disney Enterprises.
Much of what goes on for people is said to be held in the tacit domain (Polyani 1966) and is therefore not available to conscious thought or speech.	Propp (1928) and all his successors with an interest in folklore, including stories, demonstrate narrative as an expression of a wide range of oppressive counter-cultures or fantasies and their underlying emotions (Gabriel 2000). Cunliffe's 'social poetics' approach to enquiry is taken (2002). This respects the living relationship between researcher and participant and is more likely to open up the tacit domain to the researcher.

Critique	Mitigation strategies
A single shot thematic analysis of narratives does not convey the temporal aspect of the social and personal realities of organisational change.	Conducting three sets of interviews over 12 months to gain an insight into a serial and narrative themes evolving over time.
Management narratives are meaningless unless framed in a specific context.	Initially, performing a single in-depth study of one context, mental health service organisational change, and then later expanding the study to other service areas in the trust concerned.
It is impossible to generalise narrative findings across different contexts.	Narratives are collated from mental health services and then presented back to focus groups of managers from wider contexts to discuss and relate to their stories. See below for further elaboration on this point.
Socially constructing influence of presenting findings back to an audience.	Full narrative polyphony (stories, serial and themes) presented as a description without interpretation to focus groups. Small groups challenged the findings and introduced their own narratives at the focus groups.
The researcher is part of the field and therefore influences the narrative.	Fieldwork draws inspiration from Cunliffe's (2002) 'social poetics', a radically reflexive approach that respects and makes open the living relationship between researcher and researched. This kind of reflexive stance means that the researcher can be free to respond (like the participants' colleagues might respond) but also admit their role in co-construction of meaning. The feedback process mentioned above helps ensure that whatever is constructed is representative of participants' social reality as well.
Assume everything is language: that life consists of a set of concocted stories (Czarniawska 1997) or to regard everything as narrative (Gabriel 2000) and to lose sight of the importance of actual events in organisations.	Acceptance that there are other perspectives on organisations but that narrative offers a different and powerful way to understand more about organisational life. The stories, themes and serial presented here are viewed as poetic elaborations on actual events but also their constructing effects can and do lead to a physical reality, for example, someone leaving the service

5.4.1   Cultural metaphor

According to Czarniawska (1997) it has the potential to describe the reciprocal process by which life feeds materials to contemporary literature and the arts while literature and the arts returns the favour by conferring forms upon life. Interest lies in the literary forms and social construction of narrative. Rather than a model, the findings are related to a cultural metaphor, an art form that is recognisable in Western culture and that sits in the reciprocal socially constructing loop of art feeding life and vice versa.

   In summary, this first methodology section has demonstrated three main points. First, it showed that the narrative approach is capable of answering the question of what it means to managers to be implementing change. Second, it demonstrated that the critiques of the narrative approach can be addressed through a variety of strategies that when brought together offer a potentially robust synthesis of methods. That synthesis is described in the next section. Finally, I have looked to Czarniawska (1997) and Skoldberg (1994) who have shown that the narrative approach has the potential to offer a way of generalising with other organisations by way of the analogy of literary modes. Having considered some of the critiques and proposed strategies to address them, I next discuss the selected methods in more detail.

5.5   Research design and development

This section describes the research study itself starting with the research question, then a detailed description of the process of gathering empirical data and finally the stages of the analysis of those data in order to answer the research questions.

5.5.1   Research question evolution

There are two initial research questions and two questions posed by the PCT that the method has to be capable of answering. These four questions along with key themes that were later incorporated are listed below.

   The initial research questions were set as:

- What does it mean to managers to be implementing organisational change aimed at improving the quality of health care?
- What meanings are shared between the participants in how they account for being in the midst of change?

After discussing the study with Omega board members the following two questions were added:

- Do the accounts convey a change approach that is working for managers and the service?
- What do the accounts tell us about what managers need in terms of support?

These aims were refined as the study progressed and significant themes emerged. Early analysis of the data and my exposure to writers such as Czarniawska and MacIntyre resulted in the emergence of a number of key themes that were incorporated into the initial research aims:

- To explore the power of narrative approach in organisational change research and in maintaining a dialogue with participants
- To understand the nature of the ethical conflicts and dilemmas enacted in the narratives and what kind of social reality they construct
- To examine the narratives using the lens of MacIntyre's virtues-goods-practices-institution schema theory (Moore and Beadle 2006) in order to enrich organisational change theory particularly in the areas of ethics and resistance to change

As can be seen from the above, the study evolved from seeking to explore the meaning of change to managers to a focus on the moral pressures that managers construct in the context of mental health services through their narrative enactments of change and what those enactments unfold into the social reality of the organisation under reform. The reason for this focus is that the moral conflict constructions were discerned as a prevalent theme at the heart of the enacted narratives and one that has received little attention from a narrative-based change perspective to date. This focus led to an interest in notions of resistance to change and alternative, narrative-based theorising of resistance which draws in an ethical dimension.

5.5.2   Method outline – a synthesis

In this section I present an outline of the research method including the synthesis of narrative approaches that draws primarily on the work of Cunliffe (2002), Czarniawska (1997), Gabriel (2000) and Boje (2001). In the rest of the chapter the research design and process are described in detail and finally the approach taken to the MacIntyre (1985) inspired theoretical analysis is explained.

The core of the data was collected in three rounds of in-depth semi-structured interviews with a total of 37 managers over a period of 12 months. During the interviews a 'social poetics' approach was taken in order to explore metaphors, storytelling, irony and gestures that help convey meanings to the interviewee (Cunliffe 2002). All the interviews were transcribed and the data categorised into three main forms: stories of change, serials of change and narrative themes (Czarniawska 2004: 49). The stories were then further categorised into four poetic modes: epic, tragic, comic and romantic (Gabriel 2000). One serial of change, the community mental health team (CMHT) implementation, was selected for further analysis and six episodes in that serial were drawn out from the transcripts. The final stage of the thematic analysis was developed to include 'antenarrative' (Boje 2001) so that fragments of narratives that come before emplotment are included. Following the capture of the data in these different forms a feedback phase was implemented to ensure that the stories, serial and themes together represented a picture of the social reality to managers across the locality served by the trusts and then across the geographic region. Two main workshops with a total of 121 managers (70 and 51 respectively) were held. Each workshop included plenary and focus groups of approximately 12 managers per group to respond to the findings. Finally the detailed theoretical analysis which draws on MacIntyre's virtue-ethics was carried through the stories, serial, themes and feedback findings to build the central arguments and contributions.

The above outline is now elaborated in four main stages, each having its own section. The first stage is participant identification and interviews (5.5.3), the second is data processing and analysis (5.5.4), the third is feedback and focus groups (5.5.5) and the fourth is the MacIntyre-informed analysis (5.5.6).

5.5.3   Stage one: Participant identification and interviews

A meeting was arranged with the director of mental health, his deputy and the director of human resources to discuss the subject of participants. We together decided that I would interview people at all levels of managerial responsibility within mental health services from director level down to ward manager. A total of 20 managers were identified representing all service areas within mental health services. I contacted all of them and 17 responded and agreed to be interviewed. After I explained the research aims and questions, all signed consent forms in accordance with Omega's research policy. These managers were inter-viewed twice in the period January 2004 to September 2004. After the initial findings were presented back to mental health and the Omega board I was asked to interview another 21 managers from all service areas in Omega Trust. They were interviewed in a third round of inter-views from January 2005 to March 2005. Therefore 38 managers in total were interviewed, 17 of whom were interviewed twice. After the interviews were completed, the findings in the form of stories, serial and themes were fed back to focus groups of 70 managers from Omega in April 2005 and later to a focus group of 51 regional managers in September 2005. These managers were not selected by the researcher but by the organisers of the events which were the Omega management forum and SHA regional management meeting respectively.

A full description of the changes that the participants were imple-menting is included in Chapter 2. Initially I selected managers who were responsible for the implementation of a number of discrete change projects, for example, closure of an inpatient unit, redeployment of staff, redistribution of the services offered and formation of commu-nity mental health teams. All participants had some responsibility for implementing change in their service areas and a general change to ask people to think from a different paradigm of collaboration and pre-ventative approaches to mental health.

Interviews

The first stage of the fieldwork was conducted within Omega mental health services, managed jointly by a primary care trust (PCT) and two local authority (LA) social services (SS) during the spring and summer months of 2004. During this period 17 managers from Omega were inter-viewed twice; they included four senior managers, eight middle managers and five who have senior management and clinical responsibilities.

The in-depth, semi-structured interviews with the participants were the most valuable source of data from which the case has been con-structed. The interviews lasted an average of 60 minutes and were recorded on audiotape before being transcribed and subjected to ana-lysis. Handwritten notes were also taken, recording an outline of the interview, non-verbal signals from the research participants, environ-mental description and the researcher's own internal responses. Field notes from two mental health managers meetings and a number of other formal and informal meetings supplemented interview data.

The philosophical approach to the interviews was inspired by Cunliffe (2002) and her 'social poetics' approach to enquiry. This approach respects the living relationship between researcher and participant. This method is distinguished from other forms of linguistic methods and analyses because it operates on the assumption that sensemaking is an embodied, relational and dialogic process of making connections. Whereas linguistics studies the various elements of language, social poetics explores aspects of narrative frequently taken for granted, such as:

- Metaphors, images and analogies
- Instructive forms of talk
- Imaginative trips into the future or alternatives
- Gestures such as thumping the table, shrugging shoulders
- Comparisons
- Rhythm
- Emotion

Social poetics views language as ontology rather than epistemology. So rather than a device through which an extra-linguistic 'real world' is interpreted as in a discourse analysis approach it stops at narrative as a worthy phenomenon to investigate and one that conveys meaning.

The interviews were loosely structured conversations, seeking to evoke narratives the respondents tell of their experiences of leading organisational change. I started the interviews by explaining the purpose of the research. Gabriel (2000: 144) suggests starting by asking the respondent to try to describe their organisational change activity in terms of a metaphor and then tell a story that that supports their preferred metaphor. Gabriel (2000) found this to be a light-hearted beginning that allows the respondent to relax and then move on to accounts of specific incidents. In practice I found that I had to adapt my style depending on the person. Not having tried the Gabriel metaphor approach previously I tried out the idea during the pilot interviews. For some it worked well and they had a go at describing their metaphor, for others they were visibly thrown by this and I quickly abandoned the idea. For the main interviews I settled on just making it clear at the start where my interest lay and allowing them to start wherever and however they wanted to. A few did say 'Where do you want me to start?' and I might say 'Where do you want to start?' If they did not respond to this then I might say 'It seems hard for you to start on this subject, would you like to start with the difficulty?' They would often then talk about how they felt about implementing change in a general way, for example, 'Change motivates me and my staff' or 'It is very stressful for me' or 'I feel we have always been implementing change' or 'I feel upset and angry about the way I am treated by the organisation with regard to change'.

After allowing them to complete the expression of how they feel supported mainly with non-verbal signals from me they went on to give examples that were their stories of change. They usually did but if they didn't move on to talk about instances or stories, I would ask them about specific examples with something like 'Would you be able to give me an example of when you felt motivated/ angry/ upset?' and that would bring out specific stories of change. These were exceptional cases, however, most just talked and talked, in some cases without me needing to say much else other than my introduction and giving them non-verbal signals that I was listening and taking in what they had said. As the interviews progressed certain stories and narratives emerged and questions relating to these stories were asked.

With the permission of the respondents interviews were taped. I took notes on my own emotions evoked by the narrative plus interviewee gestures and body language that would not be captured on tape.

Reflection on the interview process

Most interviewees were very forthcoming with their accounts as stories of change and even the ones who were less forthcoming were able to offer fragments of narrative and meanings in between my questions and prompts even if they were not always emplotted into a complete story cycle with beginning, middle and end. These fragments would normally be missed by just collating stories alone and is partly the reason why I include antenarrative (Boje 2001) analysis in this study. Because I was aware of the concept of antenarrative before starting the interviews I did follow up on some fragments of narrative in the interview especially when I was aware of the 'party line' type narrative coming across. In some cases interviewees would offer hints of hidden meaning when I was just about to conclude the interview, switch the tape off or even as I was walking out of the room. Examples were 'I'm exhausted' or, jokingly, 'Now I'll tell you what it is really like!' In those cases, if they had the time, I would offer to stay and if they felt they could tell me more then I would listen. Knowing the tape was off I would also make copious notes capturing as much of their narrative as I could. In this way I was able to access more of the hidden narratives. The 'manager as buffer' antenarrative is a good example of this kind of narrative that tells a very different story. As Bruner (1991: 124) observes I am sure that some of the stories and fragments of narrative I heard were designed in some measure for my interest, a performance narrative. Nor was I under any illusion that I as an interviewer was completely neutral during the interviews.

5.5.4   Stage two: Data processing and analysis

The interviews were transcribed from the tapes and then each transcription was entered on a separate record and the following information recorded for each:

- Serial number
- Participant (coded for confidentiality)
- Full text of the transcript
- Story and narrative segments highlighted
- Poetic mode (epic, tragic, comic or romantic)
- Change serial episodes (for example, community mental health team, care Records)
- Theme codes (for example, finances, IT, training)
- Emotions described in the narrative
- Metaphors used in the narrative
- Emotions generated in the researcher by the delivery
- Body language and gestures
- Moral conflicts in the narrative (this was done later)
- Keywords

These records permitted the selection of narratives sharing specific modes or related to one particular serial or having particular themes in common. I will say more about the way the narratives were categorised in the next section on data analysis.

Data analysis: Narrative categorisation

The narratives collected from interviews, informal meetings and meeting observations were initially categorised in a similar way to that demonstrated by Czarniawska (1997) in her study of Swedish public-sector reform. The three categories she applies are stories, serials and themes. A second stage of categorisation was applied to the stories to discern the different poetic modes (Gabriel 2000) of epic, tragic, comic and romantic.

Like Czarniawska and Gabriel I have chosen this style of categorisation because, as they demonstrate, applying interpretive devices borrowed from literary studies to the data helps greatly with naming the range of experiences and meanings the participants are describing. I hope to show how this treatment can further understanding of the ethical dimension of what it means to managers to be implementing change and further support a challenge to the dominance of structural conceptions of change (Sturdy & Grey 2003). The categories, their relationship to each other and their relevance to the research questions are discussed next.

Stories.   According to Czarniawska (1997), stories have a beginning, an ending and a plot with related episodes that may culminate in a solution to a problem. Stories are the most localised element and come from specific parts of the organisations. They are relevant here because this study is primarily asking, What does leading the implementation of organisational change mean to managers responsible for implementing reform to services? According to Czarniawska (ibid.: 78), actors improvise against a backdrop of known rules: 'They combine traditional elements ("This is the way we do things round here") with spontaneous features ("But does it actually apply in this case?") and creative aspects ("Now we do it this way instead")'. I wanted, however, to go beyond just identifying stories in the material to gain a sense of the literary mode or poetic mode (Gabriel 2000) and therefore the overall meaning conveyed in the stories.

It has been suggested by generations of literary theorists from Aristotle onwards that in their tone and form, narratives draw on a finite range of cultural archetypes, basic storylines, made familiar to us through societal-level socialisation (McAdams 1996). Brown and Humphreys (2003) state that 'the plots associated with the epic and tragic genres in the West are some of the best known and salient of these cultural resources...' Gabriel (2000) suggests that stories are the basic unit of narrative and like Gabriel I found that the stories collected from the interviews could be classified not just as epic and tragic but also as comic and romantic. The *epic* invites the audience to marvel at the hero's achievements, the *comic* invites laughter, the *tragic* invites feelings of compassion and awe at the protagonists suffering and the *romantic* invites feelings of sentimentality and love. The classification was based on the feelings the story-teller evoked in me the researcher. Each story type, according to Gabriel (ibid.: 60), 'represents a distinct *poetic mode* or way of infusing meaning into events' and can sometimes be combined to form a hybrid for example, *comic-tragic*. As a development of Czarniawska's approach I found that Gabriel's further categorisation of the stories helped in describing the range of stories and experiences being conveyed by the story-tellers.

Against classification is the danger of overlaying my interpretation, my construction and moving away from the raw stories and meaning that the managers draw from implementing reforms. I decided to maintain the classification for four main reasons. First, I agree with Gabriel that the poetic modes infuse meaning into events but further to this is what listeners feel about and do with the stories they hear – the listener is the powerful point for change. Second, I found that when I fed the stories back to managers they could relate to them, they supported meaning to them, and helped them see how they as a peer group shared many similar feelings and meanings in the midst of implementing change. Third, I found them helpful in describing the options selected by the managers to enact their narratives in response to the situations and events they describe. Finally, the classification also helped to surface what meanings are shared across the group of managers interviewed and allowed comparison across managerial groups in the different service areas provided by Omega.

Serials.   Serials tend not to have any overall plot; as Czarniawska (1997: 107) describes it, 'A serial starts as a story but does not reach a conclusion: it is a chain of interconnected stories'. Taking the example of a classic TV serial it consists of temporally related episodes (instalments) that both vary and are repeated. A serial does not usually contain any solution: the point is it can continue forever (or as long as anybody is interested in it). According to Czarniawska, organisational changes of various types can be regarded as serials. Just as in stories and themes the actors have to take into account 'how people do things' but in this case it is a question of transforming a story (a new way of working) into a theme – something that is incorporated into the relevant routines. Usually there are a number of similar serials against which the directors and writers compete. Within healthcare, currently, a number of 'serials' are competing for the attention of the actors (and audience), for example, 'interagency working' (like the CMHT serial in this study), 'Agenda for Change' (a job evaluation programme), 'Choose and Book System' (creating the option for patients to see consultants from other UK regions) and CPA (care pathways for patients) to name but a few. The serial proceeds slowly but surely: today's episodes establish the conditions for the next. Czarniawska (1997: 79) argues that serials 'reflect the current fashion in the organisational field within which the action takes place'. Healthcare change could especially be seen to follow the serial pattern, with apparently unsolvable and paradoxical problems thrown up by new initiatives providing endless material for fresh episodes. For example, interagency working, which began in US health services about ten years ago, has now become a fashionable initiative here in the UK and embedded into the

NSF for mental health. It is an example of interagency working, the community mental health team, that forms the serial described in Chapter 7. Serials are relevant to this study because they offer an account of shared meanings evolving over time with managers who regularly work with each other through different episodes. They are particularly relevant to this study in which managers say they have experienced a never-ending series of healthcare change initiatives. By tracking a specific change, that of CMHT implementation over a period of time it helps to answer the third question posed by Omega: Do the accounts convey a change approach that is working for managers and the service?

Themes. Themes are observed in modern dramas with no plot. Czarniawska builds up thematically related episodes, such as 'budgets' and 'identity'. The objective for her is to demonstrate 'what people do and how they act in certain types of situations'. Czarniawska claims that in organisational terms, scenes built around such themes show how relevant routines are created, recreated and changed in everyday life. So like stories, themes are highly relevant to a study of organisational change. However, rather than build up scenes from introduced themes, I build up themes taken from the story content to demonstrate 'what people *say they* do and how they *say they* act in certain types of situations'. The themes emerge from similar episodes in the stories from the managers to describe those aspects of organisational life that appear to be shared and therefore what seems to be shared in terms of what it means to them to be managing the implementation of change which is the second research question. Rather than the actual routines I see them as representing common themes in their social reality which as Gabriel (2000) suggests may or may not be representative of the actual events. Themes are relevant to this study because drawing them out collates what different managers in different parts of the organisation share in terms of what it means to them to be implementing change. Furthermore, these same themes may be found in other parts of the healthcare sector and indeed in any large organisation undergoing modernising change. The value of a thematic analysis to this book is to enable the inclusion of other narratives that may have been missed with the localised stories and CMHT episode analysis. This mitigates against claims that narrative approaches favour good story-tellers (Boje 2001) and that 'antenarratives' are often missed (see below). The term *antenarrative* was originally coined by Boje (ibid.) to describe fragments of narratives that come before the emplotment of a narrative that then form a 'story' or that are stakes in the process of building a narrative – 'upping the ante'. For Boje story is antenarrative and on some occasions anti-narrative. What he means by 'ante' is that people in organisations inhabit storytelling spaces outside plot, not the tidy and rationalised narrative spaces that are the currency of many narrative analyses. To translate story into narrative for Boje is to work with counterfeits, a false currency that we can't possibly spend on credible analysis. My stance and finding is that people do exchange 'counterfeit currency' in the form of emplotted narrative but that antenarratives or 'genuine' currency for Boje also circulate that do not adhere to any kind of plot. Anti-narratives are those narratives that run against the mainstream organisational narratives and I point to examples of both in the data analysis chapters 6–9.

Boje (2001) claims that classical thematic analysis can sometimes omit antenarrative and therefore favour the good raconteur. My interest in this study is to ensure that as many facets of what it means to managers to implementing reform are illuminated. I am not claiming that even the antenarratives or stories for Boje represent the actual events but that they are aspects to include and describe in the study because for me both narrative and antenarrative circulate in organisations to form the social reality for participants. Therefore by including antenarratives in this study a more complete picture is painted of what it means to managers to be leading the implementation of reform. In practice this involved describing and tracing fragments of semi-hidden stories and those that conflict with the 'official' story in a similar way described in Boje's (1995) analysis of Walt Disney Enterprises and including them in the description.

My methodological argument is that when themes are added to stories and serials a fuller picture of the social reality of change implementation can be presented and the analysis is strengthened.

Linking of the categorisation

In summary, the *stories* are the most localised element, they come from specific parts of the organisation and some might never be repeated. The stories or episodes within stories that are repeated by different actors build into *themes*. Themes may be recognisable in any large organisation undergoing change. *Serials* tend to recognisable in the whole of the organisation because they represent fashionable change initiatives that ripple right the way through, in this case, healthcare and sometimes all government departments and agencies.

5.5.5   Stage three: Feedback and focus groups

The purpose of this part of the process is threefold: first, to counter the co-constructing effects of my preconceived ideas, encapsulated by the notion that the researcher is part of the field; second, to answer the question 'What do managers say they need to support them in leading the implementation of reform?'; and third, to ask, 'Do the needs expressed by the managers bear any relationship to what MacIntyre's virtues-goods-practices-institution schema suggests is needed for a healthy institution?'

It should be noted that at no time during the series of feedback sessions did I discuss or converse with theoretical models such as MacIntyre's virtue ethics, I just presented the findings more or less as stories, serial and themes in the Chapters 6–9. Although he was there in the background as a source, the detailed conversations with MacIntyre's work came much later as I was writing up the book.

The feedback process had five distinct steps:

1. Director of mental health meeting – 3 people
2. Mental health managers meeting – 10 people
3. Third round of interviews with a wider group of managers – 21 people
4. Focus group with all Omega managers – 70 people
5. Focus group with regional managers – 50 people

Each of these steps and the outcomes are described in Chapter 9.

Temporal component

As can be seen from the description of the method, three main interview 'dips' were taken: one in the spring of 2004, one in the autumn/winter of 2004 and one in the early part of 2005. In Chapters 7 and 8 and to some extent in the Chapter 6, we can see how narrative is built on and changes over the period of the fieldwork. In organisational change terms this is an attempt to convey the dynamic aspect of change as shifting stories and conversations (Ford 1999) and that this is an important aspect in illuminating what change means to these managers. So rather than just a single snap shot we see some of the change in meaning over time to these managers. The theme of moral conflict, however, persists over the period of the fieldwork and it is that theme, or the means to understand that theme that I briefly describe now.

5.5.6   Stage four: MacIntyre informed analysis

As explained in the methodology section above MacIntyre's concepts were a later addition to the data analysis and came through a mixture of reading the data in parallel with reading MacIntyre. It became clear that morality and the virtues held by the participants were a significant theme in their enacted narratives of reform implementation. The method I employed was to mediate a conversation between MacIntyre's narrative-based concepts in *After Virtue* (1981) and the data. The aim of this conversation was to contribute new understandings to the ethical nature of the conflicts and dilemmas enacted in the narratives and what they unfold into the social reality of the organisation in change. This process led to an illumination of the ethical or virtue conflicts conveyed in each of the stories, episodes and themes. Each section of analysis, in the main asks,

- What does implementing reform mean to this participant?
- What is the ethical or virtue conflict in the narrative?
- What does the narrative unfold into the social reality?

I then viewed the answers to these questions in the light of MacIntyre's concepts and discuss the implications in relation to methodology, theory and practice in order to develop the arguments and contributions of the book. The outcomes of this process are elaborated on in Chapters 6–9.

5.6 Concluding comments

This chapter set out the ontological and epistemological approach to this study. The research is based on the notion of change as a set of shifting stories and conversations (Ford 1999) and that we can gain access to that by collecting narratives to form a sample of the social reality. The study is underpinned primarily by the work of Czarniawska (1997) and MacIntyre (1985).

Significant early influences on the research were set out and the evolving synthesis of narrative approaches is described. That synthesis draws on the work of Czarniawska (1997), Gabriel (2000), Boje (2001) and Cunliffe (2002) to produce a method that is capable of answering the research questions and that responds to the many critiques of the narrative approach. The research process of selecting interviewees, interviewing, transcribing, analysing and interpretation have been discussed in detail. It clarifies development of the analysis to include MacIntyre's virtue ethics with a view to bringing fresh understanding of the complex dynamic of organisational change in the public sector.

5.7 Structure of the data and analysis chapters

This chapter set out the research methodology, design and process. The data and analysis of the narratives is presented in the next four chapters.

Chapters 6, 7 and 8, stories, themes and serial, are the core data chapters and demonstrate how empirical material relating to leading organisational change in the public sector can be analysed using a synthesis of narrative approaches. The analysis itself is in three stages. First, localised *stories* of change, narrative *themes* and a *serial* of change episodes are extracted from the interview transcripts and what leading change means to the managers is examined. This approach follows the precedent set by Czarniawska in her classic study of public-sector organisational change (1997). Each chapter explains how the different treatments contribute to addressing the aims described above. Second, 'poetic story modes' following the example of Gabriel (2000), are used to categorise the stories into different types of plot (epic, tragic, comic and romantic) as originally discerned in Aristotle's *Poetics*. Third, conversations are mediated between key narrative theorists mentioned in the preceding chapters to suggest what the participants' narratives are doing or constructing as well as what they are saying. The final part of the analysis focusses on MacIntyre's virtues-goods-practices-institution schema (Moore & Beadle 2006). This enables a closer examination of the nature of the conflicts described in the stories, themes and serial and the constructing influence of their narrative enactments on the social reality of the managers across the service. The analyses are presented as a triad. This reveals the range of meanings and shows the importance of having all three present to support the developing arguments and contributions. In this way the three chapters could be viewed as a three-legged stool to support the argument that virtue conflict and the ensuing social constructions have been largely neglected in theories of public-sector change and yet they feature so strongly in this in-depth case study. The moral history and philosophy embedded in MacIntyre's thesis, it is argued, offers a wider perspective on those conflicts experienced by managers and in doing so begins to identify ways in which they might be supported in the midst of reform. The next Chapters 68, in addition to confirming that I have fairly attributed meaning to managers[3] in the narratives chosen, also reports on their expressed needs and compares that to what the analysis suggests in terms of support.

Finally **Chapter 9** offers data from when the findings were fed back to the participants and wider groups of managers from January to March 2005. Essentially, three stages of feedback and subsequent collations of data are contained in this chapter. Stage one contains the initial expressed need themes from the final stage interviews with participants, stage two is additions to those by a wider group of

managers from Omega and finally the feedback from a regional conference workshop/ focus group. Chapter 9 demonstrates the ability to
maintain a dialogue with the participants that leads to them putting
forward many ideas that could be taken forward by the organisation.
Some of these have been taken forward into specific programmes and
Chapter 10, Discussions and conclusions which follows describes these
in more detail.

6
Stories: Epic, Tragic, Comic and Romantic

This chapter is the first step in answering the primary research question: What does it mean to managers to be implementing government-driven reforms to mental health services? The purpose is to convey the range of localised stories, the polyphony, offered by managers in the midst of implementing change. It explores the nature of the enacted conflicts and how this relates to current narrative-change theory. It illustrates the power of stories and narrative analysis in developing a deeper understanding of the multiple meanings to managers in the midst of implementing change. The chapter therefore has both a methodological and a theoretical purpose.

Methodologically it specifically aims to explore stories as a medium to answer the primary research question. Stories have been observed as a way in which actors construct and convey meaning (Czarniawska 1997; Gabriel 2000). Underpinning the work of Czarniawska, Gabriel and many other narrative theorists mentioned in Chapters 2–4 is Ricoeur and his time and narrative trilogy (1983–5) which builds a case for suggesting that a close examination of narratives is a fruitful way of engaging with organisational data. Since Aristotle, typologies have been developed to classify stories. Gabriel's recent study (2000: 59) of 404 narratives derived four main categories (epic, tragic, comic and romantic) and inspired the classification used here. Similar to Downing (1997) I argued that these plots and storylines have an important role in shaping the 'unfolding reality'.

Moving beyond the story categories, theoretically, the chapter begins to mediate a dialogue between the empirical data, which describes organisational change through the stories of managers, and MacIntyre's 'after virtue' thesis. A number of concepts from MacIntyre's thesis are discussed to help expand understanding of organisational change in the context of healthcare reform. Here I briefly recap on the treatment of MacIntyre's work in Chapter 4 and then draw out the concepts further in dialogue with specific stories.

MacIntyre's belief is that humans are storytelling animals and one of the purposes of stories is to carry a set of moral virtues that when enacted in practice with others bring the good life for all those that are part of the *polis*[1], or in this case the institution that is the public healthcare system in the UK. For an institution such as this, when viewed through MacIntyre's lens, the importance of individual and collective narratives is emphasised as the carriers of a set of virtues that offer internal goods for all practitioners. What is the relationship between practices, internal goods and virtues? Starting with MacIntyre's notion of practice and its relationship to internal goods, he offers this:

> Any coherent and complex form of socially established cooperative human activity through which goods internal to that form of activity are realized in the course of trying to achieve those standards of excellence which are appropriate to, and partially definitive of, that form of activity, with the result that human powers to achieve excellence, and human conceptions of the ends and goods involved, are systematically extended. (MacIntyre 1985: 187)

MacIntyre further explains the relationship between virtues, practices and internal goods.

> A virtue is an acquired human quality the possession and exercise of which tends to enable us to achieve those goods which are internal to practices and the lack of which effectively prevents us from achieving any such goods. (MacIntyre 1985: 191)

Finally the way MacIntyre envisages the collective relationship of practices is summarised by McCann and Brownsberger (1990):

> The normative character of MacIntyre's definition of a social practice ... is secured within a larger account of the moral life as a whole. There must be some telos to human life, a vision anticipating the moral unity of life, given in the form of a narrative history that has meaning within a particular community's traditions; otherwise the various internal goods generated by the range of social practices will remain disordered and potentially subversive of one another.

Without a community's shared sense of telos, there will be no way of signifying 'the overriding good' by which various internal goods may be ranked and evaluated. (McCann & Brownsberger 1990: 227–228)

MacIntyre would view the managers in this study as being on a narrative quest. Moore and Beadle (2006: 332) explain this concept in relation to the communal narrative:

It is only within the context of this continuing and communal narrative that she can make sense of herself and that she can begin to make some sense of her telos. Initially this telos is derived from experiences of early childhood, but gradually it becomes hers as she embarks on her own narrative quest.

Like Moore and Beadle (2006) I believe MacIntyre's ideas are underrepresented but highly relevant to the study of organisations and especially relevant to the public sector and healthcare right now as it tries, as an institution, to find improvements in dialogue with the narratives of modernisation.

Having outlined the main concepts used by MacIntyre I will now discuss the classification of the stories and how that classification was carried out.

6.1   Story classification

Czarniawska (2000: 60) does not classify her stories but for Gabriel (ibid.: 60) 'each story type represents a distinct "poetic mode" or way of infusing meaning into events'. This raises the issue of classification of stories and the justification for doing so in this case. How does classification help to inform my story of managers leading the implementation of organisational change in healthcare? I began the classification process to enable me to structure the stories and discuss meanings across a number of stories. Gabriel (ibid.: 60) developed his classification of organisational stories based partly on Aristotle's *Poetics* and four main modes of epic, tragic, comic and romantic. His justification is that it enables the advancement of storytelling theory and that once classifications have been made, comparisons across organisations can be made. Against classification is the danger of overlaying my interpretation, my construction and moving away from the raw stories and meaning that the managers draw from implementing reforms. As explained in Chapter 5 I decided to maintain the classification for the following reasons which I briefly recap.

• Poetic modes infuse meaning into events.
• The story mode affects what people feel and do with the stories they hear – the listener is the powerful point for change (mimesis 3)[2].
• The managers could relate to them, they supported meaning to them, and helped them see how they as a peer group shared many similar feelings.
• They were helpful in describing the options selected by the managers to enact their narratives in response to the situations and events they describe.

Finally the classification also helps to bring to surface what meanings are shared across the group of managers interviewed and allows comparison across managerial groups in the different service areas provided by Omega. I will expand on all these points as the analysis develops.

The classification offered here is based on Gabriel's unique study of 404 organisational narratives. Gabriel (2000: 59) found he could classify the narratives across four main categories: epic, tragic, comic and romantic based on the feelings evoked in the listener. Gabriel suggests that stories are the basic unit of narrative and like him I found that the stories I collected could also be classified in this way. The epic evokes in the audience a marvelling at the hero's achievements, the comic evokes laughter, the tragic evokes feelings of compassion and awe at the protagonist's suffering and the romantic evokes feelings of nostalgia and love. Each story type, according to Gabriel (ibid.: 60), 'represents a distinct poetic mode' and they can sometimes be combined to form a hybrid, for example, comic-tragic.

Stories collected from the managers at in-depth interviews during this study were initially classified using Aristotle (1963) influenced 'poetic story modes' as described by Gabriel (2000).

The stories reproduced here are selected from the whole period of fieldwork. What I do is offer a selection of the type of stories told by the managers involved. Initially I just selected one of each type (the first one) for the early feedback presentations. Following the second round of interviews, and as I became more familiar with the material, I started to discern the different nuances in each poetic mode. By including the nuances, the picture of life on the front line of healthcare change becomes more inclusive: more people are able to relate to the stories. This was confirmed when I fed the stories back to a focus group of 70 managers from the same organisation to test out wider peer group resonance with the findings. Very strong affirmation that I had captured the balance and multiple perspectives of what it means to them to be in the midst of implementing change were fed back to me by the focus group participants.

Having outlined the main methodological and theoretical interests I will briefly explain how I classified the stories using Gabriel's method before introducing the stories themselves.

The epic stories describe the hero, usually the narrator, successfully implementing change; they evoke admiration and inspiration in the listener. The tragic stories convey managers suffering loss or coping with forces beyond their control; they evoke pity, sorrow and sadness at the suffering and provoke anger at the perpetrators, identified or unidentified. They often portray the manager as undeserving victim. The romantic stories have an emotional tone of caring, love or a nostalgic quality but without the tragic component of fear. The comic stories seem to offer misfortune as an occasion for wit and evoke laughter and amusement that is often close to or combined with tragedy. Hybrids can be discerned but I classified based on the main emotional tone evoked by the story that I picked up and noted during the interview and later when I read the transcripts.

The table below provides a brief title for the stories selected from the transcripts in order to give a flavour of the range of stories being told

Poetic Story Mode	Examples of the different forms	Told by
Epic (successful change story)	Finding the flow Subversive I'm not having it	Dave– senior manager Jane – senior manager with clinical responsibilities Lisa – district ward manager
Tragic (suffering loss through change)	Cuckoo reform Wasted talent Nobody to get angry with	Jo – service manager Julie – senior manager Linda and Charles – service managers
Comic (entertaining/ farcical/ tragic)	Bite on the bottom I shred it Gone shopping	Jeanne – Omega board member Ivan – senior manager Kate – project manager
Romantic (showing care or love for another)	Rose-tinted glasses My staff need me Just absorb that crap!	Geoff – service manager Pat – ward manager Graham – integration manager

by the participants. The spread of epic, tragic, comic and romantic stories was roughly equal across the transcripts and when this selection was fed back to managers they agreed that it did offer a fair representation of the range of meanings present across the service. The table is followed by extracts from each of the stories and an analysis of their meaning through a commentary that draws on the theoretical perspectives offered in Chapters 6–9.

6.2 Epic: Three forms of heroic change success stories:

6.2.1 'Finding the flow'

Context: Dave is a senior manager in his early forties and has responsibility for approximately a third of the mental health service delivery. He is known for his dynamic and forward-thinking style, works closely with the director and has a particular responsibility for hospital, day and residential care. As the hero in his success story he explains how he tried to encourage people to sign up for a leadership course from a university business school in order to help make change happen in his part of the organisation. He describes how he ignored the resistance of those he calls 'negatrons' and 'tweenies', pushed for leadership training for his staff and gave them both support and motivation. In the second part of his story he gives an example of him implementing change by talking about the closure of a small hospital and how he handled the situation.

...you know the scepticism which I felt was disappointing in an organisation and I did feel it. So when I went out without a clear mandate from the trust board which is how I felt at that time – this was in the 1990s. When I came back in, 1999 type of time we were without one i.e. a mandate, and that was the then service managers, mental health primary care and hired help professionals.... And I went round and said 'This is the product!' [i.e. the leadership course], 'I've got some money if you can arrange it. I've worked with the hospital's trust and we've got to put these programs on probably temporary, over the next couple of years, 25 places...are you interested in it?' Then came people's resistance, sceptical or you know.... Primary care were very interested, so I'm pleased, feels like a river: you flow when the doors open. If you get resistance, I'm not going to waste my time, I'm not going to work with people who are not going to work with me. But based on the view that over a period of time the 'negatrons' and 'tweenies' will come on board at some point so people see it, this is a good thing, so I'll jump on the band-wagon. So I work with primary care and

I got a lot of staff through primary care…I made sure that all the people I was working with in charge of the sisters went on this [leadership] program…Scepticism from the managers and people like that so I said 'Well?' [i.e. lets not be put off]…so that was my influence there, so I got a lot of my sister charge nurses through, community health team leaders and service managers through. Eventually that did take place, but…, it was like managers thought 'All right I might send my staff in but what's the clear direction?' You've got to take the support.

I asked if he had a specific example of implementing organisational change and he then went on to explain how he built on the above when handling the closure of a home for the mentally ill and the transfer of their care into the community:

…I think people were a bit apprehensive first because I asked for opinions, I discuss and consult with people about issues, I don't always, well it's very rarely I have a top down approach, it's usually about open consultation, discussion; how are we going to do it? Let people bring their ideas up and then try support them in doing it, because if they have ownership then there is going to be change, they don't have ownership and it's imposed then you sometimes come to brick walls and I think it's about explaining, communicating and talking to people, and giving them reasons why you want to do it. If you explain the reasons for it people are more acceptable to change and getting the actions done rather than saying, I want this doing now and when. That is not my style at all…

…I'm here if anyone wants to talk about an issue…

…When issues came up we were like a laser beam. People understand providing they have been listened to…

…In some cases the change opened up new career opportunities for staff…

…It is like spinning plates, we have an open system and I have got a team of change agents around me who are working on the changes. A lot of the change is small but staff are involved.

In the first part of the story we find in this manager's narrative what it means to be leading the implementing of change: persuading staff to attend a leadership course. This is a heroic tale of someone who believes in leadership education as a way of supporting the implementation of change and feels pleased to find the flow: *'feels like a river, you flow when the doors open'* and not *'wasting his time'* when he experiences resistance to education. This is almost diametrically opposed to Lewin's (1952) counsel of working on the resisting forces to weaken them.

In the second part of the transcript the manager expands on what he says he did in an example of him applying the leadership training to lead the implementation of change, in this case the closure of a ward: asking for opinions, consulting, listening, bringing ideas up, supporting people, building ownership, explaining, and being there if anyone wanted to talk about an issue. The 'laser beam' metaphor offers a sense of the intensity of his focus on listening to issues as they come up. 'Spinning plates' sums up what it means to this manager and I am left with an image of him dashing from one plate to another, working alongside his leadership-trained 'change agents' to keep all the plates going. It is interesting to note that this metaphor is usually used to signal someone rushing around with a schedule that is really too much for them but in this story he manages to keep everything spinning and is successful in implementing the service transformation.

So successful reform implementation, to this manager, means leadership education, something he believes is worthwhile and going with those that open the doors to that education and hoping that those against leadership training will eventually come on board. What is noticeable is that although conflicts emerge in the story he finds a strategy to deal with those conflicts, that is, going with the flow, and still maintains his belief in the value of leadership education. The sense is that he knows where he stands and from a Ricoeurian viewpoint we might judge this manager as successfully mediating with an 'identity narrative' between his character (*ipse*) and self-hood (*idem*) to say 'this is me, here I am, this is what I stand for'. In dialogue with MacIntyre, the narrative has a personal unity from the past to the present and a transmission or social construction potential of the virtues of (leadership) education and going with the flow. His narrative was inspiring to listen to and might, if I was a staff member, make me think about going on his recommended leadership course and trying out his 'going with the flow' style.

In this story we also hear about some meshing with other personal narratives: *'I asked for opinions, I discuss and consult with people about issues, I don't always, well it's very rarely I have a top down approach, it's usually about open consultation, discussion; how are we going to do it? Let people bring their ideas up and then try support them in doing it'* and creating a limited form of communal narrative unity with *'I have got a team of change agents around me who are working on the changes'*. The question arises whether this was what everyone wanted or whether it was just what he wanted. This quote, 'I *think it's about explaining, communicating and talking to people, and giving them reasons why you want to do it. If you explain the reasons for it people are more acceptable to change and getting the actions done rather than saying, I want this doing now and when. That is not my style at all*', conveys that the change is what he wanted and was supported by a case for doing it. There was no sense that others' stories had influenced his thinking, despite the consulting, and that their narratives were meshing with his to create a communal narrative.

What might this story do to the social reality? According to Pedersen (2006) mythic stories of heroic adventures do not generate new stories of heroes but rather tragic stories from employees. The next tranche of stories deals with some of the tragic stories that emerged from other managers. My analysis is that this story is ultimately about an individual who has an approach to change that he believes is right and that it would encourage others to take an individualistic approach to change. The virtue clash in the story is his belief in leadership education versus no education from the '*negatrons and tweenies*' and he overcomes it by ignoring them and finding people who go along with his ideas. MacIntyre would argue that the individualistic moral tradition encompassing as it does freedom of choice depending on what the market offers is ultimately corrupting of practice and is less likely to result in 'internal goods' for the practitioners and possibly tragedy as Pedersen finds.

The data contains a number of epic stories similar to this one with the hero or heroine describing how they have successfully implemented change in the organisation by finding the flow and gaining buy-in to the change from the people affected. As an alternative to this way of 'finding the flow' with others were stories about managers finding their own flow (with others in this case). Still of the epic type, the next form of successful change describes a manager using what she terms 'subversive' tactics.

6.2.2 'Subversive'

Context: Jane is a senior manager in her late forties with clinical responsibilities. She has a dual role which means she sits on the management team, manages a group of clinicians and carries her own caseload of patients. She is greatly respected in the organisation, is not afraid to challenge policy and is often asked to represent the trust externally as a specialist and review manager. She is describing her approach to implementing a change which started with a small group of people with a common interest in a certain type of mental health disorder.

After attending a presentation where they were told what they should be doing to implement mood disorder interventions, they instead did their own thing. Jane starts the story by offering an opinion on the split between *'evidence-based management'* and *'doing our own thing'* that met in principle.

> *I think it's this split between how management see the organisation and what it's actually like at the coalface and that's certainly not unique to this organisation, because since I met with you last I've done a Health Care Commission Review which was absolutely fascinating and there was the same very different organisation, but yet so many aspects that resonated and particularly this thing about this split between working clinically, it's like you've got these two sorts of currents you've got your top current that's going one way and then there's this sort of clinical one that goes on and flows on and thinks we'll be here anyway whatever happens. The patients don't change and the clinical issues don't change, and it's not necessarily that that bottom current is flowing in the opposite direction, but it may be going slightly differently. It's not that things are standing still and not changing or progressing at the coalface it's doing it to a different agenda to the agenda that drives the rest of the organisation*

You're in a position of experiencing both these currents.

> *There are areas in which I know I've set up my own little current to achieve something and a group of us have done this for people with mood disorders and we've been very successful. Like metaphors we've like flowed off along our own channel which has been supported in the organisation but in a strange sort of way and now we're flowing back and almost flying ahead of the current, in terms of sort of engagement developing a service which is very much engaged with people with the disorders.*

Making your own path down the same river.

> *Yes it's being subversive but to achieve a goal that I feel is what the spirit of the service is about.*

In practice what was happening? What were the managers saying and what did you do in your subversion?

> *It started off as an interest in mood disorders and somebody else needed to change their role as an outpatient nurse, they wanted to change the role of the outpatient nurse to be more challenging and as we talked we saw the common goals and then I was aware of other like-minded people and we got together a group of people who had no common base, apart from their interest in mood disorders who came together and that group changed over*

time and eventually became a coherent little group who came from very different places in the organisation. We had various ideas about how we wanted to develop services for people with mood disorders, we wanted to establish better practice to make sure people who had skills were able to use those and we also were very keen to develop a partnership style of working. I think what we all had in common was that we saw our clinical work as being working in partnership with patients, clients or whatever we personally called them and we wanted the service to develop in that way and then we had the opportunity to go into the Clinical Governance Development Programme, which basically was I think six days that we had away working with some training, but more than that it gave us the space and time out of the organisation to meet up, plan out what we were doing and to achieve various steps on the way towards our goal. We were fairly subversive in that we sat and listened to the presentations which were very useful and were then given tasks and then we just did our own thing.

'Rivers' and 'flows' also feature in this story and are added to with 'currents' to describe what it means to be leading organisational change for this manager. She says that she has deliberately set up her own little 'subversive' current to achieve something with others and claims to have been very successful – to the point of almost flying ahead of the main (government-driven) current of change. In this story we get more detail about what 'flows' and 'currents' mean: she names the management current as *'evidence-based management'* and her own as *'clinical'*, flowing in different directions but not entirely opposed. Because of her position, straddling management and clinical, she can see both currents and the sense is that they do not really flow together.

For Jane, she sees her clinical role as working in partnership with the client and used time away on a Clinical Governance Development Programme to develop that way of working with her group of like-minded professionals who all had a common interest: *'I think what we all had in common was that we saw our clinical work as being working in partnership with patients'*. In this account, they did their 'own thing' on the course and used the time away to plan out the steps to their goal. She claims this insurrection was successful.

MacIntyre might argue that the evidence-based and community-of-practitioners approaches are based on different principles and moral traditions, and therefore are incompatible. This manager finds a way of the two meeting in terms of outcomes by doing her own thing with a group of like-minded others. She is like the leader of a peaceful rebellion recognising there is a conflict of approaches but finding a quicker way down the river to meet and get ahead of the evidence-based approach in terms of what they both want to achieve. So a shared sense of telos (purpose) exists but very different virtues, one acting on evidence and the other acting in partnering, they don't clash head-on but they do remain separate with a sense of competition between them.

What might this story construct into the social reality of the organisation under change? I felt inspired by her story, it was like I was listening to a leader of an underground movement, who was working both with the management as a spy and returning to her band of outlaws, the latter were the heroic ones who found a way to beat the system without directly opposing it. The virtue of clinical partnership wins through in the end but to get there you have to be subversive and do your own thing. Again this runs counter to the notion of the communal narrative and would suggest a proliferation of people being subversive and doing their own thing in the face of prescriptions on how to implement change.

In this excerpt the social poetics (Cunliffe 2002) of the interview can be observed: the interviewer reflecting and building on figurative language, the metaphor of the 'river' and the trope of 'subversion' being used by the interviewee. The approach, which will be observed in other transcripts, allows the interviewees to continue their story and supports them in expressing what it means to be implementing service change.

Some managers reported a style that was predominately 'hard line' as described in this next form of story of managing successful change.

6.2.3   'I'm not having it!'

Context: Lisa is a senior manager in her late thirties who manages a number of mental health wards in one district. She is slight but is known for her forthright style and in this story is describing how she implements change to the way services are managed. This is another epic change success story that seems to be about her deciding what needs to be done and then ensuring it is done by confronting people when they don't do as instructed:

I said I was going to introduce an annual leave rota and we'll count how many people want to be off at any one time and I want you to request your holidays. So they again started playing off, me against whoever, well you're not accountable to me and they went to their next manager within the teams and said I'm not having it, I'm managing this service and I don't agree with having four people off...

...I know full well he says he's done things that he hasn't done. So for instance fire risk assessments, 'Yes we're on the way with them', so I go

and monitor it or whatever and it's not been done. I said 'Look you told me you'd done it' he said 'Did I say I'd done it?' I said 'Yes you did'.

According to Lisa, implementing change to services means walking the job spotting what is wrong based on experience and telling her staff what needs to be done, in this case implementing an annual leave rota, and then being assertive about what is to be done. In this third epic mode of successful change my sense is of a manager as a parent figure confronting her unruly children who 'play off' another parent to try to get their way. Lisa is 'not having it' and she asserts her authority over her children. She claims success with her approach.

What does this kind of story construct? Lisa's story was admirable from the point of view of her bravery in standing up to staff who were older and often with much longer service. What is at the heart of what it means to this person to be implementing change? Again a central virtue clash is enacted: the manager deciding what should be done versus staff deciding or being included in what should be done. For Lisa, to get things changed the manager has to decide what needs to be done and then assert his or her authority: 'I'm managing this service and I don't agree with having four people off!' MacIntyre points to the shrillness in modern debate, due in part to the lack of a communally negotiated approach and virtues of practice. This, he says, results in assertion and counter-assertion. Are we hearing a reflection of that here? Or are we hearing a story of bravery, using title power as sword to make much-needed change? The virtue of prudence manifested as care for what other people feel and think seems to absent from this particular story. The hero does not question the rightness of what they are doing under the circumstances and constructs heroic and individualistic notions of leading change.

Other managers told stories of a similar nature that were about introducing 'boundaries', 'parameters' and 'guidelines' and then patrolling them to ensure they were adhered to. They all claimed success either in terms of motivated staff or just the fact that the boundaries were being adhered to.

6.2.4   Conclusion to the epic stories

Summing up, the three forms of epic poetic modes appear different in what it means to these managers to be implementing change. In this trilogy, we have one meaning that is about going with the flow and focussing on issues, another that is about subversion and finding your own flow, and a third in which it means spelling out the change and confronting people when they do not do what they have agreed to do. What the stories have in common is a narrative of the right way of leading change and that by using different strategies they manage to uphold what they believe is the right way to implement improvements to healthcare practice. In this way they do have what MacIntyre (1985) describes as 'personal narrative unity' and what Ricoeur (1983–1985) would call 'narrative identity'. A communal narrative is present to some extent in the first and second stories but it is not meshing with all who feature in the stories.

As stories carrying a set of 'virtues' they construct heroic and individualistic notions of leading change that could, it is argued, proliferate the idea that being true to yourself is the best way to implement change. MacIntyre argued that modern moral debate is in a state of disarray because we collectively possess no means to judge one argument against another. He says '... there is nothing to such contemporary disagreements but a clash of antagonistic wills, each will determined by some set of arbitrary choices of its own' (MacIntyre 1985: 7). Whether by design or default, in these stories, the managers manage to avoid the need to enter the arena of disagreement or debate in a variety of ways: by just going with the flow with those who agree, hoping that 'others will come on board'; by subversion; and by assertion. What are we seeing here? Do these managers instinctively know what MacIntyre suggested, that there is no point in trying to reconcile opposing wills? So much for what the stories are saying, but what do they collectively construct into the social reality? We are left with the question of whether these stories collectively construct the notion of debate avoidance when leading change. Together they carry 'virtues' of doing your own thing, persevering with it and avoiding any kind of disagreement or debate.

'Virtue conflict' as drawn out from these three stories is a strand that weaves through the analysis and I will build on this theme and other themes that converse with MacIntyre's ideas as this book develops its own story.

The next set of three stories continue to reflect what it means to managers to be implementing change but the meanings they convey are very different: they are about loss and sit within the poetic mode of tragedy.

6.3   Tragic: Three forms of loss

In the first round of interviews stories were told by managers of staff grieving the destruction of communities of practice and old ways of working that seemed to work better for them and their patients. The changes have been brought about in response to implementing specific services as specified in the National Service Framework for Mental Health (DoH 1999). This tragic storyline continues in the second round and seems to have exacerbated to the point of people leaving the organisation in the first of these three tragic stories:

6.3.1 'Cuckoo organisation'

Context: Jo, a service manager, is in her mid-fifties and has seen many changes in her career but says she is finding recent demands for organisational change particularly difficult to reconcile. She has had to implement a significant change to the way the mental health services she is responsible for are delivered. The changes are required by the National Service Framework for Mental Health, a government policy document that describes what the service should be providing. Relocation of her team has also been necessary. She starts by describing how she feels and then moves on to describing the relationship between the organisation and the clinical work she manages.

> *I keep getting illnesses, no immune system, even though I look after myself I go to the gym, eat healthily, try and have holidays doing the normal self-care stuff... talk to staff and really good supportive relationships within our service, so I feel as though I'm in a really good balance with the rest of my life. There's this thing about having to manage, in the olden days I was a bridge to the organisation so we got on with what we were meant to be doing so I bridged – there was this two-way process of linking in with the wider organisation, but now the organisation is like a cuckoo it's just consuming it.*

So what does the nest represent?

> *The nest is the work, getting on doing a good clinical job and the demands of the organisation is eroding our time, energy it's getting rid of staff our staff have left. It sounds very emotive, the staff have said you can't sustain this if I've got to book a room and that room isn't free, then I'm not having that kind of uncertainty in my working environment. I mean it sounds very emotive.*

That's how it feels?

> *Yes, one of my staff is trying to get secondment out for two years into a different field, another one is saying she wants to reduce her hours because she's just not coping...*

Two very clear metaphors are used in Jo's description which describe what implementing change means to her: Jo originally feeling like she personally was a two-way 'bridge' to the wider organisation and now feeling like the organisation is like a 'cuckoo' eroding time and energy and getting rid of her staff. In social poetic style I enter the metaphor of the cuckoo and nest and she tells me more about what the nest means to her – it is the clinical work, doing a good job is what she values. What she describes might be seen by MacIntyre as the virtues of practice that offer a nest for the 'internal goods'[3] – the eggs. In this short excerpt we have a sense of a very dramatic and in her own words 'emotive' story of the government agenda of change arriving in her nest of work like a cuckoo chick and tossing her eggs, internal goods, out of the nest. I felt the sadness of the loss she was expressing to me in her story and through seeing her close to tears as she explained how ill she felt. The framing of the organisation as the villain, the murderer even, is highly emotive and conveys the depth of her feelings around the changes.

The cuckoo is a very powerful metaphor for a bird that appears only to care about itself and is ruthless, willing to steal and murder to get what it wants – a nest for its own chick to be raised in. Willmott's (1993) notion of the ideological colonisation of workers' affects and subjectivities has some resonance with this metaphor. I find the metaphor interesting and illuminating in its depth – as first the cuckoo lays its egg in the nest and the nest-owning bird just sees another egg and raises it as its own; only when the cuckoo chick hatches is the destructive force truly unleashed. Similarly the modernisation and managerial programme of change seemed reasonable, just another government initiative, but later its ideological force is revealed and the tragedy unfolds.

What this story is doing in my opinion, like Propp's[4] (1928) folklore of oppression under Stalin, is conveying the feelings of oppression and an inability to cope with a ruthless 'cuckoo' type virtue set that is successfully competing against a virtue set that this manager sees is about her 'work, getting on doing a good clinical job'. 'Bridging' with a cuckoo would indeed be impossible given the massive difference in ethics they uphold. Conversing again between MacIntyre and this data we see what might be an example of a breakdown in what he describes as the 'narrative unity'[5] (1985: 226) and a corruption to practice (1951: 223) when two different ideologies meet at the point of practice. Her story evokes anger and outrage and is experienced as tragic. Other managers in the same environment told similar stories of loss.

What does this story construct into the social reality? It demonises the source of the changes and demands on her, in this case the 'organisation', and exhibits an explanation of the organisation, as cuckoo, being responsible for eroding our 'time and energy' and making people get sick and leave. On a human level I felt very angry on her behalf at the 'organisation' doing this to her and her staff even though I was aware of it being her *story*. I argue, therefore, that this kind of story has the potential to construct anger and cynicism towards change amongst her colleagues and peers and unfold organisational change meaning tragedy and suffering to loyal staff into the social reality. As Ricoeur (1983–1985) observes the reader or listener completes the cycle (mimesis 3) and has the potential to act on their interpretation and therefore narrative can become ethics in practice.

In this next story another manager describes a second form of loss, the loss of the talents and self-esteem of the workforce.

6.3.2 'Wasted talent'

Context: Julie is a senior manager with considerable experience both as a manager and as a clinician working with people suffering from severe mental illness. This story emerged in the second round of interviews after Julie had read some of my initial findings. The initial findings did include the tragic 'cuckoo' story above but she felt I had missed something important with regard to organisational change, that the skills of the workforce were being wasted. She felt the organisation could be using their staff much more effectively in the process of making changes. This had, according to her, been going on for some time, it was not a recent phenomenon but it was significant enough for her to want to highlight the issue in the context of recent changes. She did not say 'here is another tragic story' but in this moving story the tragic loss both to the organisation of her skills and for her personally, the temporary loss of her self-esteem, are conveyed.

> *I was talking to somebody earlier in the week and I think both of us are very articulate, skilful people in our own ways and don't fit the standard mould, will challenge things and we can be uncomfortable but we would say that this organisation appears to be unable to identify and use the skills, not skills in the formal sense as you are trained to do CBT[6] or trained to prescribe their medicine, but the personal attributes, it doesn't say, 'Oh so and so is really good at doing that. Should we ask them to do that?'*
>
> That hasn't come through strongly [in my findings to date]?
>
> *It's a huge issue, it really is.*
>
> Making the most of the skills and the talents?
>
> *People have to be pushed into boxes and if you don't fit in the box and they can't push you into the box to fit you're difficult, you're an embarrassment,*

maybe embarrassment is too strong a word but that feeling that you have be managed instead of saying 'Well what's this person saying, how could we use this?'

Is that how you felt at times, pushed into a box?

Very much so, well I don't get pushed into boxes so I'm a problem to the organisation for various reasons I think for various reasons I now understand why I don't fit into the organisation. That has been very useful in terms of psychological assessment...which allowed me to understand and gain insight into why I didn't fit in, which then allowed me to say to other people 'This is why I don't fit in'. I also have the skills which I should be using, but they still struggle to do that and I see that with other people as well, there are other people who have particular skills which should be nurtured and developed.

...pushed into a box and yet you have other skills you could be offering.

I thought for years there was something wrong with me, that I was stupid and why didn't I relate to people and yet I lived with this dissonance with the evidence I had on one hand working with teams and closely with people and elsewhere.

I was thinking of self-esteem.

People would never have thought I lacked self-esteem, but until I...these particular things quite serendipitously everything fell into place and it made sense and I could then manage that, but I think that must apply to other people within the organisation as well.

So what does that mean for you?

I've wasted my talents for years.

Organisational change for this manager is about being pushed into a box rather than being called upon to use her talents, and those of her colleagues, in the pursuance of the change agenda. The clash of virtues in Julie's story is conveyed in this quote: '*that feeling that you have been managed instead of saying "Well what's this person saying? How could we use this?"*' She sees the organisation as managing change by putting people in boxes rather than trying to use the skills and talents as conveyed in what people are saying. She herself says she felt this pressure to be placed in a box, suffering for a long period as she struggles to understand what is happening to her.

What does leading the implementation of change mean to Julie? It means tragedy and loss: a waste of her and her colleagues' talents for years. The narrative is also tragic for the organisation in terms of 'wasted talent' in the midst of change. An indication in her comment that she is making sense of the situation after many years of feeling that there was something wrong with her: *'everything fell into place and it made sense'* seems to indicate a turn to the epic mode.

The box metaphor and my *self-esteem* comment said in the moment as they occurred to me offer further examples of the social poetics of the interview process. They demonstrate the co-construction of meaning present in the interview. With regard to the latter comment she seems to relate to this and says *'People would never have thought I lacked self-esteem'* implying that she did feel she lacked self-esteem for some of the time. Her comment that this might apply to other people in the organisation does come through in other similar stories. 'Skill blindness' from the organisation recurs in many of the managers' stories of implementing change and is drawn out in Chapter 8.

What is the story unfolding into the social reality? At the start she reports that she has discussed this topic with a colleague and they have come to some level of agreement on this being how it is. My view is that this story sits side by side with the previous story in demonising the 'organisation' in change as the cause of the tragedy, in this case by putting people in boxes rather than seeing how their talents could be used to implement change. The organisation is portrayed as treating people like objects to be pigeonholed. Again I felt anger towards whoever was doing this to her and her colleagues and can imagine it constructing anger and cynicism towards change in others if this is the outcome. But who or what is the 'organisation' responsible for these tragedies? In this next story we are offered a view on this.

In the final tragic story example, we hear the story of the loss of the entity or person to be angry with at the way change is managed in the organisation.

6.3.3   'Nobody to get angry with'

Context: Linda and Charles are both experienced service managers who manage large groups of practitioners who offer specialist nursing and therapeutic treatments. They are talking about a recent review and reorganisation of the services they manage. They work fairly closely with each other and I interviewed them independently whilst they covered for each other. The review looked at what each team was doing and how the teams use resources leading to a reconfiguration into a new organisation model in South Omega. Coping with debt combined with making changes leaves both these managers feeling exhausted and angry. Linda says:

> *...my main memory at that time was a lot of the nurses being up in arms because of the threat to their jobs and situations that was the big issue at the time. At the time those people went to reapply for jobs and you know they were all having interviews as to their first preference, I mean they weren't going to be made redundant but it was like you know you have to be fitted in to this new organisation, what's your first preference, what's your second preference and the acting managers would, whether they would actually accept people who wanted to do it you know, there was a lot of anxiety around them. The service modernisation group was a group that I think was overseeing it all, seeing not just the management of that but the whole change.*

Yes, so it was a service modernisation group.

Senior managers, so [X], Omega-wide head of service was on that until she went on maternity leave and I took over standing in for her for a while.

So you were in that group as well? And how did you find working in that group?

It took me a while to get my head around what was going on, I mean this was before I'd taken on this job so I've been you know, fairly unexposed to higher level management work and most of it wasn't directly relevant to me so there was lots of things to do with social services and contracts and employment and all sorts of things that were out of my area, but I enjoyed being a part of it actually, beginning to get a bit more of a sense of a wider picture, to be given a feeling that there's just so much that needs doing and not the time and resources to do it thoughtfully.

That's still there that feeling is it?

Yes, quite a universal feeling at the moment is that everyone feels they have too much work to do. What's happening is that you're having to not do some of it...people are there every weekend, the senior managers are there trying to cope with the...government...it's a very saturated or over-saturated...

It wasn't always like that?

No.

No, that's happened since these changes then?

It's not just the changes. I think the whole problem of the debt that we've been in for a long time. That dates back to when we amalgamated with South Omega, so as I said the fact that all these changes happen within the context of reducing cost I think is the biggest, so there's a sense of like, nothing ever gets better, it just seems to get tighter and tighter.

... nothing gets better, it gets tighter, financially and timewise?

Time, space, financially and what I haven't even mentioned yet is as part of you know the [initiative Z] savings, Omega is required to save 20 per cent and what they've decided is everyone must save 1 per cent and then they'll look at bigger projects that might save so they're looking at closing down the physiotherapy gyms or closing down a regional alcohol service or one of the things they're looking at is psychological therapies across Omega so I have been charged with reviewed psychological services across Omega. This is partly in relation to this having to make [initiative Z] savings but it's partly in relation to the CHI, Commission for Health Improvement and that's a very powerful body that's you know, everybody lives in fear and trepidation of them coming to visit and inspect you and one of their action points which is a must do, is the need to address the waiting lists for psychology and the resources ...

... I feel angry but there is no one to get angry with because it is like we are all part of it – I'm exhausted.

Whereas in the last story it was the organisation, here 'we are all part of it' conveys a sense that they just can't stop themselves from angering themselves. Charles, the other service manager from the same office, offers his perspective on this latter issue in a separate interview:

Around all this it's very frustrating not being able to personalise the source of the lack of respect so I've been feeling really not respected, in my position as a senior Y, manager, human being, long-standing member of staff, long-standing reputation, but even just as a human being trying to do a job there is a huge lack of respect, but there's nobody to focus it on I can't name one particular person who's doing that to me. If that was in real life I'd want to tackle it head on if you were my line manager was doing that to me I'd deal with it, have an arbitrator if necessary but deal with it, voice the complaint, ask for a response, what's the way forward? There's nobody to take that to because it's, we're all in it. I know I'm not singled out, we're all in it.

The story conveys a number of issues but running through the narrative is anger at the something that they are all a part of that is not respecting them as senior managers and as human beings needing time and resources to do a good job. The emphasis is on tightening finances, inspection and performance management and that they seem to be all part of constructing that change. For them it means that there is no one person to focus the anger on. Foucault's panopticon metaphor (1984) seems relevant here as they police themselves but feel angry with that invisible policing. The policing is around effectiveness, standards, financing and performance and the outcome for the first manager is 'I'm exhausted'. Here again we have exhibited explanation in the narrative – current pressures for organisational change result in my exhaustion.

Once again a clash in virtues can be discerned as the central drama in the narrative: respect for doing a good job versus being overloaded with 'must dos' and financial constraints. This account of all being in something that they are unhappy about, aware that they are angry about it but apparently unable to voice their complaint or anger at the way they are being treated, will be explored further in Chapter 10 as I explore the cultural metaphor of reality TV and the *Big Brother*[7] phenomenon.

6.3.4   Conclusion to the tragic stories

What collectively do tragic stories like this construct into the social reality of organisational change for managers? When stories convey exhaustion, disrespect, staff leaving, and talents wasted, parallels with oppression, bullying and slavery come to mind. One manager reported to me that the healthcare sector 'can only function by bullying at the moment'. My view is that this kind of story evokes a mixture of anxiety, fear, anger, mistrust and cynicism towards change especially when it is supported, as was the case with Linda and Charles, by visible signs of stress and exhaustion.

In terms of virtues what do they construct, what is the moral tale in these stories? MacIntyre argues very strongly that when money, status and power (or in these managers' language 'effectiveness', 'finances', 'standards' and 'performance') become central then corruption to practice occurs and people suffer loss of the 'internal goods' such as wellbeing and job satisfaction. The public-sector context relates very closely to the kind of communal virtue ethic narrative that MacIntyre espouses. Mangham, I think, puts it well: when summing up MacIntyre he says 'the self must have a sense of purpose, be socially grounded and constructed in a consistent and continuing narrative in pursuit of the good' (1995: 293). I think most public sector managers would sign up to that ethic. The corruption of that ethic by private sector ethics has been recognised by writers such as Brereton and Temple (1999). In this case therefore, the moral construction might be that organisational change embedded with private sector ethics and managerialism is not healthy for people who hold a public service ethos. And what about the service and the patients? The managerial level social construction of the impact of reform on health and wellbeing for the patients is a question that we move to in Chapter 9 when we ask 'Do the narratives construct reform as improving services for the patient?'

These tragic stories also raise a final point. MacIntyre holds up the manager as a significant character (along with the aesthete and therapist[8]) of corrupted and fragmented morality in modern society. MacIntyre condemns the manager's 'profession' as an agent of moral degeneration in society. Du Gay (1998) and Brewer (1997) have criticised MacIntyre's stance in this area by defending the practice of management as honourable and ethically sound. MacIntyre's argument is that because part of a manager's role is to improve efficiency and effectiveness, managers have a corrupting influence on the ethics of practice. In these stories we see managers suffering for their moral stance with regard to practice, then enacting a narrative of their suffering which it could be argued constructs a moral backlash against reform. So MacIntyre's argument as a whole may hold in the private sector and this public-sector example in terms of outcome, but his rationale in the area of effectiveness and efficiency interests seems to break down in the context of the public sector. Some managers become unwilling agents of managerialism but are not advocates of effectiveness and efficiency, despite the hegemony. Rather they appear to form an underground resistance movement – good soldiers[9] (Hasek 1973). Comedy is one way of fighting back and in the next section we look at some examples.

6.4 Comic: Three forms of entertainment/farce

6.4.1 'Bite on the bottom'

Context: Jeanne starts her story by describing the dialogue at a board meeting where she was trying to make a case for a service to meet a specific and local mental health service need. Jeanne is in her early fifties, has an executive role on the board and is a champion of the needs of under-represented groups. Being an ex-nurse she also understands and is close to the concerns of clinicians on the front line of care. She is someone the board regularly consults on matters associated with the mental health service needs of the local population.

> *I was in a meeting discussing the serious issue of* [not meeting a mental health need for a marginalised and vulnerable group of patients]

and I said well surely this fits into one of our targets. Y said 'Well no it doesn't'. We just left it and went back to looking at finance [associated with restructuring and cutbacks to save money]. *We have these different aims and they are mutually exclusive.*

I feel frustration that our overriding purpose of caring for people is ... survival at best ... every time we start looking ahead someone changes the goalposts. Z said to me 'They would not know a patient if one jumped out and bit them on the bottom.'

Who are they?

The government I suppose.

OK.

What is the name of the organisation this year? is a common joke. I think the changes that have taken place in structure will not have affected working practices on the ground ...

... Even if all the PCTs raised the issue with the SHA the government would not shift. We feel powerless – it is harder the closer you are to the service delivery. Nobody has said this but the sense is let's just overspend and meet the needs

The clash of purpose or telos is more explicit in this instance: 'we have different aims and they are mutually exclusive'. According to this manager the board 'just left it' and went on to look at finance. Why did they just leave it? Were the needs – meeting targets and addressing local mental health problems – just too difficult to deal with and finance an 'easier' and perhaps more pressing agenda item for them? Were they being bullied into focussing on targets with no room for personal leadership as Blackler (2006) suggests? MacIntyre (1985) argues that the telos and virtues of finance, efficiency and effectiveness are incompatible with striving to provide equality of care to and wellbeing to all. Since they are based on different premises and perfectly logical in their contained arguments all that can be done to achieve resolution is assert one above the other. In this story we see finance being asserted over equality of care and the frustration this executive feels about this situation. The narrative suggests that these two ideological horizons are reflected into Omega's boardroom and find no resolution.

I suspect this narrative might be enacted in other healthcare trust board rooms around the country where effectiveness/ efficiency/ performance management (managerialist) virtues meet the virtues of improving the equality of care for people in need – the original ethos of the NHS and the public service ethos that motivated many people to work in healthcare. Government is framed as the villain and wins over 'good' people trying to promote equality of care. We see dramatic resolution when the villain becomes an object of ridicule, like a cross between Fagin[10] and a buffoon in a farce, he is laughed at for not even recognising his customer because he is too busy counting his pennies. The financial position of Omega like many other healthcare trusts is dire and stringent measures are being taken, including service reduction, cutting posts and the closure of wards. The board seems to have no way to resolve the moral argument put forward by the managers other than by moving on to something they feel they can deal with. (Arguably they cannot deal with that either.) However it is argued here that the narrative enactments of people out of tune with that decision are far-reaching and actually work to achieve the opposite.

The enacted narrative in this case is comic, subversive even and could be interpreted as another example of Propp's (1928) idea of the counter-culture folklore in a situation where they feel powerless, an oppressed group that expresses its power in their jokes and stories. According to managers[11] from trusts across the UK this kind of story is prevalent across healthcare (and the wider public sector). The last 'let's just over-spend' comment offers an ironic (and possibly satisfying) twist in that whilst the board (and government) are framed as prioritising finance, the people on the ground prioritise meeting needs like heroes in an epic resistance battle.

Taken literally organisational change means an ever-widening gap between the virtues of practising healthcare for people on the front line of care and the financial interests of the board/government. In terms of what the story might unfold into the social reality, once again we can imagine cynicism and anger but also amusement around organisational change. For peers and colleagues it might mean it is not worth taking organisational change too seriously, after all the villain perpetuating change is really a sad, mean comic character and out of touch with our reality. This story could be seen to help inspire the good of a telos and virtues of caring for all people equally whilst the virtues of efficiency and effectiveness are rejected.

Through the next comic story we get a sense of what it means to be handling 'must dos' that seem at odds with what a manager sees as important.

6.4.2 'I shred it'

Context: The service manager, Ivan, recounting this story is responsible for a group of practitioners who provide one-to-one therapeutic treatment for people suffering serious mental health conditions. He is explaining how he handles the continuous flow of practice changes he is asked to make:

> *I couldn't quite see the relevance to my work at having to ask somebody about their allergies or other physical questions. It's that kind of thing we're supposed to respond to and be relevant and so we change our practice accordingly and as a result of that I tell my staff, 'Look what we're having to do here' and they stormed in angrily saying 'That's ridiculous' so we go back to the source and she says 'Well it's a national requirement'. So we have to do it then. We get a lot of this it feels like the old cliché of bureaucracy gone mad…audit could be done by an administrator. I choose to leave gaps between paragraphs, but you're not allowed to leave lines and it's this kind of pedantic attention to detail, unnecessary in my point of view.*

> By meeting all the detailed requirements it takes away from your central role?

> *That came out of the bombardment of having to attend to so many requests, how many more piles of paper do I have on my desk that are connected with ongoing things can I cope with and as a result I sometimes put a letter at the bottom of the pile and hope they'll go away or get forgotten about or people will forget they've asked and then six months have gone and nobody's asked so I shred it.*

> That's the reality for you?

> *If I were running a business I would be horrified to hear that, so I can see other sides to this.*

This account conveys what it means to this manager to be handling change to services that he does not believe in. The story was accompanied by the poetics of gesture and movement: he picked up a piece of paper representing a 'must do' change to practice and placed it under a pile of other papers on his desk then extracted it and traced an arc of movement towards the shredder with his hand. He laughed and I could not help smiling – I sensed some of his relish at being able to shred what he considered to be another bureaucratic and irrelevant 'must do'.

Like the previous story, this one could be interpreted as an expression of resistance driven by a personal belief in what is worthy to be spending time on – certainly not the national requirements that increase bureaucracy: '*it's this kind of pedantic attention to detail, unnecessary in my point of view*'.

The essence of the story contains a clash of virtues associated with the level of bureaucracy that is required to run a service. For this manager what it means to be implementing reform is finding ways to reduce the number of things that they believe are unnecessary.

What kind of social construction and virtues might this story unfold? The story itself contains some reactions from this managers' staff group *'they stormed in angrily saying "That's ridiculous"'*. The source of the change is framed as a kind of meddling bureaucrat. The edicts, partly due to their nature and partly due to their volume, are not to be taken too seriously and not to be acted upon immediately. The way you handle change is to ignore it for a while, hope that it will go away and you can then shred the edict. The virtue of keeping things simple and not being distracted by 'unnecessary' disruptive influences to practice such as the next great change idea from meddling bureaucrats disconnected from our reality seems to be the moral tale. A twist in the story is apparent when this manager brings a different moral perspective as though he was running a business and aware of what an employee was doing. Nevertheless even that ability to take the moral stance of the owner of the organisation is insufficient for this manager to change his approach to managing the implementation of reform.

The final story in this comic trilogy reveals more than the usual dose of accompanying tragedy.

6.4.3 'Gone shopping'

Context: Kate is a senior clinician turned project manager who came up with an idea to improve practice in support of and in line with government reform policy on multi-agency working. She explained how she had put a lot of work into a project to support changes to the way multi-agency mental health teams share information and are managed. The change was to share patient information, especially for patients with complex needs, with all the clinicians that might be involved in their case so that all had access to a growing computer-based single case file and multiple collecting of patient demographics could be stopped. Previously all the different clinicians involved would collect demographics and keep their own case files which would occasionally be shared orally at case meetings. This meant that clinicians were often unaware of treatment given by other clinicians and so could often duplicate or annoy the patient by collecting information that had been collected at previous sessions. All the work had been done locally but now a national IT programme (Connecting for Health) was threatening to take over. Her work had been done by involving the clinicians, IT people and administrators and, she claims, had their buy-in. All this hard work had been done with minimum support and she felt very proud of her efforts. Unfortunately when the work was presented it was seen as not fitting with the national priorities and was effectively discarded. She felt it was still a vitally important piece of change to improve services for the service users. We take up her story.

> *The green paper is Victoria Climbie*[12] *... it was the big enquiry for a child you know, being concerns and numerous professionals who'd visited this family and had concerns but they hadn't linked ... and that enquiry was suggesting that agencies needed to work better together. Initially that's a link between education and social services and left health a bit, you know, not clear where it fits in, but because, I'm thinking aloud a little bit here, but it seems to me that sort of patch based working that comes up from a child that's actually very, very relevant to adult work, certainly where it overlaps with carers. You've got to develop working system arrangements and value continuous [clinical?] knowledge and the ability to understand local need. Data managed at a very local level I think would be good.*
>
> Around local knowledge?
>
> *... well, education is being given a lead, and I'm just thinking, because it's very very difficult to see where ours fits in with this national programme completely, it doesn't fit really, no it doesn't.*
>
> No because it's a completely home-grown database?
>
> *That's right yes. But in terms of giving the clinical team a sense of their own, well it's about having a sense of responsibility isn't it, that for a manageable group, for a professional to feel able and enable, you got to have some sense of 'I know who I'm responsible for' and it's a size, a case load or whatever is within my ability to support it. If it gets beyond ... supportive for any individual then you get meltdown really.*
>
> *I nearly sent an email saying 'Gone shopping – you guys have taken control away'.*

She did not send the email but she was tempted just to see if anyone did really care about her work in the organisation and if they would react. She went on to explain her own analysis of the situation in a second interview:

> *People have gone from high-energy states to learned helplessness. If you take the parent-child metaphor, gradually the child starts to express the world in its own way and you want the child to be rebellious, to find their*

own tune within the boundaries set by the parent. Through battling you get to a more mature relationship. But if you force me I'll lose interest, I'll go along with it but… We learn to go through the motions now, jumping to someone else's tune rather than our own tune. Rather than being able to decide based on local need, someone else has decided. If you have an intrusive parent, there is no listening, no dialogue… we are totally helpless.

The social poetic of the parent-child metaphor in this case is made very explicit to convey what it means to her to be in the midst of leading the implementation of government-driven reform. Stepping back again, what is this story doing? It is highlighting what is a clash of values for her: *'You've got to develop working system arrangements and value continuous (clinical?) knowledge and the ability to understand local need'* and this she sees as not fitting with the national programme: *'It doesn't fit really, no it doesn't'*. The story is given emotive power through the Climbie reference and generates feelings of anger: 'How could they do this to you when you are trying to prevent children like VC from being abused?' After her work is brushed to one side by the national programme she fantasises about testing the organisation – would they react if she announced she was going shopping? Gabriel's idea (2000) is that fantasy offers a symbolic refashioning of official organisational practices in the interests of pleasure rather than oppression. In feeling helpless the resort is to comic folklore of resistance, imagined in this case but nonetheless a clear message of 'Do you really care about what I've got to offer?'

MacIntyre's suggestion (1985) is sharing personal narrative quests to form an evolving communal narrative that carry the institution's telos and virtues. That telos and virtues set determines how a group of practitioners should conduct their collective practice. This seems very close to what Kate is describing in her vision of how different disciplines could work together supported by the system. The national system, decided on by 'someone else' for her, does not fit with her vision and she 'loses interest'. Her quashed attempt to implement in practice what she believes is the right way to practise her vocation is enacted as a comic-tragic narrative.

What might this narrative unfold into the social reality? You can be pro-active, creative and innovative in the process of organisational change but in the end your work might be discarded without recognition. For me it breeds anger and cynicism towards the big change initiative, 'Connecting for Health' in this case, rather than the virtue of innovation and risk taking which is what the government wants from practitioners. Her later analysis of the social reality is 'We learn to go through the motions now jumping to someone else's tune'.

6.4.4   Conclusion to the comic stories

In each of the above stories a clash of values or virtues can be discerned and the enactment has a comic edge to it. This choice of emplotment adds amusement and, it is argued, strengthens the cynicism and anger that the tragic stories construct towards what change means to our managers. Demonisation of government reform agents turns to ridicule of the villains through the use of humour and the message is not to take reform too seriously, in fact you can 'shred it', tell them you have 'gone shopping' or even get a patient to bite them 'on the bottom' and it will not make a difference to the way reform is managed. Just learn 'to go through the motions' keep your head down because even if all the people in all the trusts raised the issue 'the government would not shift' so 'just overspend' and 'meet the needs'. The moral message that these stories would unfold into the social reality seems to be that covert rebellion is virtuous under this kind of reform approach.

In the final series of stories I review three that I categorised as romantic.

6.5   Romantic: Three forms of care

6.5.1   'Rose-tinted glasses'

Context: Geoff is a service manager in his late forties and is greatly respected at all levels. He, like many of the managers I interviewed, works long hours trying to marry reform needs with patient needs. He contrasts how they currently look after mental health sufferers who are difficult to engage and how they used to do it before they implemented the NSF guidelines and recommended roles and responsibilities. He had just explained that since tightening up roles and responsibilities they have found that more of the 'difficult to engage' group of patients have been left without care.

> *A lot of people who are just described as being very difficult to help, very difficult to engage with in services and traditionally a lot of people who have been helped in the more, things like therapeutic communities which are disappearing, the nearest one to us is closing down.*

By tightening up on your roles and responsibilities, who you can take care of, has highlighted a need for care for other patient groups, or user groups, I don't know, what would you call them?

Patients!

Patients, but some of them might not be patients yet. They might just be out there suffering.

Yes because people with personality disorders are often heavy users of lots of other services, such as prisons, police, social services, housing, bene-fits you know, probation and they get bounced around because they're often very difficult people, angry, not feeling looked after and so on. So the government is actually emphasising the need to develop interagency ways of helping people like this and understanding how to help these people, which is very positive, but a long way down the road.

I'm just trying to understand. That group of people, previously were they supported in any way?

There was a lot more flexibility before I think, so people sort of did their own thing, they may have done it guiltily without telling their managers or whatever but I think those people were held in different ways and now there's a lot more of them, often to the detriment of the staff because these people are very difficult to help and work with but they're very worried, they're often the ones that are self-injuring and suicidal ...

So they kind of bent the rules a little bit to support those people?

You get certain people who are, I mean, are the ones that will end up ... and no one coming down on them saying you must only do 12 sessions and then discharge because that's increasing as the pressure is to justify what we're doing and make sure we're not carrying massive caseloads, a lot of the CPNs carry horrendous caseloads and quite rightly they're looking at managing their caseloads a lot more efficiently and fairly. Essentially what's happening really is the service is being cut in terms of making sure the staff aren't burnt out by doing too much ... that's positive and also the services are being cut by the additional time that goes into additional bur-eaucracy ...

Geoff is less vociferous than most in criticising the new ways of work-ing and destruction of the communitarianism of the 'good old days'. The extended care that people showed for the users who were tradition-ally hard to engage is conveyed in this story and also an acknowledge-ment of the detrimental effect on staff who would take on 'horrendous caseloads'. The story constructs a picture of what health-care 'mod-ernisation' in process means to this manager. The service for the *'very difficult to help'* mental health patients who are *'often the ones that are self-injuring and suicidal'* has effectively been cut. Staff need to look after themselves and spend time on the bureaucracy of implement-ing an integrated service and attending each others' meetings which will eventually mean a better service but 'a long way down the road'. Modernisation virtues of practitioners' self care and bureaucracy (for a worthy long-term cause) clash with the virtue of communitarianism of the old days where these people were 'held' by caring staff willing to bend the rules without regard for personal wellbeing. Neither seems preferable but the story paints a romantic picture of patients getting a better deal as opposed to the modernising state where the staff get a bet-ter deal – or do they? What does this story unfold into the social reality? The price for modernisation is a temporary loss of service. Normal ser-vice or a better service will be resumed some way down the line. A tale of the disappearing good old days being replaced by a service in which staff have clearer roles and responsibilities but no time to 'hold' people. The morality message of the modernising healthcare sector is look after yourself, limit what you do to your job description and pay attention to the bureaucracy and things will improve – or will they?

Many of the managers I interviewed referred to the way the services used to work and created a kind of romantic imagery of the 'good old days'. In this story that romantic image is tempered with a sense of the NSF offering 'positive' change in some respects so that staff have manageable caseloads and that in the long term it will be better for the patients; however, it is acknowledged that time is a 'long way down the road'. The conclusion made by managers who tell this type of story is more or less the same: the service actually worked better pre-reform for patients in that they were 'held', they were cared about and staff were prepared to bend the rules to support these people. What is different here is that this person's story is about a manager coming to terms or convincing himself that the change will be beneficial. He has recon-ciled the virtue of setting limits to the care being offered and accepted that the service has effectively been cut. For others this reconciliation has not happened and they still grieve for the old days and the way they used to work together to care for people. The point here is that no reported morale debate has happened for the manager instead she con-vinces herself of the positive aspect of the change – it has been asserted as the right way because it is in the NSF and policy implementation guidelines.

This story appears to show practitioners originally committed to their community with little thought for themselves and their workload. Their interest was to 'hold' people in the community by bending the rules if necessary. This sounds like the kind of meshing of narratives that MacIntyre describes as having the potential to bring purpose, virtues in practice and wellbeing for all. Czarniawska suggests that with reform we have modern identity narrative being plotted against the individual's life history (1997: 48) as opposed to the communal narrative that this manager seems to be describing as the identity of the service in the good old days. By modern identity, Czarniawska means the outcome from the spread of liberal individual ideology so despised by MacIntyre (1985). Reform in this case is manifested in the story as a tightening of individual roles and responsibilities, the collective role and responsibilities seem to have gone missing.

It is as though this manager is convincing himself of the right in the new way of doing things. This manager's story is however being taken the way of setting individual accountabilities through the 'modernisation' project spearheaded by the guidelines in the NSF. In this story and others they are being moved away from caring for people in the community with shared discourse of it will be better in the long run for the patients if they set limits to the care they can offer. Taking a MacIntyrian perspective, it could be argued that this manager has become an agent of a liberal individualist ideology in the running of mental health services.

The romance in this story has a duality: first, the manager romancing about the good old days, and second, the romance of the modernisation discourse seducing this manager into a union that will bring a change for the better in the long run.

What might this story unfold into in the social reality? It says reform may not be working at the moment but with the virtues of 'no pain without gain' and looking after ourselves we will be able to look after our patients better. For now we have to leave them to self-harm and commit suicide because we have got to meet up, integrate and get on with the bureaucracy of making it better.

The next story has also got a connection with roles and responsibilities but is a different form of romance – the loving care shown for people who work for the storyteller.

6.5.2 'My staff need me'

Context: Pat is a ward manager in her early thirties and reform projects to her mean extreme stress. During one such programme of change called 'Agenda for Change[13'] she describes reaching the point of feeling that she just could not cope any more. The whole programme was tightly controlled with a set of 'must do' deadlines and salaries could be affected by the outcomes. She knew that what she really needed was to take time off and recover but the care she felt for her staff outweighed her personal needs:

> *If it were not for my staff needing me I would have gone off sick definitely.*

This manager cried whilst she told me her story of the dilemma she felt inside. I just listened and gained a sense of the strength of loyalty she felt for her staff during this period of significant demand and the cost to her personally. Loyalty to staff by managers and vice versa was a common theme in the stories told of organisational change and is brought out in the themes section.

What is this type of story doing? For this manager the virtue of being there for her staff, meeting their needs, was paramount, overriding her need to recover, and gave her the incentive to come in to work. The message is: I am not prepared to sacrifice what I believe to be the right thing to do which is to be there for my staff. This type of folklore has a sense of 'you might make me ill but I will not be beaten' and again is reminiscent of the counter-culture of the oppressed as described by Propp (1928). The implementation was running at the time of my fieldwork and many managers reported feeling under pressure with tight deadlines to meet. Kallinikos (2006) speaks about the roles and responsibilities that the institution defines to meet its own ends and therefore directs people to operate towards the ends and external goods, as defined by those roles. Like in the last story, through being an agent of change the manager can unwittingly be an agent of the ideology underpinning that change. Taking the MacIntyre line, practice is therefore corrupted unwittingly by the practitioners who adhere to managerialist solution constructions to service improvement. Reports from my managers suggested that some people came out of 'Agenda for Change' winning financially while others lost out and had their jobs downgraded. Many reported that it pitted people against each other and created competition, fear, anxiety and mistrust. The job panel reviews were designed to be objective with reams of criteria documentation to assess jobs and people against. Some claimed the pressure to deliver reduced the whole process to a fiasco and turned the impossibility of objectivity into something like a reality TV assessment of whether someone should be given the grade or not.

In this story, like the last, we have duality in the romance: seduction in the aims of the change – it being about equality of pay and on the face of it very appealing. For managers the reality of implementing change meant competition and suffering. Here we have a story of a manager pushing herself to attain the 'internal goods' feeling good about caring for her staff through the virtue of courage to push against her own needs.

Along similar lines, the last story in this chapter has the underlying theme of protecting or buffering staff from all that goes on above.

6.5.3 'Just absorb that crap!'

Context: Graham, a senior manager in his early forties is responsible for overseeing the integration of two teams, one from local authority county council social services and another from healthcare services. In his view, protecting staff from the politics going above and a deluge of policies and bureaucracy that are delivered into the mental health services from two different institutions as 'must dos' is the theme of this story. Here the account goes on to give an example.

> *You've got to just absorb that crap! Because they don't need to see that rubbish. They don't need to see that, so you're absorbing that then, presenting a sort of smooth management... That's a bit too ideological that. It's more about presenting it as upbeat perspective of the dilemmas and the obstacles that are being considered by those above, to the integrated teams through dissemination of information to them which is major turmoil on the photocopier, but at least they have the information and through the monthly integrated team meetings, again is where both agency staff are treated equitably. I've just thought of another example of where we've got parallel things.*

> Please go on.

> *We've got two appraisal systems. Well, technically yes, on paper what we are actually doing is using the best. Which is actually the local authority one, I mean in terms of positive attendance we use local authority reporting forms and we have if you like unwritten permission to do that because we have an integrated agenda.*

> So you're taking the best from each of the two systems?

> *So long as it's consistent with the...organisations policy, what isn't necessarily important is how it's recorded so long as that policy is complied with. In terms of health and safety our record of incidents etc, is on health documentation and it's reported to local authority if their staff are involved*

and local authority health and safety lead comes to the locality health and safety meeting.

And they're okay with it, that they are documented on health authority forms, yes?

Yes, we have two different lone worker policies but the commitment of the agencies is that the, this new electronic computerised gadgetry which is being commissioned by the health will be rolled out to local authority personnel as well. So again these bits and pieces that are gradually being dragged through, which do allow much more explicit integration to happen. Insight to the chaos in [my area].

That's exactly what I wanted – your insight

So you can come back in four months time and find out that we are exactly the same!

The joke in this last comment offers a possible insight into what it means to him to be in the midst of change – nothing really seems to change. When I returned for the second round of interviews a different manager, Madeline, who sits outside the integrated teams offers their perspective on the kind of protective role described above and questions whether buffering is really a caring option:

The stress is so vast but even in their best efforts to be a buffer, they do end up dumping more than they realise….they're not getting the support they need they are not able to contain it and so they're acting it out in destructive ways.

Two alternative story modes are apparent: the romance of protection and the 'destructive' nature of protection. In the first manager's account, what it means to be managing change seems to be to take up a buffering role and present an upbeat image of the bureaucratic debates going on above. This could be seen as a partial isolation of his staff from the raw debate going on above him and across the two institutions. The manager goes on to describe being asked by his two line managers from the HA and LA to use two different appraisal systems but actually choosing to use only one of them because he considered it the best and most consistent with both policies therefore absorbing the stress of the dilemma himself.

The virtue being conveyed here could be said to be caring for staff by not overloading them with policies and bureaucracy by buffering them. For Graham, gradually reform is being 'dragged through': 'So again these bits and pieces that are gradually being dragged through, which do allow much more explicit integration to happen' but the impression is of pulling something along that does not want to move and it is slow going – come back in four months and nothing will have changed!

The second manager questions the viability of the buffering virtue and offers another storyline that runs against the first, and offers what could described as antenarrative[14] (Boje 2001): an alternative story, a story with a destructive outcome. Following through on this antenarrative with other managers did reveal a range of stories, some claiming that buffering was an essential managerial activity in change and others claiming that bullying was the outcome of this so-called protective role, further that the buffering was happening at all levels in the organisation due to the level of requirements for change in the form of initiatives, measures, policies and frameworks.

What then, in the context of organisational change, are the virtue clashes conveyed in these stories? First of all there is a virtue clash between managers: some believe in the buffering and protecting and others believe that this is ultimately destructive and far from protecting staff it is a form of bullying. Second, there is a clash between what the government believes will help to make practices change (a blunderbuss of policy initiatives) and what these manager believe will work with their staff (a controlled flow of information and demands and a filtering of what they believe is important). We are not hearing the kind of communal narrative unity described by MacIntyre (1985) as the carrier of a set of virtues that will bring wellbeing to the institution through excellence in practice. The narratives clash and exhibit disunity. MacIntyre argues that this kind of narrative disunity is characteristic of the modern institution and signifies moral disunity that is corrupting of practice and the 'internal goods'. He sees managers as co-authors of the divided institution because they unwittingly act as agents of the effectiveness and efficiency goals of liberal individualism which in this case, we might argue, are embedded in the healthcare reform agendas. He also positions managers as moral representatives of modern society because of their status and power over so many people. As moral representatives along with Aesthetes and therapists, he claims they are partially responsible for our morality as a society being in grave disorder. Other writers (for example, du Gay 1998; Brewer 1997) have sought to bring MacIntyre back from this position and see managers as having a great deal of moral integrity whilst others (such as Mangham 1995) to some extent agree with MacIntyre and call for further understanding of his ideas in the context of the institution. That call has recently been reiterated by Moore and Beadle (2006).

What then does Graham's buffering story, his colleague's bullying version story and the general narrative disunity around change unfold into the social reality of healthcare under reform? My view is that together they unfold further disillusionment and cynicism towards change amongst staff and provide ammunition to ridicule reform. I imagine being an apprentice in this community trying to form my values and feeling lost in a sea of conflicting narratives, virtues and values. One manager, an 'apprentice', new to the service conveyed her impression after four weeks in her post:

So are we seeing here under reform pressures a microcosm of what MacIntyre describes as the modern institution in moral disarray? Are we seeing, as he claims, practices being corrupted by efficiency and effectiveness drives of liberal individualism loaded into the reform agenda wittingly or unwittingly? My view from the stories I gathered is that to an extent we are and it is damaging to people, their practice and ultimately their patients. Does it have to be like this? Perhaps the irony here is that the aim is to 'integrate' two institutions, to try to create a communal narrative in the interests of giving a better service, but, as MacIntyre argues without the resources to enter into a moral debate the different parties just end up 'dragging' through, asserting their will on the situation.

6.5.4   Conclusion to the romantic stories

Clashes of values or virtues run through the above romantic stories. In the first clash we have caring for people without caring about the cost from the good old days of the NHS versus the situation now where we have to care for the cost to us individually and financially to the organisation of caring for people. The second clash involves a manager who considers the greater good of staff needing her to be above her personal needs to recover from the stress of her implementing change. In the last story we have a virtue clash between managers: some advocate the buffering and protecting role and others describe this as ultimately destructive and far from protecting staff it is a form of bullying. Finally there is clash between what the government believes will help to make practices change (a blunderbuss of policy initiatives) and what these managers believe will work with their staff: a controlled flow of information and demands and a filtering of what they believe is important and ultimately no change to their community of practice.

This choice of emplotment conveys that what it means to be leading reform is to have care and concern for others. For some it has a flip side which means this approach can be destructive and oppressive.

These types of stories unfold a great deal of confusion about what is the appropriate way to interpret the reform agenda. Taken as a whole they strengthen the cynicism and anger that the previous forms of stories construct towards what change means to our managers. There is a sense that staff should be infantilised during change, 'don't tell the children all that is going on it will only upset them' or 'I need to be there to protect them at all costs'. Hunter (2000) argues that government policy is in danger of creating a 'managerial infantilism that cannot deliver the modernisation agenda'. So these romantic stories partially construct the virtue of infantilisation in the midst of change. Another side to the romantic stories is a construction of reform meaning oppression under a well-meaning but bullying exterior. Caring for your staff by protecting them from reform initiatives is virtuous but actually that virtue has an inbuilt vice of oppression. So the message might be that in pummelling the service with government initiatives, managers become bullies through protecting staff from all the initiatives. I imagine that for some people it would generate fear and paralysis and for others reactions like anger and subversion and mistrust achieving the opposite of what reform is trying to achieve.

6.6   Conclusion to the stories

Downing (1997) argues that managers choose to enact their stories of organisational change using different emplotments. I took further inspiration from Gabriel (2000) who discerned four main poetic modes from 404 organisational stories: epic, tragic, comic and Romantic. I used these four categories to convey the different types of stories that managers enact in the midst of change and through the stories draw out the meaning of reform to managers. The epic conveys a successful story of change, tragic loss in change, comic makes fun of change and romantic is a story of love or caring in the midst of change. In all the narratives I looked into what the managers were saying was at stake – what I found invariably was some form of virtue clash, antagonism derived from opposing social and moral traditions and standpoints. I also wanted to understand what these stories might unfold into the social reality of reform for these managers. In other words what, collectively, do these stories do?

The table below shows my interpretation of the virtues at stake.

In the heroic stories the managers choose to uphold their own virtues of reform practice and in the three examples they do this either by going with the flow, being subversive or asserting their will. In the practice of implementing change, the epic stories convey a journey to uphold the virtues the manager believes in and to ignore, subvert or challenge virtue sets that differ with their own. Together they carry 'virtues' of doing your own thing, individualism, persevering with what you believe to be the right course of action and avoiding any kind of disagreement or debate. This type of heroic story would educate others in the benefits of taking the individualistic approach. Some critics have argued that this has been the Labour government's approach to reforming healthcare (for example, Hunter 2000) and if so are we seeing a reflection of their ideological horizon in these claims of successful change?

For some the option chosen for enacting their narrative of reform is tragedy. The tragic stories of change convey a clash of virtues where the manager loses their ability to work by their virtues and feels oppressed

Poetic Story Mode	Examples of the different sub-modes	Central virtue clash in the story
Epic (successful change story)	*Finding the flow*	*Leadership education vs. no education*
	Subversive	*Evidence-based management vs. partnership-based clinical work*
	I'm not having it!	*Manager decides vs. staff decide*
Tragic (suffering loss through change)	*Cuckoo Reform*	*Doing a good clinical job vs. individual self-interest*
	Wasted Talent	*Using skills and talents vs. putting people in boxes*
	Nobody to get angry with	*Respecting that humans need time and resources to do a good job vs. efficiency measures and effectiveness standards*
Comic (entertaining/ farcical/ tragic)	*Bite on the bottom*	*Meeting needs vs. meeting targets*
	I shred it	*Manager and clinician led vs. bureaucratic edicts from government (locally led vs. centrally led)*
	Gone Shopping	*Locally managed case data and accountabilities vs. nationally managed case data*
Romantic (showing care or love for another)	*Rose-tinted glasses?*	*Caring for people without caring about the cost (good old days) vs. caring for the cost of caring for people (modernisation)*
	My staff need me	*For the greater good (staff needing her) vs. personal needs (recovery from stress)*
	Just absorb that crap!	*Buffering (bullying) staff with selective communication vs. open communication channel*

by a virtue set that is imposed on them from above. In trying to uphold virtues such as 'doing a good clinical job', 'using skills and talents' and 'respecting that humans need time and resources to do a good job' they suffer a loss. Their virtues correlate strongly with MacIntyre's notion of making virtues and excellence in practice the end so as to offer 'internal goods' rather than chasing the 'external goods' of money, status and power. In these stories people seem to suffer loss of what MacIntyre describes as 'internal goods' of practice such as wellbeing and job satisfaction and other losses such as valued members of staff. In this case therefore, the moral construction might be that the reform agenda is not good for the wellbeing of people who believe in using the skills and talents of people to do a good clinical job and who respect that they need time to do it. These stories unfold meanings of anxiety, anger, mistrust and cynicism towards change into the social reality especially when it is supported by visible signs of stress and exhaustion. They are also likely to generate a good deal of anger from people who believe the virtues of the protagonists as 'good' and managerialistic reform virtues of efficiency and effectiveness as 'bad'. According to Downing (1997: 28) this type of good vs. bad plot construction is 'primary' or 'core' and expresses anger. He argues that the primary plots offer 'simple frames of reference or sense-making for actors involved in major organisational change'. He also suggests that 'during unfolding events, stakeholders are implicitly framing the social drama in one of a number of generic plot formulas derived from romance, tragedy, irony and melodrama.

The comic mode is chosen by others to enact change. The comic stories of change could be seen as part of the folklore which expresses a counter-culture against change. A level of disengagement from an imposed virtue set or fantasy of disengagement is present in the comic stories. This choice of emplotment adds amusement and strengthens the cynicism and anger that the tragic stories construct towards what change means to our managers. It seems that the moral message in these stories is that given the government is a villainous old fool and not to be taken seriously then covert rebellion is virtuous and is for the greater good.

The romantic stories convey to some extent a blind upholding of a virtue such as protecting staff by buffering all the bureaucratic wrangling or overriding own needs to recover to care for them. I argue that these romantic stories partially construct the notion that infantilisation of staff in the midst of change is appropriate. Caring for your staff by protecting them from reform initiatives is virtuous. For some that virtue has an inbuilt vice of oppression. So the message might be that in pummelling the service with government initiatives, managers become bullies through protecting staff from all the initiatives. I argue that for most people this would only generate further anger at and mistrust in reform and achieve the opposite of what reform is trying to achieve.

Bakhtin and Medvedev (1928/1978: 30) suggest that we should look to the wider ideological horizons reflected in narrative. If we do that it is clear that in many cases the virtues at stake are embedded in political and moral traditions from many different sources, for example, devolution vs. centralisation, communitarian vs. market. MacIntyre suggests that these different stances cannot be just brought together and resolved because their moral baseline is fundamentally different and therefore justice or a decision as to which way to go is impossible to make. How do we know if they are incompatible in this context? We can't know for certain but in this study, not one manager, in recounting stories of implementing reform, describes a story where they have achieved the feat of bringing different moral stances together to form a synthesis, or a meshing of narratives where common virtues are agreed and acted upon. This is how MacIntyre summarises the situation:

> The suspicion – is that all those various concepts which inform our moral discourse were originally at home in larger totalities of theory and practice in which they enjoyed a role and function supplied by contexts of which they have now been deprived. (1985: 10)

MacIntyre also suggests that we are left with fragments of moral traditions that people use haphazardly to convey and argue their moral position. MacIntyre references a multitude of moral traditions and their sources (1985) which we can see reflected in the above clashes. What is important for me is MacIntyre's claim that these virtue clashes have roots in different philosophies and they are not compatible. If he is right and the roots are deep, these managers are unlikely to be in position to dislodge those roots and replant the trees somewhere else or if they have grown large to splice them to form a new hybrid tree. But similarly trying to knot branches together at the canopy level would not be a satisfactory outcome if they are trying to create a safe, solid and reliable tree (or service in this case) that is better than any one of the trees. So in a way what managers are being asked to do is create one solid tree from a mix of well developed trees and saplings. What MacIntyre is arguing is that because moral debate has lost a single telos and an accompanying set of virtues and has become corrupted with different kinds of argument, especially liberal individualistic politics, we have created an ugly and 'shrill' debate.

What has been argued elsewhere (e.g. McNulty & Ferlie 2004) is that the government ideology is weak: simply because it keeps shifting and changing with the popular management theory or other fads. It plays with different concepts like growing small new saplings then finds they bend and break as soon as any pressure is applied. A new one is grown as soon as the last one begins to collapse. This is not just a criticism of the current government. Managers in this study often told a story of structural changes that run in five to ten year cycles such as devolution (small local health authorities) and centralisation (large regional health authorities) and this becomes very frustrating for them. After they have just recovered from the pain of one restructure, another comes along that recreates the previous structure. This would seem to further support MacIntyre's argument that we have lost the resources to have a narrative-based moral debate about how best to organise people and institutions to practise their craft for the wellbeing of all. What seems to happen instead is assertion and counter assertion ad infinitum. As a devolved structure appears not to be working the assertion that centralised structure would be better wins the argument and vice versa, hence the seesaw effect. This situation could be described as 'unstable' and as such highly anxiety provoking for people in the situation especially as they have to continue to achieve 'the day job' and this in itself is highly complex. Add to this the narrative and moral disunity that we see in these stories between the swings then, and as MacIntyre suggests, do we have an institution (and society) that is living 'after virtue' in a state of moral disarray?

Up to now we have looked at localised stories of reform implementation and what they mean for managers individually and collectively. I now look at one specific change driven by the Department of Health edict for mental health services to form multi-agency community-based teams. This team is called a community mental health team. It is constructed in Chapter 7 as a serial of change (Czarniawska 1997) containing episodes described by the managers involved in the reform process.

7
Serial: Community Mental Health Team Formation

The primary purpose of this chapter is to answer the question 'Do managers construct reform as working for them and service users?' and to do that by looking at one specific reform, that of the community mental health teams (CMHT) formation. After the localised stories of change I turn to a specific serial of change. The analogy of the serial in the context of public-sector change, according to Czarniawska (1997), can be viewed as changes that are being freshly introduced and in this way we can observe the characters and themes evolving just as in a TV soap opera.

> A serial does not have any plot, it consists of related episodes (instalments) that both vary and are repeated. A serial does not contain any solution – the point is that it can continue forever. Organisational change of various kinds can be regarded as serials of this type. Public Sector change could especially be seen to follow the serial mode, with apparently unsolvable and paradoxical problems providing endless material for fresh episodes! (Czarniawska 1997: 78).

Serials are relevant to this study because they offer an account of shared meanings evolving over time with people who regularly work with each other through different episodes. I believe them to be particularly relevant to this study since many managers said they have experienced a never-ending series of healthcare change initiatives. The concept of multi-agency working is at the heart of this particular change initiative to form community mental health teams. The belief behind the concept is that by co-locating the mental health professionals from the different disciplines together in a single team they will provide a better service (improved access and higher quality of care). Further, it is believed that rather than people needing expensive in-patient treatment they can be treated early and in the community thereby saving on treatment costs. That is the theory that has become government policy in the form of a National Service Framework (NSF) Department of Health (1999) along with Policy Implementation Guidelines (PIGs) Department of Health (1999) for mental health services. The accounts below are from managers who are in the process of translating policy into practice and are under a great deal of pressure from DoH to prove they have recruited people and set up the teams.

7.1   Community mental health team serial

Stories of managing the changes associated with implementing the CMHTs are conveyed in many of the managers' accounts. As explained in Chapter 2, under the National Service Framework for Mental Health, the modernisation aim of this particular reform is to transfer the care of MH service users away from inpatient and outpatient facilities to care in the community. The hoped-for outcome is reduced costs and an increase in the quality of care provided. The CMHTs are often linked closely to housing support agencies, voluntary and community organisations and other agencies that can support people suffering from mental illness. The NSF and PIGs describe the need for multi-agency teams offering a flexible and responsive service to the mental health needs of the community. The state of play is that the professionals from main agencies have now been brought together formally, including the two main agencies, the local authority (LA) and the mental health service provider Omega, to deliver community mental health care as co-located subregional teams. In the region served by Omega, three CMHTs have been formed to cover three distinct geographic areas. Prior to this, community mental health existed in various forms with professionals usually, but not always, located in the offices of their home organisations. There was informal liaison between the different professions involved in supporting people suffering from mental health disorders but little in the way of formalised joint roles and responsibilities and no shared budgets.

This chapter contains episodes from both the first round of interviews in early 2004 and the second round in the latter part of 2004.

Five episodes form this serial including a final compilation:

1. Beginnings: GPs fight tooth and nail
2. Bringing the policies of two institutions together: trench warfare

3. Managers spanning health and social care
4. Under way with depressed crew and a holed ship
5. Dog's dinner: the compilation episode

7.1.1   Episode 1 – Beginnings: GPs fight tooth and nail

Context: The mental health NSF and PIGs ask for the co-location of community psychiatric nurses (CPNs) within CMHTs so that agency partners work together to offer care in the community. CPNs, prior to the implementation of CMHTs, were usually located in GP practices. The GPs referred patients directly to the CPNs and they carried out assessments of need. The CPNs would also have a close relationship with other practitioners in the GP practices in addition to the GPs, such as counsellors and practice nurses. The change meant that GPs would instead have to refer patients to the CMHT. It was important at the very start of the project that GPs agreed to this change. According to this manager the GPs resisted this change vehemently to stop 'their' CPNs being lost. Phillipa, one of the senior managers who has clinical responsibilities and a key role in the CMHT formation, takes up the story:

> P: *...we must have been the last area in the county ever to develop fully functioning CMHTs which we only did last year and the reason that we took so long to do it was that we were opposed by GPs. And what I have to say may sound rather jaundiced but I guess I have 12 years or more of negotiating with GPs and they don't like being told that the way that things are running to their satisfaction is actually not the way things can carry on running! So my biggest experience of trying to manage change has been trying to work with GPs which I've been doing ever since I've been [working in Omega]*
>
> MC: What were the GPs concerned about?
>
> P: *Their ability to access somebody quickly for their patients when they needed it in their surgery would be lost. And it would go into some face-less, nameless and amorphous body and their patients would get sort of dropped into a hole somewhere –and their experience before had been that people didn't communicate very well and they didn't know what was going on. That was their core anxiety. They like to retain control and they felt that what their CPNs were doing was delivering a very good service, and they didn't want that spoiled, they only looked at their needs. So they fought tooth and nail against any change and without the CPNs coming into the CMHTs we couldn't run the CMHTs. In the*

end the changes were forced through with very bad grace despite huge amounts of effort ... to keep saying 'Stop them!'...

The tape stops at this point. I reflect to her that an 'amorphous body' is the impression I have of the CMHTs from the stories others have given me so far. She agrees that in their current state they do appear this way.

The storyteller seems to claim the moral high ground by saying the GPs *'only looked at their needs'* – the implication being that she was looking at the greater good of the service and the patients. The GPs value having the CPNs close by, in their surgeries, whereas the manager is trying to implement the CMHT policy guidelines which advocate the creation of a co-located team to deliver the service. What the story is doing is conveying a clash of virtues which in this case is managed by *'forcing through'* the change. This is what leading the implementation of change means to this manager: forcing it through, asserting the policy despite huge amounts of effort to stop it by the GPs. This episode frames the GPs as the villains in this early phase of the change and one of the managers in a later interview described them as *'the* blockers' to the formation of the CMHTs even though their concerns seem to be well founded. As observed in Chapter 6 no moral debate occurs in the story, just assertion of policy will.

Six months later another manager, Alan, who has both local authority and healthcare services staff under him, reports that the GPs are given more reason to doubt the efficacy of the CMHTs with closure of referrals into the team to all but the most severe.

GPs are experiencing major anxiety over the waiting list closure

One of the other CMHT managers, Simon, reported a shift in the relationship; he smiled and said

We have tamed the tail and stopped the GPs wagging the dog.

In a later focus group, another six months down the line (see Chapter 9), one of the key concerns raised by Omega managers was the need to build better relationships with GPs!

The second episode offers an explicit description of a clash of traditions and virtues that have to be managed in the process of leading the implementation of change.

7.1.2   Episode 2 – Bringing the policies of two institutions together: Trench warfare

Context: Having overcome the 'villainous' GPs and 'rescued' the CPNs from their surgeries the CMHT implementers have to come to terms with bringing not only different disciplines together but also the policies of different institutions. This episode covers accounts that offer narrative related to what happens when the professionals are brought together as a team and they have to deal with the practicalities of working together to deliver a coherent service. The term 'trench warfare' was used by one manager in the pilot interviews to describe the battle to bring the different philosophies of health-based care and social care into a workable team unit as CMHTs. Steve, a senior local authority manager, offers his thoughts on the issue:

> S: *What I continually find interesting is the cultural difference between the NHS and the local authority. That's not to say that one is kind of better than the other. There are clearly differences. There are differences in accountability in that the local authority's accountability has been through elected members. The NHS has a different kind of accountability. Social services have been traditionally involved in providing community-based care of one sort or another, so looking after people living in the community. The NHS has a different line of accountability – a lot of it has been hospital-based. I hesitate there because clearly GPs do a vast amount of community-based primary care, caring for people in the community. I suppose the other thing is that the NHS on the whole provides treatment-related care and that can be focussed on the illness. Whereas social services will see the illness as only one part of the issue and there will be a number of things that will contribute to a person's situation in the community. Illness may be one of them, but there are other factors – family, poverty or a whole range of things, unemployment, education – and our training in social services has been if you are assessing someone's needs you would look at all those things and so the challenge in working together is to ensure that assessments of people in the community whether done by a social worker or a nurse are holistic and take account of all the issues and don't just focus on 'giving the pills', just the physical. If it's a mental health problem, just the psychological. My theory is that there are people in both health and social services who are very good at doing holistic assessment and in arranging the appropriate care across the board. But equally in both instances there are people who want to focus on providing the treatment. I think*

that is a kind of tension that still exists, and in some degrees is healthy but it needs to be addressed and probably needs a fairly fundamental kind of shift.

MC: That's what you are seeing.

S: *I think so and I think that there is still some confusion in the minds of some people as to what the roles are.*

MC: Do you experience that confusion?

S: *On occasions, yes – it's associated with the whole issue of community care. If you are going to care for people in the community you have to do an assessment that recognises what the key issues are and if they are solely to do with treatment then that's fine. Unless you are absolutely certain about that the treatment is not going to be successful, I think. I think that there are some people who come into either nursing or social work who really want to be much more into the treatment, the stereotype of a nurse is that they are into treatment and a doctor for instance, but the issues are wider.*

MC: It's a really interesting aspect to me, that difference.

S: *What's interesting and it's not unique to mental health but I think probably it's fairly important in terms of mental health that the issues to do with unemployment, poverty, family relations are really fairly crucial. If you break a leg and you're poor, social services can probably arrange for someone to do your shopping and so on until your leg is better, but if you are mentally ill it is more than just sitting waiting for your leg to heal, it's a much longer process.*

MC: What is the feedback from the CMHTs?

S: *The difficulties that occur are in effect [those of] using two systems – particularly for the managers, so they have to manage two supervision systems, personnel systems, work to two personnel officers, complaints procedures, that sort of thing.*

The dual-systems issue is also raised by another manager from another locality, Kate, who adds further explanation of the problem:

K: *I suppose at the CMHT manager level we are integrated team managers ... The problem that brings is that because we are not integrated above or below we are working with two sets of policies, two sets of procedures, two sets of IT systems, two cultures. Those things aren't integrated and when you are trying to take a team along the process and sell ideas to them and concepts to them etc. you are fighting a bit of a losing battle because all the other things aren't integrated. It's like you are integrated on one level but not on another*

The narratives highlight what it means to be leading the implementation of change for managers who have to knit together the systems from two very different traditions (health care and social care) and make them useable. Outcomes seem to range from 'confusion' on occasions at one end to full-blown *'trench warfare'* at the other. War metaphors such as in this instance *'fighting a losing battle'* were very noticeable when managers talked about this subject and caused me to speculate about what they were fighting for. Were they were fighting for 'justice' for their patients? Or justice for themselves and the practices they believe in? If so the problem as MacIntyre suggests is *'Whose justice and which rationality?'* (1988). Here we see what it means to these managers to be implementing a government policy of multi-agency community team-work. There is considerable complexity in what they are trying to achieve and what it means to them. What I am doing here is trying to isolate one aspect of their stories and illuminate it from the perspective of MacIntyre's virtues-goods-practices-institution schema (Moore & Beadle 2006) so as to add further understanding of the difficulties they face in the midst of reform implementation. Their accounts develop a collective picture of attempting to bring the multi-agency service provision concept/policy into a meaningful practice on the ground and the issues that arise when agencies are not integrated above and below.

The above represents a small fraction of the material on the cultural clash and as a theme in a serial about the change to CMHTs it has many avenues that could be followed. My interest is in what they say they do to manage the clash. One manager explained that for one particular change, that of creating a joint mental health worker post, it took two years of meetings to produce a draft job description and could take quite a lot longer to get it signed off. The message seems to be that they have great difficulty in bringing the two traditions together to produce what would have been a challenging task in any one of these organisations and in this case seems insurmountable. Charlotte, a CMHT manager new to the post, seems to confirm this situation:

C: *The problem that I've really had has been with senior people at the organisation because they aren't integrated and they all have their own agendas and they all want to tick off boxes to show they have done something. So you have demands from the trust and obviously they want to tick off boxes, but I'm not certain that they appreciate that you get demands from social services who also want you to tick off boxes. So it's like you've got two levels of work with that. This all sounds very negative doesn't it? I'll find a few positives along the way.*

MC: When did it start, where did you start to get involved with the
integration?

C: *I suppose officially the team became integrated two years ago and that
was when I was appointed and I was the first integrated manager. So
really nobody got any idea what that was about.*

MC: So you were setting a precedent for that area. So what happened
when you came on day one?

C: I hadn't any idea what I was doing.

MC: No guidelines or anything.

C: *I was versed with being in health for 18 years, having done nothing else.
I was not versed in social services or county council, had no induction,
and had no policies for procedures, no senior social worker to back me
up or give me any advice on anything. All I can say was I started on
the Monday and really had no idea. It was my first middle manager
post I suppose.*

People in posts means ticks, means integration and therefore government reform target met – or so it seems. This episode tells a very
different story, an antenarrative, of teams a long way from being fully
integrated and functional. The message coming through in this manager's story and many others like it is that the desire for ticks in boxes
pushes people into posts (boxes) and not only is there no integration
between the boxes but the managers seem to have little or no knowledge of what to do to make that integration happen and in this manager's case nobody to provide backup support and advice. Blackler et al.
(1999) describe this kind of situation as a tension or friction. His call is
to better understand what the professionals need and how they cope
when they do manage this kind of complexity. Czarniawska (1997)
constructs these situations as paradoxes, for example if you want to
push people apart, force their integration. Her suggestion is that 'by
confronting such paradoxes we bring crisis to existing institutions that
enable them to change'. Conversing between MacIntyre's ideas and this
episode, he suggests that when different moral traditions (e.g. medicine and social care) are brought together we (as Western civilisation)
have lost touch with the resources to reconcile. For MacIntyre those
resources are highly dependent on narrative as the medium through
which to resolve the debate, since narrative carries the moral standards and virtues by which we can together determine how we practise
and what that practice is working towards. MacIntyre's neo-Aristotelian
ideas suggest that what institutions, separately and collectively, need to
recover in order to bring wellbeing for all (in society) is the ability to

practise with virtues that derive from a meshing of personal narrative quests that then form a joint quest and telos that brings internal goods of wellbeing for all who practise in the institution. This for me is not really very different from the aims of the NHS: healthcare that leads to wellbeing for all citizens regardless of their ability to pay. When we see narratives conflicting in terms of what people believe is the right way to practise their craft then we see a breakdown in the narrative unity of the CMHT. The example of it taking two years to formulate a draft job description would seem to support MacIntyre's argument that we have lost the ability to (easily) resolve moral debate about how to practise.

Exploring the theme of conflicting moral traditions further, in the next episode the focus is on one particular manager who is coming to terms with what it means to her personally to be managing a CMHT that has started to take on patients and is operating in the 'no man's land' between the local authority and the healthcare services.

7.1.3   Episode 3 – Spanning health and social care

Context: This episode develops from the previous episode into a personal story told by one of the CMHT managers, Vivien, who is an ex-nurse. It is representative of the difficulty managers say they are having in coming to terms with their new roles which require them to span both health and social services. The temptation for this manager is to 'bunker down' on the side that is known and most identified with:

> V: *Supposedly, you're employed by health – and for me I'm from health, so my loyalties are automatically there...I'm not employed by social services, they don't directly line manage me but I manage their staff and their budgets. I actually feel the same amount of loyalty to them. Certainly for me that has challenged me at times because there has been many times I have wanted to turn round and tell them to, you know 'Go away!' So I would sort of say, you know, 'Why, how come you can demand that of me?, because you don't employ me, you're not helping me. In that sense you're nothing to do with me!'. So I've found that at times a real challenge because like I say I'm a nurse that is where my core skills lie.*
>
> *I'm for an integrated way of working and a multidisciplinary way of working, but not integration to the point where each profession loses the skills because I think each professional group has something very different to offer and give and it's about having a team made up of all of those so that you can dip in and out of them and be flexible enough to meet the*

person's needs. I don't think it's about merging all those skills together into one person, not at all ...

...I think I sort of chunnered to myself inside you know sort of thing, have a moan to myself and carry on. Like I say loyalty to the team undoubtedly, but it's hard to have loyalty to an organisation that doesn't fully support you, doesn't pay you.

Some days I feel like just going back to putting on my blue uniform so that I can feel again the backing of an institution and the nursing profession.

What is this narrative doing? It conveys the personal struggle of a manager positioned between two institutions, one that pays her and one that does not but still makes demands of her. When this episode was recounted to a group of managers, one nurse-turned-manager said, *'All us ex-nurses feel like that at times'*, indicating to me that as managers they no longer feel they are in a position to cope with the challenges they face. The clash in virtues is one challenge I am highlighting here because it seems so prevalent. This story highlights that the clash in virtues is not just at an institutional level but also at a personal level as this manager tussles with the virtue of needing to be loyal to both organisations but tending towards the one that pays her rather than the one that doesn't and that she feels least supported by.

In the midst of this she is in no doubt that she stands by her team: *'Like I say loyalty to the team undoubtedly'*. Many other stories from the managers convey a similar loyalty to their staff despite all the other clashes they experience. It is as though this is the one of the few virtues they can still hold on to and live by in the midst of implementing government-driven reform. For me it constructs a social reality of the frailty of the CMHT concept, a reform concept that in my opinion needs sophisticated resources available to managers, the kind of moral debating capability MacIntyre describes and more, in order to bring together two very different institutions, two philosophies of care, and create lasting organisational change.

In breaking new ground this episode illustrates that professionals also need to feel they have the backing of mentors and a profession to support them in facing the challenge of stepping out into 'no man's land'. With neither of these apparently available their stories construct the manager as standing on very shaky and dangerous ground: *'it's hard to have loyalty to an organisation that doesn't fully support you, doesn't pay you'*. Feeling vulnerable when they look up, instead they look down to their staff to provide the needed stability and loyalty. The 'moral' message and virtue construction is, 'be loyal to your staff always'. My sense is of a *'band of brothers'* fighting in no man's land in a war they feel ambivalent about and their commanders have left them to it. All they can do is rely on each other, cover for each other and show loyalty to each other to the end. Imagine watching this in a real TV serial. The audience would feel anger towards their commanders, feel inspired by their comradeship and perhaps be asking why would such talented, skilled, caring people be forced into such a vulnerable situation?

To continue the theme of the personal and collective struggle in the midst of change we now look at a particularly disturbing episode of CMHT implementation that spans a group of people who are working within the new structure.

7.1.4   Episode 4 – Underway with a depressed crew and a holed ship

Context: Many managers reported professionals from different agencies having worked together informally and it all working well, but now trying to formalise the relationship has meant the service seems to have taken a step back. This has already been referred to in the romantic stories in the previous section. Setting up formal roles and responsibilities seems to have reduced the flexibility that they had before. Managers tell of staff grieving the destruction of a community of practice and old ways of working that seemed to work.

In this next episode Rosalind, a duty manager in one of the new CMHTs, compares how community mental health used to work with what they do now under the new structure and roles. She breaks down in tears as she explains the tragic story of losing something very special in terms of a community of different practitioners, each with their own knowledge and specialisation, and that together they understood local needs and could meet them in a flexible way without being overburdened with bureaucracy, controls and management. Having implemented the change to CMHTs she starts by describing what she does in a typical week now:

> R: *Typically, Monday and Tuesday are the only days I see any patients and I also do a lot of supervision, I do supervision groups and so on, and then this Monday there is an accommodation meeting and I'm stuck in the middle of one of those, there's the two CMHT meetings on a Monday so if B can't go to those I have to go to those, I'm in a conference all day on Tuesday so no clinical work there. Had I not*

been at the conference I should have been at a meeting at the university in the afternoon, another one of those added-on things. I do two groups to keep me sane, on Wednesday, an evening group and a lunch time group. All morning is taken up with meetings and the afternoon's supervision. All day typically, all day is meetings and supervisions. One in three I get the afternoons and then Friday mornings is admin, and then on top of that, these are all just regular things, on top of that I'm going to...commissioning group, and various different meetings that get...reference group, operational managers meetings. Clinical government development teams days, head of speciality all day. We're trying to attract a consultant psychotherapist to tackle the trusts issue about making requirements for junior doctor trainings and psychotherapy and treat that as something I'm very interested in because its psychotherapy. But if we get anybody interested trying to arrange the visits and getting everybody involved and you know and it all sort of happens as soon as possible. So things like that, having time available to respond to those ad hoc things when you're also you know, always doing supervision at 2 o'clock on a Tuesday and 3 o'clock on a Wednesday, always seeing certain patients at certain times and running certain groups and so on.

MC: So you do the groups to keep you sane, what drives you insane?

R: *The biggest things I would say being [crying]...losing what we've built up, you know I can cope with the accommodation thing and everything else and there's a sense of worthwhile work that's being done by people who feel valued.*

MC: You have developed skills as a community to be able to support people and losing that, is that it?

R: *[still crying] For me that's the thing that's it, partly because it's happened very recently meeting with Y [a senior manager] and so on and I didn't you know. I say it's driven me insane all the accommodation issues and the building and everything but it's always had a sense of that will get better. This can't go on we've got to...it has to, it will get worked though and get better. But it has a feeling of real...the feeling that some of the senior managers don't, it's a big problem for me, they don't see it from where we see it. I think you know generally the lack of, just a lack of understanding which isn't surprising.*

She continues grappling for words to express how she feels and does not quite get there but her tears convey the grief she feels. Another duty manager, Phillipa, who has also experienced the change to a CMHT structure and roles, describes her feelings:

> P: *...there is nobody to get angry with for breaking up a service that worked and replacing it with a service that feels like it may never work.*

An episode of despair and loss which conveys change meaning bearing such feelings of loss and anger without receiving any kind of understanding from senior managers *'they don't see it from where we see it'* and without an outlet or target for their anger.

For these managers the virtue at stake seem to be the integrity of a community of practitioners who have built up a practice together to provide a service that they believe worked better than what they have now in the new form of the CMHT. The meetings and accommodation problems are bad enough but what drives her insane seems to be the loss of her 'community of practice' which sounds close to what Lave and Wenger (1991), Hutchins (1993) describe, where knowledge and learning is shared amongst a community of practitioners all working together to complete a task or in this case deliver mental health services in the community. These managers seem to convey a natural understanding of that concept and a belief in the value of that to their patients. The grief of losing such a precious resource, one that has probably taken many years to grow, is understandable. A story that suggests it has been broken up by the reform process is something equivalent to someone taking an axe to their work of art that has taken years to refine into a beautiful whole. And then having it replaced with someone else's lump of machinery, promising efficiency and effectiveness and hundreds of meetings to work out how to get it going. Added to this, not having anyone to identify for this outrage means their anger has no outlet. Psychologists argue that when anger has no outlet it turns to depression or 'anger without enthusiasm'. Whether that is the case, depression, was talked about by one of the senior managers, Anna, who oversees many of the practitioners who work in the CMHTs:

> A: *I'm having to deal with a depressed service...As a profession we have been clinically depressed for two years...I am thinking of retiring now for the first time...We were sinking but we have now put bungs in the ship.*

A real sense of what it means to her to be implementing reform is contained in this simple sinking ship metaphor. Reform has been threatening to sink the ship, a community of valued practitioners, crew morale is in a depressed state as the integrity of the community is gradually eroded, corroded even to the point of being holed. Some hope of saving this ship is offered with the bungs in place.

The episode is one of near tragedy, virtues compromised over an extended period, two years, during which time their has been no one to around to understand their plight and no one to get angry with for putting them in danger of sinking. Adrift at sea in a sinking ship without communications! Some are prepared to stay on the ship but the latter manager has had enough and is thinking about retirement – her last sailing maybe.

MacIntyre's observation on a manager's work in sustaining communities as part of institutions seems highly relevant to this episode:

> the making and sustaining of forms of human community – *and therefore of institutions* – itself has all the characteristics of a practice, and moreover of a practice which stands in a peculiarly close relationship to the exercise of the virtues... (MacIntyre 1988: 194, emphasis added)

Moore and Beadle (2006: 372), drawing on MacIntyre, link internal goods to practice and an individual's purpose – this is how they puts it:

> The virtues enable the individual to achieve the goods internal to practices, and the achievement of those goods across a variety of practices and over time is instrumental in the individual's search for and movement towards their own telos.

Just a brief recap on 'virtue' as defined by MacIntyre:

> A virtue is an acquired human quality the possession and exercise of which tends to enable us to achieve those goods which are internal to practices and the lack of which effectively prevents us from achieving any such goods. (MacIntyre 1981: 191)

MacIntyre, in drawing attention to the central dilemma, notes that, 'practices are often distorted by their modes of institutionalization, when irrelevant considerations relating to money, power and status are allowed to invade the practice' (MacIntyre 1994: 289).

According to MacIntyre:

> the ability of a practice to retain its integrity will depend on the way in which the virtues can be and are exercised in sustaining the institutional forms which are the social bearers of the practice. The integrity of a practice causally requires the exercise of the virtues by at

least some of the individuals who embody it in their activities; and conversely the corruption of institutions is always in part at least an effect of the vices. (MacIntyre 1985: 195)

We do have a distortion in the narratives about practice, the story being for the purpose of cost but also to improve the quality of practice. So if we are to use MacIntyre's virtues-goods-practices-institution schema we have a vice (money) mixed with a virtue (practice enhancement) and the outcome is, according to the latter manager, a depressed service and according to the first manager a service that may never work. Whether the service will work in reality is not the issue, their social construction, powerfully and passionately expressed in their accounts is that this specific reform, CMHTs, which they have all been part of implementing 'may never work'.

The next section can be viewed as a compilation of the CMHT serial so far.

7.1.5   Episode 5 – 'Dog's dinner' – the compilation episode

Context: Jane, the senior manager with clinical responsibilities who offered the subversive story recorded in Chapter 6 describes her thoughts on the progression of implementing the CMHT policy. Her clinical work encompasses the CMHT and so she has been keeping a close watch on how they are forming.

To cater for viewers who miss some of the episodes of a soap opera, the TV companies sometimes broadcast extended compilations of all the episodes in one block of TV – the equivalent of a marathon. The transcript below is a little like that: it compresses many of the previous episodes into one marathon blog.

> J: *I think we've made a total dog's dinner of establishing the community mental health team ... We've made a dog's dinner in that, the cost of that dog's dinner if you like has been the relationship between primary and secondary care where we've accentuated the separation between primary and secondary care, and we've reinforced a sense of specialist that is detached from primary care. So there's been an external cost in the whole system as it were. We've confused, frustrated, angered, all sorts of things, many staff by getting them to change their roles in the ways that they can't really see why they're changing them and appears to be only because there has to be a CMHT role not because it achieves anything.*

Then it's in practical a way which means that we've missed the deadlines we've said we'd have for doing various phases of it. We've moved people into rooms before the computers are attached, we've not listened to people who've said there are too many of us to fit in that room and we've got them in a room and then we've discovered that there are too many of them to fit into the room. We've failed to provide the training to support new roles; we've failed to help people understand why changing the way that the teams work and the development for example, of the model and what that's about. We've failed to work through the practicalities of that so we didn't understand what volume of demand ... but we've also failed to give any sense of how people can relate that back to the service professionally. We've failed to connect the crisis resolution, home treatment service with the CMHT in a coherent way, so that people can understand, the people who use the service, or people that work in the service can understand the connects and see it as a whole system whereas what we've actually got is a repeat of the old system, it's just a new name for cross referral. We failed out the people in the old crisis service and some things have managed to change in terms of their personal identities that they were in the crisis service because the crisis service worked in a particular way and that was a way they valued. They build their identities around ... so we said right the crisis service is stopping, it's going to be a different kind of service and we didn't appreciate what that meant to those people and I could go on, and I've deliberately painted a fairly negative set, I mean clearly there have been positives along the way, but in all those instances they're all little bits where each individual one would have been ... with more capability, to keep using those phrases and where there is a kind of slippery slope with the whole thing ending up. So at the moment I wouldn't want to be totally negative about it because its working through and it will come out but there has been a heavy cost in systems terms, in personal terms and in motivational terms, well I suppose that's part of the personal, but in motivational terms and probably along the way in some sort of way in financial terms, through the way that we've done that and there is little doubt although there is not a lot of hard evidence, there's little doubt that all of that has impacted negatively upon individuals who use the services.

The social reality for this manager runs very close to other accounts in terms of the value clashes and the effect on relationships. Her metaphor for what it means in terms of the outcome of implementing government policy of CMHTs is *'a dog's dinner'* and she goes on to explain in detail what the cost of that dog's dinner has been. It is not pretty and by her own admission she is painting a fairly negative picture and concludes *'there's little doubt that all of that has impacted negatively upon individuals who use the services'.*

Much of what she cites suggests that managers have not been in a position to manage the clashes in virtues. They have been under pressure to put new structures in place like the CMHTs because this is what the targets require (even then they missed some of those). This has left staff in new roles and *'they can't really see why they're changing them and appears to be only because there has to be a CMHT role not because it achieves anything'.* It seems managers have bypassed the work of addressing the virtue clashes at every turn leaving people feeling *'confused, frustrated, angered'.* I would argue that this is a micro example of what is being played out across healthcare as restructuring becomes one of the main forms of modernising solution. However the debates emerge on the other side largely untouched, so managers never really get the chance to work out as a peer group what is important and where to focus spending, energy and time. Instead finances and their personal resources are sucked up by the reform machine. The greater tragedy is that, as Czarniawska (1997) points out, the serial of changes continues without resolution. In fact she highlights this as one of the key features of a serial is that there is no resolution, the same actors continue to play out different scenes, whilst the audience is still prepared to sit and watch. In this example we have the problem of hospital care for mentally ill people not offering them quality of life and no longer affordable. The solution constructed by policy makers is community-based care and the formation of teams to deliver that care in the community. Policy demands that new teams are formed and so the health professionals, paid actors, respond on cue to the latest script in the latest change initiative. But this is not a TV serial, the script happens to involve real life and death decisions. Would engagement in moral debate before the script (NSF) is released to the actors, as MacIntyre's thesis suggests, improve the situation?

In the next part of the same interview with Jane I ask about day-to-day management of the change.

MC: What do you feel you do that helps to move the change along?
J: *I don't know that's an interesting question. Part of what I try and do, the, what actually happens on a day to day basis is lots of individual decisions, either about aspects of the day to day running of the service or about decisions about investment or change whatever. Lots of individual decisions, most of which are pretty prosaic and part of daily life rather*

than very exciting major things and what I try and do is I try and rein-
force working with them, senior colleagues and through contact with
other people, try and reinforce a sense of where are we going with this
and what, how does this relate back to the vision? I have in my head
always, a sailing metaphor which is about the vision being some sense
of where you're heading, but there being a whole set of forces of wind
or tide, all sorts of things which you have to ride in order to get there
and sometimes you appear to be going in entirely the wrong direction,
but you need to do that in order to get to your goal. If you forget your
goal then you just go where the winds and tides take you, but if you've
got a sense of how you are, where you are trying to get to then you try
and make interconnections between wind and tide and your technical
resources and all the rest of it in order to move forward. That's a meta-
phor that means something to me because I enjoy sailing and it means
something to me because it feels as though quite a lot of the time, there
are some very powerful forces whether they're about this years targets
or planetary position or whatever, which are driving you in all sorts of
places and the real knack is trying to see how you can build an intercon-
nection between this bit of that and that bit of this and even though it
appears to be taking your eye off the ball you can be using it to move
forward.

As can be seen from this transcript and the subversive one in
Chapter 6, what it means to Jane to be moving change along is to work
out with colleagues where they are going and then sail there. The policy
and targets are equivalent to 'powerful forces' like wind and tide and
to be used for moving forward to the destination. She develops the destination, the vision, with her colleagues. The sailing metaphor moves
the focus from virtue conflicts to purpose, end point, goal or telos to
describe what it means to her on a day-to-day level to be managing
the implementation of change in this challenging environment. Again
we see a very strong connection with MacIntyre's neo-Aristotelian idea
that through a communal narrative we create a 'narrative quest' as individuals and as a community. The telos offers a general direction and
is being continually refined along the way. MacIntyre emphasises the
importance of a shared vision that is about the greater good for all. The
greater good being defined as *eudaimonia* or the blessed life, a fulfilling
life for all members of the institution and the *polis*. This manager story
offers us an insight into what it means to be leading the implementation of change in healthcare and how the individual telos can or cannot
interconnect with the organisation. Has she discovered the contents

of the 'magic box' and is she applying them in her practice of leading change to services?

As the different CMHTs across the region develop their teams another manager, in the second-round interviews, observes their separation in terms of mission:

> *We have got to have all the CMHTs rowing in the same direction – at present they are all doing their own thing.*

From this quote is could be argued that the services lack a common telos. This theme is brought out strongly in the first part of Chapter 8 as many managers offer a construction of a similar lack of vision and overall leadership.

7.2 Conclusion to the CMHT serial

In the episodes of this serial, managers construct reform as not working for staff or users. Like the actors in a TV serial they are following a script in the form of a National Service Framework (NSF) and Policy Implementation Guidelines (PIGs). They act out the script but have their misgivings, their rebellion, their subversions and their opinion on whether the script is working. The script is like the narrative and the rest antenarrative that runs against the narrative. What might this kind of antenarrative serial construct in terms of the social reality? One outcome highlighted by a very senior DoH advisor to me is that this type of serial is 'dangerous' and he was even fearful of me disseminating the findings. The concern was that it would breed cynicism towards the reform agenda. My experience was that cynicism was already rife and has been noted by other healthcare researchers (Greener & Powell 2003). Recent feedback from a senior manager was that in his opinion, one of the reasons that reform is floundering is that the government is not taking the social reality of cynicism into account. I agree with this analysis and I argue that 'virtue conflict' and its compatriot 'narrative disunity' and their manifestations recorded here offer policy makers a deeper understanding of the nature of the cynicism under reform and social constructions that fuel it. I also argue that by introducing MacIntyre's brand of narrative-based moral philosophy to illuminate the findings, organisational change theory is offered the extra dimensions of 'virtue conflict' and 'narrative disunity' as important aspects that have, until now, been left largely unexamined. They also offer practitioners a better understanding of the challenges to be faced when leading the implementation of reform and an avenue to gain a deeper understanding of change initiatives that fall by the wayside. Given the well-planted antecedents of some of the virtues at stake I also argue that this challenge has been severely underestimated until now. I argue that these managers and clinicians, like many others in the public sector, are in virtue-to-virtue combat for the moral high ground of healthcare practice. Due to the fierce battle conditions many have already fallen and left the service.

My further analysis, drawing on MacIntyre, is that many healthcare managers (at all levels, including policymakers) given the task of leading change tend not to enter the moral debate to identify what is important and therefore where to focus its valuable resources. Trusts are financially punished for not meeting targets, and therefore fear going against the prescribed (managerialist) script. This fear makes it hard for managers to act on their own view of the virtues or their own telos. In my view this is an essential task and similar one to that highlighted by Burgoyne et al. (1997) and Blackler et al. (1999) as important. Their argument was about discussing meanings in general before moving on to activities. In this book I argue for the importance of specific meanings: what it will mean for the virtues, the morality, of the organisation and the purpose for which the organisation was created. Restructuring is often offered as the solution to the affordability and quality issues of healthcare but as we can see in this serial of change implementation the virtue clashes are still enacted during and at the other side largely untouched. As the process of change happens the unresolved clashes construct a considerable amount of cynicism through the enactments of virtue conflict. The enactment of this serial, taken as a whole, amounts to a tragedy: that so much money, energy and emotion are spent on so much that these managers claim has had little impact on the quality of services and negative effect in some cases. A further tragedy is that while the cynicism, anger and fear are growing some patients have to wait until the restructuring ceases so that they can receive treatment from the people who are embroiled in the change process. Treatment from a cynical, angry person full of distrust is not in the best interests of the patient.

I accept it is early days for this particular intervention and we may never really know what impact the CMHTs are having given the complex web of factors that influence any social or health intervention. What has been found here though is that the current social construction of what it means to implement a specific reform programme, from a manager's perspective, is tragedy. From soundings taken through focus groups and conferences I have found that other managers from healthcare and other public-sector services report similar tragic serials of change. I am arguing that this is in part the outcome of a reform construction and solutions which bypass a moral debate that includes looking at how the change might affect virtues of practice and the purpose of the institution as it sits within wider society. Further, given MacIntyre's radical analysis of society as a whole – that is, we are living in a time after virtue – then it is an inevitable outcome. Serial policy initiatives that fail and are resurrected with different names (Jessop 2000), it could be argued, are symptomatic of unresolved moral debates. We see swings from assertion of one initiative to counter assertion of another the second wins on the basis of the previous failure. The newly asserted initiative then fails and all the while the moral debate is being avoided and not surprisingly, since it would be like asking Truman in the 1998 film about a reality TV show, *The Truman Show*,[1] to break out of his artificial village life. Eventually he finds courage and a ladder, climbs up and knocks on the fake ceiling, realisation dawns, and we, the audience, all cheer inside. He climbs out and finally stops the abuse of being tricked into acting out entertainment for TV audiences.

Returning now to Czarniawska (1997) and her analysis of serials, she constructed from research into the Swedish public sector and which formed the inspiration for this serial. Her conclusion is that the public sector truly belongs to places and situations where literary tradition and real life notably transect; hence we see soap-opera-like serials of change. 'Life feeds materials to art while art returns the favour by conferring forms on life' she claims. Following this line of argument I argue that reality TV has taken over from the TV soap opera as the new genre of TV 'art' and so is insidiously conferring form on life. I argue that it might already have happened and that we are all watching the 'reality TV of public-sector reform' as it is played out in the media on a daily basis. The reality TV participants and their strategies – that is, to have a game plan or not – and the absurdity of the minutiae that are commented on are just some of the parallels that I will explore later in Chapter 10. Given cycles of reforms that in their eyes do not deliver on expectations, what do managers need in order to support them in making reform work? With Chapters 8 and 9, we explore this question.

The next chapter presents a third type of analysis, thematic, which adds to the picture of social reality according to these managers and supports the arguments I am making in this Chapter and in Chapter 6.

8
Themes

In Chapter 6, we saw localised enactments of implementing change from different parts of Omega mental health services. In Chapter 7, episodes were constructed from the participants' accounts of implementing the community mental health teams. In both of these we heard many different versions and different meanings of change implementation and through the analysis a strong theme of virtue conflict enactment and their social constructions of reform. But what about other narratives that are not emplotted and enacted as stories or that do not form a serial of change? This chapter brings together fragments of narrative that speak in different ways of change under a set of themes. According to Czarniawska (1997: 79) themes are 'sure to be found in large complex organisations of many kinds'.

The purpose of this chapter is threefold: first, to contribute further to answering the question 'What is shared in the way managers account for change?'; second, to demonstrate the importance of a third kind of narrative analysis: one that picks up what might have been missed from the stories and serial analyses; and third, to strengthen the arguments developed in Chapters 6 and 7. The approach is inspired by Czarniawska's (1997) use of themes to elaborate meaning and philosophically underpinned by MacIntyre's understanding of the relationship between narrative, goods, practice, virtues and institutions (1985). Together they suggest that a close examination of aspects of narrative is a worthwhile way to examine organisational change in public sector institutions.

According to Czarniawska (1997) themes, like serials, have no plot, but are thematically related scenes such as 'personnel' and 'communication' and the objective is to demonstrate 'what people do and how they act in certain types of situations' (ibid.: 78). In this book the themes are induced from the data and the objective is to develop further understanding of what managers share in what it means to be implementing change. The analysis is in three parts. First, themes are drawn out from recurring or similar narratives from different managers in different parts of the service. Second, for each theme, I ask what implementing organisational change means to these managers and what their narratives are unfolding into the social reality of their organisation. Finally, I examine their constructions in the light of MacIntyre's virtues-goods-practices-institution schema (Moore & Beadle 2006) in order to strengthen the arguments put forward in the preceding chapters.

The value of a thematic analysis to this book is to enable the inclusion of other narratives that may have been missed with the localised stories and CMHT episode analysis. This mitigates against claims that narrative approaches favour good story-tellers (Boje 2001) and that 'antenarratives' are often missed. 'Antenarratives' as a concept means narratives that either run against the typical narratives or that are not coherent in terms of plot or that are fragments of a story that when investigated further reveal a new story – stories hidden from the investigator. My methodological argument is that when themes are added to stories and serials a fuller picture of the social reality of change implementation can be presented and the analysis is strengthened.

This chapter is in two parts. The first part describes the themes that emerged from the data in the first round of interviews in early 2004 and the second part describes the further themes that emerged in the latter part of 2004 and early 2005. The earlier themes were still apparent in the second-round interviews but the second round brought to the foreground some of the themes that were in the background in the first-round analysis.

Four themes emerged from the data in the first round of interviews:

1. No change authority, no vision
2. *'Under siege'* from the barrage of *'must dos'*
3. *'Comedy theatre'*
4. Improving change management practice

A further three themes emerged from the second interviews:

1. Policies not meaningful on the ground
2. Financial and 'must do' pressure increasing
3. Gaps in understanding

8.1 First-round interview themes

8.1.1 Theme 1 – No authority, deferred vision

Many managers expressed the reactive nature of their work in the implementation of change and a feeling of no authority guiding the change process. Brendan, a very experienced senior manager with responsibility for about a third of mental health services, put it like this:

> There's a very common, I don't know whether complaint is the right word, but the common difficulty is the feeling that there is no clear kind of authority. They've not been able to set up or release anyone with the time to devote to overseeing these change processes, they tend to happen in a very reactive way without time to think them through.

Others said they want more in terms of leadership steering the change programme and to give them more clarity of what is required of them. One of the ward managers, Kate, explains how she feels:

> Nobody has a whole overview – a feeling that there is no clear authority overseeing the changes.

A district ward manager, Sheila, who had recently moved into the post, expresses her difficulties in managing the implementation of change.

> It was difficult, I didn't know what was expected – I was still learning a lot. I wasn't sure what I was supposed to be doing. Feedback was 'Have you done a, b, c?' I was a bit disappointed – I had no feedback in the form of guidance.

Others talked about the vision for the service changes that is contained in an Omega document produced by the local implementation team (LIT) and how it seems so distant for them under the current circumstances. Alison, another district ward manager, gives her opinion.

> They have to agree it's [the vision] appropriate and obviously you always have to do within financial constraints, but the financial constraints are so extreme at the moment that you're having to compromise and compromise and compromise and because all bits of the service are doing that, it feels like vision has gone out of the window. Suddenly there's no room for vision because actually we're just surviving – it's all about just surviving and trying to save money everywhere and making huge compromises to

keep afloat, and that's how it is – it's no one individual's fault but it makes visions seem deferred.

One of the CMHT managers, Charlotte, said:

No time to work on the vision, too busy dealing with the 'must dos' and the day-to-day muddle.

Two key meanings emerge from these transcripts excerpts. First, change authority is absent in the organisation, and second, the vision is present but because of the current pressures it has been 'deferred'. These were very common constructions in many fragments of narrative and therefore, I felt, worthy of further examination. My view is that when these meanings are present in an organisation they unfold anxiety and stress. To be left alone without authority, a leader, a parent figure for support and guidance and to have a plan of where you are going but that plan has been put on hold whilst you respond to a barrage of 'must dos' feels like a 'survival' fight or flight situation and many do use the word 'survival' to describe their situation.

Fundamental to MacIntyre's thesis is the concept of a common purpose or telos. The telos is developed through a communal narrative and it might be argued that the LIT has produced this. In this theme we have narratives that construct meanings of there being little or nothing in the way of authority and no time for implementing the vision even though it exists and they believe in the principles of the vision. The overriding priority seems to be survival. This is compounded by the message of no authority in terms of prioritising change and managing stakeholder interests. This seems to support Blackler's (2006) analysis of CEs just acting as a conduit for the policies of the centre and perhaps shows what it means to managers further down the hierarchy on the end of the conduit.

We saw in Chapters 6 and 7 how virtue clashes are enacted in the participants' narratives. A significant finding is that in none of the accounts do managers enact resolving the virtue clashes. From CE down, participants' accounts do not convey the authority or capability in whatever form (virtues, standards or criteria) to resolve change priorities. For MacIntyre, virtues carried in narratives of practice help institutions decide on the priorities. We might ask at this stage: Who has the authority over the narratives and therefore over the morality that helps decide on priorities? In the constructed absence of this authority it seems like it is open day for narratives and therefore open day for the morality of the priorities of mental health services under reform.

8.1.2 Theme 2 – Under siege

Following the theme of no authority and deferred vision I take up a related narrative theme of managers feeling under siege from a continual 'barrage' of 'must dos'. Many people were saying that they feel at capacity, yet demands continue to increase.

The service has to respond to many requests from the government, Strategic Health Authority (SHA), Health Care Commission (HCC), PCT board, social services, the service users, and so forth. Each time I visited Omega it seemed as if a new 'must do' was being talked about, freshly hatched from one or more of the above sources. For example, the main concern at one managers meeting I attended was the need to improve star ratings. At the next meeting it was a directive to implement care pathways. Each time these topics consumed almost the whole meeting.

One manager with clinical responsibilities, Clare, describes some of the 'must dos' that are part of the overall reform agenda that she is attempting to implement.

> *Can we have an audit on this, usually by seven days time – so many because we're going through a huge change period. In [department Z] we're having to develop systems of operation and admin systems so other colleagues across Omega are asking 'Have you got permission on that, can you send me a paper on that particular measure'. Then it's more the organisation of things, we had to do a risk analysis and that had to be done again within a very short time. We had to do clinical pathway analysis and there are so many I forget the title of them and I forget what it's about. Sometimes I feel that some of these things are not really important, they're not central to our work and then again we have Care Programme approach saying 'Have we done a carers' assessment' and it's something about asking the troops to find out if their care co-ordinators have they done it? That's an example of different types of pressures; I would say there's two or three new requests like that per week and they're all coming from different sources and in themselves they seem very laudable and yes I can see why I have to do that, but as a recipient of all these requests, it's just too much. I do try and delegate, but even the act of delegation requires sitting down and talking to people and twisting people's arms.*

One of the senior managers, Geoff, responsible for one particular group of vulnerable patients with complex needs, offers his view.

> *We can't change what is putting people under siege but we can offer windows to move people outside the service and give people a breather, to do something different, a taster of 'life on the outside'.*

This kind of non-negotiable stance *'we can't change what is putting people under siege'* in response to the 'requests' along with the language of *'must dos'* was a common construction as if as managers they have no way of questioning the reform agenda placed on themselves or others. The *'under siege'* war metaphor is completed with this offer of what sounds like the armed services version of a holiday, a 'rest and relaxation' (R&R) break, a holiday in 'life on the outside'.

In another interview with Jane, the service manager, who offered the subversive story and the compilation episode of the CMHT serial, she highlights two issues that she feels are important in the midst of change: capacity and capability.

Capacity ... it feels people are desperately busy, people are caught on the treadmill and don't have time to get off it. If they could just get off it they would be able to do much more and change the way things are in a constructive way, but there is a real sense that people are overwhelmed by the day-to-day pressures so that's the capacity, but I think there is a capability one about the skills and flair of people and the organisation hasn't nourished them so that they've not been able to, I don't know what I mean by this word flair, I don't know what the right word is but is certainly about not just conduct, doing what has to be done, but being able to kind of use some subtlety in it and see how it interconnects with the next things that have to be done ... beyond it rather than this immediate task and the subtlety of selling something. It's not really subtle, but the subtlety of having to focus on a target that has to be done at this moment, this year, to deliver it and at the same time won't people see it as something other than just a must do that has to be done, but something that has a larger point, and I do feel that we struggle with that capacity and capability issue and we don't have the option of throwing money at the problem. We can't either buy additional capacity or bring in additional capability if you will, free people in training and development, so the money thing is an absolute pain and in reality, I don't know what the word is. It closes things, it necessarily does because we haven't got the money, but also you don't even start thinking about things that you ought to think about because you haven't got the money. It reinforces a, it's part of the treadmill business, it reinforces the short-term issues because you have to go on doing it, it's way ... hopelessly inefficient and therefore costly but you have to do it that way because you can't afford to make the change that's needed in order to use the money efficiently. So, very undermining within the organisation, one thing that the rest of the organisation knows about mental health is that it is overspending and it is reinforcing the PCT's financial position and very negative messages about mental health therefore. So we've a real combination of pressures there of the key people who engage and need being caught by ... the task, the limits of their skills and the confines of the resources.

These excerpts are not a story and not part of a serial but a general theme of managers trying to express in their narratives the feeling of being 'under siege' in the midst of reform. The narratives construct frustration towards a system that appears to reinforce its own ineffi-ciencies through having to respond to short-term targets and demands. The pain of needing but not having time out to reflect and use flair, capability or whatever to make the service work better comes out very strongly in these narratives and many others I encountered.

The value of connecting the 'must dos' to *'something that has a larger point'* echoes MacIntyre's idea of the need for a telos that connects prac-tice, virtues and goods. The longing for that is apparent in *'won't people see it as something other than just a must do that has to be done, but some-thing that has a larger point'.* If people do see the larger point, the last theme suggested it is *'deferred'* or that the vision has *'gone out of the window'.*

MacIntyre suggests that a focus on external goods such as money, status and power corrupts practice. In these accounts it is a lack of money or drive to save money rather than the drive to make money: *'The money thing is an absolute pain and in reality it ... closes things ... you don't even think about the things you ought to think about'.* The narratives construct the need to think about the money rather than excellence in practice and how to achieve excellence through the reform proc-ess. MacIntyre argues that excellence in practice, what the clinicians want and what the government says it wants, can only be achieved through the virtues being the ends rather than money, status or power. These narratives strengthen MacIntyre's argument that external goods as ends do corrupt certainly the social constructions of practices under reform and suggest like Chapman (2004) that targets actually work against reform to achieve the opposite of an efficient and effec-tive service. Chapman argues for a holistic approach to service reform. MacIntyre's idea is focussing on virtues as the ends and a communal narrative that transmits the virtues and a telos of wellbeing for all. I argue that the current social reality of cynicism towards reform is in part constructed through enacted virtue conflicts. The irresolvable nature of the conflicts means that managers are effectively being asked to take on mission impossible. I further argue that it is a moral obliga-tion to help managers understand the wider picture and the influences that are generating the 'must dos' that are putting them under so much pressure and that seem to be achieving the opposite of their original aims. These findings also tend to side with the argument that questions whether change can be 'managed' at all and that it is just a 'managerialist' social construction (du Gay 2003; Sturdy & Grey 2003). MacIntyre argues along different lines but with the same outcome: that management does not qualify as a practice in his opinion because its telos is effectiveness and efficiency working towards achieving external goods rather than excellence in practice, internal goods for practitioners and wellbeing for all.

When feeling 'under siege', what do people do to cope? We saw in Chapter 6 how managers use the poetic mode of comedy to enact their narratives of handling change. The next theme elaborates this option. A number of managers referred to as the only way of coping under the circumstances.

8.1.3   Theme 3 – Comedy – Laughing off the pressure

The comic stories did reveal one option for enacting narratives of implementing change selected by the managers. Here we look at the theme of comedy in more detail. The following extract is a quote from a service manager, Catherine, who is describing how she has come to terms with the pressures and conflicts in her situation.

> *I have come to terms with my anger now and for me it is the institution and society rather than me personally that has failed to make the (NSF) change work successfully. I view the process now as entertaining, like watching a piece of comedy theatre. The latest scene being poorly managed relocation of teams, leaving some people without any place whatsoever or others, myself included, dislocated from the group they need to work with. I see others taking failure personally, feeling stressed and taking sick leave. I try to help them see it from my perspective.*

This manager's 'perspective' brings in an added dimension to the comic story mode: that of sitting in the audience and watching scenes from a 'piece of comedy theatre'. However, she is not just sitting watching, audience participation is very apparent, as she herself is included in the action. It is 'society and the institution' that has failed to make the changes work she says. A significant proportion of managers interviewed suggested that the best way to cope under the circumstances is to see the bureaucratic wrangling and ever-changing serial of policies and initiatives as a piece of entertainment that they can watch and laugh at.

If some managers do see what is happening to them as comedy theatre then what kind of comedy theatre is it? I think I was given one answer to this question when I was invited to rehearsals of a pantomime production for performance at the Omega social club. The scriptwriters, a mixture of executives and managers, had created an adult satirical version of Cinderella. The dialogue poked fun at government bureaucracy and changes affecting Omega. Some very senior managers were involved in the production and although unfortunately I did not see the final production it apparently received a very warm reception at the Omega social club.

Propp, in his study of Russian folklore (1928), argued that songs, theatre and poems were used as a means to express the other side, the hidden antenarrative (Boje 2001) of an oppressed society. For Propp, folklore expresses underlying feelings of discontent against oppression, exploitation and social injustice. Since then Western folklorists have contested this with the view that any group even the so-called dominant social classes may express protest and it does not necessarily have to be about counter-culture (Dundes 1980). It may, according to Dundes be about conscious or unconscious (in the Freudian sense) shared fantasies.

Gabriel (2000) develops Dundes' ideas to make a case for *fantasy* being the 'chief force' of the *unmanaged organisation*. Gabriel's idea is that fantasy offers a symbolic refashioning of official organisational practices in the interests of pleasure rather than oppression. The pleasure was very apparent in the people involved in the production and the viewing of the final piece at the social club. Cinderella was chosen (whether consciously or unconsciously) by a group of managers as the vehicle to express their shared symbolism and it can be viewed as their collective expression of what it means to be in the midst of implementing reforms. The Cinderella story offers access to some of the tacit meaning to the participants: like Cinderella they are left with the dirty job of cleaning up while the others get to go to the ball. The focus is on the basic practice of cleaning and staying with that, like Cinderella, and yet with good nature suffering the oppression of her mocking ugly sisters representing the ugly and corrupt aspects of work they have to deal with. The contrast of the goods of wholesome practice (satisfaction) and the goods of going to the ball (status, power, show) mirror the internal and external goods as described by MacIntyre and the two competing ideologies of working for the collective good and aggrandising self. The storyline of Cinderella winning the prince's hand in the end demonstrates a belief in the rightness of their approach and constructs hope for their colleagues that they will receive the greater reward in the midst of the ugly reform agenda that puts the external goods of efficiency and effectiveness above the internal goods that derive from a focus on excellence in practice.

This construction of taking up the audience position and distancing or dislocating themselves through comedy was one of the main surprises for the director of mental health, when I fed the findings back to him, suggesting that it was an antenarrative in the hidden sense. Boje (2001) suggests that antenarrative offers a stake (ante) in meanings hidden to the organisation, which upon investigation tell another story. This construction of a division between audience and the play of change implementation closely mirrors MacIntyre's analysis of institutions and society in general succumbing to the influences of market and liberal individualism. In MacIntyre's view managers are unwittingly or wittingly 'authors of the divided institution' (1985: 194) as they try to implement efficiency and effectiveness measures contained within reforms. For him they are implementing an embedded methodology that frames money, status and power as the telos: 'external' goods that are ultimately corrupting of practice. MacIntyre suggests that we have lost the resources to recognise that this is the morality that we are narrating into our institutions and that it is a divisive morality, with winners and losers (in the market place). In this case the constructed divisions are audience and actors and society/institution and the manager. In contrast MacIntyre positions his neo-Aristotelian morality as having a focus on internal goods derived from excellence in practices that together work towards a telos of equal chance of wellbeing for all members of society. My view is that this is what the NHS still holds as its purpose, in its rhetoric at least.

In the next theme we explore excellence in practice further by focussing on narrative extracts that construct the notion that through training or study practitioners can improve management practice in the area of implementing change. We look now at how this notion relates to MacIntyre's ideas.

8.1.4   Theme 4 – Improving change management practice

A few of the managers I interviewed did report success through the route of education or courses that helped them improve their change practice as managers. Three extracts below illustrate this theme.

A degree in health service management helped Dawn, one of the district ward managers, to gain clarity in the midst of change.

MC: ... what happened to make it come clear for you?

D: *A couple of years ago I did a degree in health management and part of that which I found really interesting, was the strategic management and strategic implementation which covered all the sort of project management type stuff and I found that really interesting and its been sort of, that was all the theory though obviously and I suppose in the last six months to a year I've actually started really seeing how it works in practice.*

MC: Can you give me an example of that, of where you've seen the theory and how you've seen that working in practice?

D: *Well, looking at having sort of time-tabled action plans or development calendars that sort of thing, so you know you're setting an end date and putting, tasking things in between really. I've found being involved in the outline business case process really interesting because again that sort of reflects some of what we did on the course and so it starts to make sense at a practical level as well as a theoretical level.*

So for this manager what it means to be implementing change (successfully) is using the theory from her degree that covers project management, time-tabled action plans and business cases and to see that theory working in practice. One of MacIntyre's central planks in his thesis is that by focussing on improving excellence in practices, practitioners will be rewarded with internal goods. This narrative offers a hint of this and constructs the virtue of education being good for change practice.

In this second extract a leadership programme from a university business school offers Dave, the manager who tells the 'Finding the flow' story, a shared way of understanding issues with his staff as they arise and so enabling them to make decisions on what to do. He starts by talking about what the leadership programme meant for him.

It put light bulbs on, I didn't think about that, but it affirmed well, and to be able to conceptualise and talk to staff, and then staff go on that training and come back, and you start to talk about issues and a whole range of things. So people know that the framework that we're trying to work with, and how I'm trying to work, so hopefully it starts giving people permission to be able to say well, hang on we don't quite like working like this at the moment or even just slipping off in this direction, so we start using the common language and understanding. So that was the model and as part of getting this job I knew there was going to be lots of change going on within the service because you have to be modernised.

For Dave, sharing a set of models helps understanding and builds a common language amongst his staff. Challenging and improving change practice all seem possible to him when people have all been on the same programme. This is what implementing change means to Dave: to be able to discuss the process of change in the light of shared concepts of change practice. Again we have a different kind of narrative that constructs the virtue of using a shared set of concepts and models, in this case from a leadership course, to improve the practice of implementing change. MacIntyre emphasises the importance of a communal narrative that carries an evolving purpose and an understanding amongst members of the institution of the way to conduct virtuous practice. Dave's narrative is essentially about developing a shared narrative around change practice and constructs the virtue of education in achieving that.

In this final narrative extract a solution focussed leadership course helps Kate, one of the heads of service, to deal with concerns quickly and move on in a positive way. She explains the turning points for her when facilitating her management team to find solutions to reduce the waiting list so that they came into line with government targets.

There were several turning points so, within the meetings. One of the turning points was the, okay why are you a 2 not a 1, so it was actually not why are you worried? Why are you as low as 2? But why are you as positive as 2? So that is an interesting spin and I think another turning point was that the options that [senior managers X and Y] had gone for in terms of the future vision was their preferred option and they had obviously, as I say...I mean I probably would have done it differently if I'd known that [senior managers N and R] had gone for something different, but basically they all feared that [senior managers N and R] would say we shouldn't do any long-term work at all and they would have huge anxieties about that because you know, there are clients that need long-term work, I mean they haven't gone for that option, what they gone for is the option of managing much more tightly the lengths of therapy, and everybody was, there was a sense of well, you know, people were expecting the worse but people got better than what they expected and they could see the advantages of it compared to now, it's progress compared to now, so I think that was a turning point. Yes those were probably the two turning points and I think the fact that with the style of doing it made it absolutely okay for them to be really negative at the start ... but in a contained way, rather than just every-body sitting there ... there was a slot for being negative and then moved on to something else ...

... I'm very much flittering with it because it's only four months ago that I did the course and at the end of the course when they were asking for evaluations and said would you reference somebody else and I said well you know, wait and see really because often you go on courses and feel enthu-siastic when actually it doesn't translate. At the end of last week I was saying well you know, I was half pushed to say it hasn't been useful but I'm sure that it made all the difference in those last two meetings and I've used it in a couple of other settings as well so now what I'm saying is let's see in another two or three months whether I'm still using it or whether it's something that actually as time goes on whether it's not ... something you go on and they're a five minute wonder aren't they so I'm very consciously using it whenever I get the opportunity at the moment and then I'll sort of take stock and think well you know, was that good?

In the latter part of this narrative there is some caution in the sus-tainability of the model applied, however, in all three narratives the outcome is constructed as successful in terms of supporting the man-ager in improving the way change is handled in organisation. The managers themselves seem to benefit from improving their imple-mentation of change practice. What implementing change means to these managers is that through training or education they can improve their change practice. These are, however, all very different pieces of development and there is a sense of luck and coincidence especially in the last account. These narrative samples could be seen as being in tune with what MacIntyre describes as an aspect of a virtuous organ-isation where practitioners focus on excellence in their practice and in doing so receive the 'internal goods' of feeling good about their work and what it will do for their patients. Together these narratives unfold the virtue of training and education and applying that in the work-place in the context of organisational change. They do also unfold the notion that practitioners can just try anything that seems to work and that it is a matter of luck, or fashion or whatever comes their way. There is little understanding conveyed in the accounts of the premises and ideologies embedded in the different methods (project manage-ment, leadership, solution focussed). It is the method rather than what they are based on and the moral standards for the organisation as a whole that appears important. MacIntyre is highly scathing of many

of these managerialist methods that for him promote liberal individualism and a focus on efficiency and effectiveness in order to achieve
the goal of a competitive market with winners and losers rather than
wellbeing for all. The NHS was set up to satisfy and still holds to the
principle of equality of care for all regardless of ability to pay. For me
therefore there is superficiality about the virtue of training and education being transmitted in these narratives that the last account starts
to question:

> *something you go on and they're a five minute wonder aren't they so I'm
> very consciously using it whenever I get the opportunity at the moment and
> then I'll sort of take stock and think well you know, was that good?*

Will this be for the good of the people served by public health services
and our society? This question raises the issue of managers as moral
representatives of the institution and society. MacIntyre's views on this
were very strong in his original 1985 thesis, *After Virtue,* to the point of
suggesting that managers are unwittingly or wittingly authors of the
morally fragmented and divided institution and as moral representatives of society they rank alongside therapists and aesthetes as being
responsible for the lack of moral cohesion in society. Strong condemna-
tion that has been challenged (for example, Brewer 1997 and du Gay
1998) but not completely dismantled (Beadle 2007) and viewing now
these narratives, and the ones in the previous chapters, in the light of
his ideas, I think we can see some of what he was getting at. This leads
me to suggest again that theories of organisational change have paid
insufficient attention to the morality of the change process in the eyes
of managers because it is the morality and the virtue conflict that in
my opinion is one of the sources of greatest angst amongst managers.
This theme shows them to be grasping at straws, at methods to try to
make change work, resolve the conflicts instead of what MacIntyre suggests: having a moral debate informed by a set of communal virtues
that inform the methods chosen to achieve excellence in practices that
are working towards a telos of wellbeing for all. Moving to discussing
action informed by this research, my tempered view is that by making
space for managers to ask the question, '*Will* this be for the good of the
people served by the public health services and our society?' there is an
opportunity for them to explore the embedded morality and ideology
in the change methods before applying and making decisions that build
a more cohesive morality into the change process and produce a better
outcome for all concerned. This, as MacIntyre observes, is not easy: he

believes that since the enlightenment the resources and ability to have the moral debate have been gradually eroded. An alternative starting point for me, and I think a moral obligation for healthcare leaders, is to increase understanding of the wider ideological horizons reflected in the methods that they choose to apply in the midst of change. This approach was piloted with a group of managers towards the end of my studies and produced some interesting outcomes that I report on the conclusions as a postscript to this book.

8.2   Second-round interview themes

In the second round interviews I fed back the findings from the first round and asked if they gave a reasonable and balanced representation of what it means to them to be implementing change. Participants were consistent in their agreement with the findings and were keen to tell me more about what was going on for them since the last interviews and add any further points that they felt were important to include. These last few themes arise from those second round interviews and add in some of the dynamics of their social reality as it changes over time. A sense of the increasing pressure for change and the increasing frustration felt by managers at not being able implement the changes they feel are necessary to make the savings being asked of them is apparent.

We have seen how the policies that these managers are implementing contain financial drivers (money) in terms bringing the trust into financial balance, status from the star ratings and power from choice agenda. We now look at the theme of policies in more detail. They became more prominent in the accounts as the fieldwork progressed. One particularly strong aspect was how they were constructed as not meaningful on the ground.

8.2.1   Theme 5 – Policies not meaningful on the ground

Many managers spoke of change policies and frameworks not being meaningful to them and or their service area. One particular example stood out from the data with a number of managers citing the poor local fit of the National Service Framework for Mental Health (NSF) and Policy Implementation Guidelines. The NSF and associated PIGs happen to be the overarching framework for change to mental health services, and many of the other smaller reforms to mental health services spring from the framework. Charles spoke for many when he describes the mismatch between an NSF model (apparently optimised for the inner cities) and the local area which is mainly rural with many dispersed villages, a few market towns and one small city.

> *I think that's one of the other issues about the national service framework that's been there all the way through is the need for...and a lot of the models in it are inner city needs and models. So people disengaging with services, yes it happens in (the Omega area) but they don't do it by moving three streets into a different neighbourhood and a different community team base and they do it by sort of not wanting to go to the limited services we can provide perhaps and they do it in a different way. So a lot of the benefits that were being shown initially seemed to feel like inner city sort of benefits, and one of the difficulties we've had with implementing the NSF is that the models that then came out, the PIG as you probably heard of, and the piglets..*

Yes I've heard of the PIGs, policy implementation guidelines.

> *Piglets are the like, the subsequent chapters of it. One of the problems we've had with is an issue that now has got an actual official name, fidelity. Fidelity to the model, where we've been saying we can't just take this model and plant it down in (the Omega area) and expect it to work because of the geography of the area, because of the size of the population is nothing like the size of inner cities, so you don't have the economies of scale. So, you know a team in an inner city might be 12 staff but you scale it down to what we need here and you get two or three and setting up teams of two or three staff is not a good way of doing things. So we've had to look at how we adjust it to meet our needs, and we've now got to even demonstrate that we are still getting the outcomes by adjusting it and...have set up some panels are going to look at fidelity, that we've got to demonstrate.*

Through this narrative we see that what it means to Charles to be implementing change is to have to work with policies that do not make sense in Omega's geographic area. Off tape he also explained the enormous amount of time and energy spent on negotiating with the SHA on the fidelity concessions that were necessary to make the policy anywhere near workable in the geographic context. What change means to managers in this theme is that much of the centrally produced policy and implementation guidelines are not meaningful on the ground. Despite this they have to try to demonstrate that they have implemented the policy and that it is generating the specified outcomes. Much of the policy they are describing is highly prescriptive in nature: it gives very specific description of how teams should be constituted and what they should be doing. The Strategic Health Authority checks out the 'fidelity' of what these managers implement so they feel pressure to at least implement a structure even if it does not work. This account like many others constructs a social reality of government change policies failing to be sensible or meaningful to their context and also the injustice of being measured against fidelity criteria that do not fit with the needs of the population in the area. The construction is oppression and an exposition of a top-down generalised policy, principles and virtues that have not been instantiated for different localities.

Brian, another service manager describes in practical terms the difference that Omega service can offer is different to what an inner city service can offer:

> *... obviously if you're in the middle of Birmingham it is going to be different. You might be talking about a ten minute bus ride for clients or whatever, you know, whereas here our furthest bit in one direction is probably an hour and a half by car and then the other way it's another hour and a half so if you had to go from one end of the area to the other it's like a three hour drive, so that obviously affects what you are offering. It would be different to an urban area.*

The clash of virtues in these narratives echo the 'Gone Shopping' clash of locally managed IT versus nationally managed IT programme reported in Chapter 6. The issue here is of centrally developed policies not being workable in different contexts, in this case, a policy that assumes a city and densely populated, context as opposed to a rural sparsely populated area.

Cath, a service development manager, explains her view on the policy issue.

> *Yes. It's hard, it's a big organisation, geographically it's massive and also the actual, I mean people say that the department of health do so some lots of new things to do, I don't think it's the department of health, I think it's the strategic health authority that interprets that and the department of health hasn't changed in approach in that since this government came in, in fact some of the things prior to this government coming in have been very, I mean the mental health service plans were in the first service advice to come in as a national policy so we should be on the front marker.*

You mean the national service framework and the NSF's and the policy implementation guidelines?

Yes, so we're inundated with loads of them [policies] and half of them are insipid. The basic principles of them aren't changing at all, things such as user involvement and challenging culture, challenging stigma, not just service user involvement but partnership working with clients, flexibility, it's been there for years. Like this star rating thing, I was shocked when people were saying we didn't know what we had to do, but if you ... with the principles what you would have had to do, mainly you would have had to look at how you demonstrated it in a different way because they ask for it in different formats, but their actual expectation hasn't changed in the last four years, eight years.

These narratives report the participants' social construction of governments' attempt at numerous policies guidelines to secure excellence and consistency in mental health practice. The government could be viewed as trying to achieve some narrative (and for them practice) unity with regard to structure, roles and practice, however, these narratives illustrate that monolithic prescriptions of how policies should be implemented create opposition, anger, and a 'dog's dinner' rather than excellence in practice. Chapman (2004) supports this finding – he says that the government approach actually achieves the opposite of what is intended. The virtues-goods-practices-institution schema suggested by MacIntyre has a very different emphasis in some fundamental ways. The fundamental difference is that the narrative unity is not one of telling practitioners what they should be implementing in practice, but a narrative unity in the virtues of practice, those ways of conducting the practice that bring internal goods. Those ways are carried as a set of virtues in the narratives of the institution. The narratives of the institution form through the meshing of personal narrative unities to form communal narrative. Cath refers to 'principles' in the policies that have been around and that have not changed for the last eight years. The principles mentioned are *'user involvement, challenging culture, challenging stigma, not just service user involvement but partnership working with clients and flexibility'* So in the MacIntyresque organisation in change my research would be reporting narratives that construct these 'principles' as virtues of the institution. Here instead we have a kind of rebellion narrative or anti-narrative (Boje 2001) that rubbishes what is added to these basic principles in subsequent policies and that criticises policy that is not appropriate for their rural, sparsely populated context. *'We're inundated with loads of them (policies) and half of them are insipid. The basic principles of them aren't changing at all.'*

In the social reality of healthcare undergoing change that we have sampled, what chance do staff have to understand what it means to be delivering excellence in mental health practice? The primary aim of healthcare reform is excellence in practice (and equal access to that excellence) along with affordability of services. Where will staff draw on narratives of the institution that carry these principles? I did not seem to find them when I asked what it means to them to be implementing reform. MacIntyre's rather pessimistic stance is that because we have been deflected from our ability to maintain a unity in moral debate by the liberal individualistic influences from the enlightenment onwards then we are unable at this point in history to properly reconcile the collision of different ideological horizons and moral traditions that are battled for daily in the workplace. I feel more optimistic that it might be possible to (re)construct the moral debate on the 'basic principles' in the context of service reform through facilitated peer group debate in certain localities with new or forming communities of practice. However, in my view, those people engaged in the debate also need to be informed on the antecedents of the reform solution constructions they are grappling with. I argue that this is one of the missing elements in organisational change theorising which has potentially profound implications for (re)forming public institutions such as the NHS. In my view this would reconnect the people to the social and historical context of their practices. If MacIntyre is right, and practice is being corrupted by the efficiency and effectiveness solution constructions of liberal individualism, then this is urgently needed not just in healthcare but in all our public services.

This theme has really only considered excellence in practice. I now move to another salient theme in the second interviews of narratives that address finances, affordability of services and an increasing pressure to balance the books.

8.2.2   Theme 6 – Financial and 'must do' pressure increasing

Managers had mentioned financial pressures in the previous round of interviews but requirements to reduce spend further had been announced since those interviews. In addition the 'must do' pressure seemed to be increasing to meet targets. Mike, a manager with clinical responsibilities explains his point of view.

> *It closes things, it necessarily does because we haven't got the money, but also you don't even start thinking about things that you ought to think about because you haven't got the money. It reinforces a, it's part of the*

*treadmill business, it reinforces the short-term issues because you have to
go on doing it it's way ... hopelessly inefficient and therefore costly but you
have to do it that way because you can't afford to make the change that's
needed in order to use the money efficiently. So, very undermining within
the organisation, one thing that the rest of the organisation knows about
mental health is that it is overspending and it is reinforcing (Omega's)
financial position and very negative messages about mental health therefore. So we've a real combination of pressures there of the key people who
engage and need being caught by ... the task, the limits of their skills and
the confines of the resources.*

Many of the managers interviewed spoke about wanting to do things
more efficiently as part of the reform process and make changes to
practice in a similar way to Mike. His narrative conveys a sense of being
held in a way of doing things because of the squeeze on finances, feeling closed *'because you have to go on doing it it's way– hopelessly inefficient and therefore costly but you have to do it that way because you can't
afford to make the change that's needed to in order to use the money more
efficiently'*. Trying to implement change in this case means feeling
unable to use their skills to create a more efficient service – the construction is change does not seem possible in the present confines of
the resources. Being under further financial pressure in the context of
reform, according to this manager, means that they feel they have to
continue to manage the organisation inefficiently because they can't
afford to make changes.

MacIntyre argues that money is an external good and that when it
becomes salient as an aim of the institution then practices can easily
become corrupted. Here in these narratives we see a corruption in the
form of stemmed desire and ability to improve practice. Here the money
is not an external good that is about profit but nevertheless it forces an
emphasis on costs in a similar way that a drive to make money would
do. Blackler et al. (1999) draw similar parallels with the private sector
environment and compares healthcare to a fast-changing business in a
highly competitive market in the private sector. The difference here in
this narrative construction is that the expectation in the reform agenda
placed on the service is for fast change however finances are being
squeezed at the same time and change seems 'closed'.

Another factor which managers claim in their narrative to be inhibit-
ing change is communication and understanding. In this final section
we explore this theme in detail.

8.2.3   Theme 7: Two *'currents'* or *'atmospheres'* with a widening gap in understanding

This theme describes what many managers referred to as a widening communication gap between middle managers and senior managers. The theme is brought out in the second round of interviews because some managers felt it had not been sufficiently emphasised in the first round findings. The metaphor of currents going in different directions is used by Jane in the second heroic/ subversive story. This is how Jane describes the gap in her story.

> ...it's like you've got these two sorts of currents you've got your top current that's going one way and then there's this sort of clinical one that goes on and flows on and thinks we'll be here anyway whatever happens. The patients don't change and the clinical issues don't change, and it's not necessarily that that bottom current is flowing in the opposite direction, but it may be going slightly differently. It's not that things are standing still and not changing or progressing at the coalface it's doing it to a different agenda to the agenda that drives the rest of the organisation.

The difference between the currents reported here appears to be a disjuncture in the narrative unity and therefore different understandings of what it means to be implementing change. What is described as the 'top' current runs to a 'different agenda' to the 'clinical' current. So how are the two currents socially constructed individually? Here is how Jake, a service manager, describes the gap in understanding as it relates to his experience of implementing change:

J: *Because the implementation [of change] is the most difficult thing to me and people can write strategies until they are blue in the face but thinking about the steps and activities that will work towards the implementation, there's a gap, a knowledge gap in the managers.*

MC: That's what you've experienced

J: *Yes, so it was like, it seems to be knee jerk reactions rather than, or we have to get everybody together to argue where no decisions are made or somebody will make a decision where they've not got the power or understanding to make to decision, so the decision making and the progressing of any plan is very difficult, because people aren't used to working with structure. X [senior manager] has got an overall, I mean his outline business case is another thing but he seems to have an overall strategy but*

> *it's not communicated in a language that the people on the ground can understand in terms of an overall agenda and where they fit in to that overall agenda, it certainly begins to become quite compartmentalised, then the changes made become quite compartmentalised rather than unified.*

The construction here is a common one in the data: that of the senior managers implementing change with knee jerk reactions, producing strategies that do not relate to practice and making decisions without an understanding of what is happening at the coalface. It constructs a chasm in terms of understanding '... *strategy ... not communicated in a language that the people on the ground can understand*'. In the final sentence there is a constructed call or need for changes to be unified rather than compartmentalised: '*the changes made become quite compartmentalised rather than unified*'.

The manager here talks about a 'gap' in management understanding of the implementing steps on the ground. I believe that this is what Blackler et al. (1999) encountered they applied activity theory to offer a better understanding to practitioners of their situation in the midst of reform. He says, 'The activity system theory breaks down when applied across different professional groupings'. Activity theory is based on the assumption that all involved parties can discuss and work towards the object of practice. What we find here is that there are some fundamental differences in what people see as the object and of the way they go about working towards their different objects. One participant from the CMHT serial offered a metaphor which seems to sum up narrative disjuncture across the organisation: '*We have got to have all the CMHTs rowing in the same direction – at present they are all doing their own thing*'. I argue that in this case there is similar disjuncture up and down the organisation as well across the organisation. The disjuncture as observed here is a narrative disjuncture or put simply, people talking differently about change and what it means to them to be implementing change. Taking MacIntyre's premise that morality is transmitted in the narratives of the institution and applying it to this analysis we could argues that morality is fragmented and divided across and up and down the institution.

According to MacIntyre (1985) the disjuncture in narrative unity of any particular tradition is a problem for the people who knowingly or unknowingly uphold that tradition. Czarniawska does allude to these difficulties in her study of public administration and describes them as 'frictions' (1997: 79) or 'paradoxes' (1997: 93) but does not explore their nature beyond a statement about the meeting of different ideologies. She does, however, acknowledge that they are a very common construction amongst those in the midst of public administration reform. What I have attempted to do in this book is explore these frictions, paradoxes and tensions (Blackler et al. 1999) through the lens of MacIntyre's thesis and offer a different and new perspective on organisational change in the public sector. I now draw the different strands of this chapter together into a set of concluding comments that say how they contribute to this perspective.

8.3   Themes conclusion

The purpose of this chapter was threefold: first, to contribute further to answering the question 'What is shared in the way managers account for change?'; second, to demonstrate the importance of a third kind of narrative analysis: one that picks up on what might have been missed from the stories and serial analyses; and third, to strengthen the arguments developed in Chapters 6 and 7.

Salient shared constructs of what it means to be implementing change to the participants are offered in this chapter as a set of themes. They add to the stories and serial to form a more detailed understanding of change through the narratives of the managers interviewed. The key meanings constructed by the participants that we have explored in this chapter and the arguments they support are listed below.

We see here in these narratives what it means to managers when trying to implement a reform agenda that itself contains different forms of morality into an institution that has become morally fragmented. Anderson (2005), Brown et al. (2005), Bryant and Cox (2004), Collins and Rainwater (2005) do consider multiplicity in organisational change studies but do not address the consequences for the morality of the organisations they study. Pedersen (2006) asks us understand more about the consequences of these interactions and the contextual interaction of these many voices. Pedersen's interest seems to be in further stories that emerge as a consequence of the interactions. Downing (1997) favours the exploration of how the conflicting stories can be managed. My theoretical line has been to understand more about the constructed morality of the institution that contains the organisational change stories and the nature of the conflicts contained in the stories. Further to articulate the support needs constructed by managers and compare that to what MacIntyre's thesis suggests is required to achieve excellence in practice.

	Meanings	Argument
1	**No change authority, no vision**: change authority is absent in the organisation and the vision is present but because of the current pressures it has been 'deferred'.	In the apparent absence of change authority it is open day for narratives and therefore open day for the morality of the priorities of mental health services under reform.
2	**'Under siege' from a barrage of 'must dos'**: people at capacity, yet demands continue to increase. Frustration towards a system which appears to reinforce its own inefficiencies through having to respond to short-term targets and demands. The pain of needing but not having time out to reflect and use flair and capability to make the service work better.	Conflict and virtue conflict in particular is the norm for the participants. I argue that the current social reality of cynicism towards reform is in part constructed through enacted virtue conflicts. The apparently irresolvable nature of the conflicts means that managers are effectively being asked to take on mission impossible. I further argue that it is a moral obligation to help managers understand the wider picture and the influences that are generating the 'must dos' that are putting them under so much social pressure and that seem to be achieving the opposite of their original aims.
3	**Comedy Theatre**: the best way to cope under the circumstances is to see the bureaucratic wrangling and ever-changing serial of policies and initiatives as a piece of entertainment. Taking up the audience position and distancing or dislocating themselves through comedy. What kind of comedy do they choose? A Cinderella pantomime.	The morality that managers are narrating into the institution is a divisive morality. It constructs the government and its reform policies as a comedy – managers sit in audience laughing at the pantomime. Or if they participate then they construct themselves as holding the moral high ground, like Cinderella they focus on doing a good honest job and believe that they will eventually receive the rewards. In the meantime, if you take the reforms too seriously you will suffer.

| 4 | **Improving change management practice:** constructs the virtue of individual or collective education being good for change practice. Through any old odd collection of training or education you can improve your change practice. Practitioners can just try anything that seems to work and that it is a matter of luck, or fashion or whatever comes their way. One person questions 'the five minute wonder' of solutions focussed quick fix methods and thinks 'well was that good?' | This theme shows managers to be grasping at theories and methods that happen to come their way to try to make change work. It is the method and the fix rather than what they are based on and the moral standards for the organisation as a whole that appears important. I argue that theories of organisational change that inform management education have paid insufficient attention to the narrative transmitted morality of the change process in the eyes of managers. This is important, firstly because it is virtue conflict in the midst of change that we have seen here forms a source of major angst amongst managers and secondly because the resulting enactments, as we see in the stories and serials, construct anger, cynicism and distrust towards any kind of practice reform. |
| 5 | **Policies not meaningful on the ground:** implementing change means they feel oppressed by a series of top down generic policy and implementation prescriptions that do not cater for geography and other significant variations. Being measured against 'insipid' policies that in their eyes do not work brings narratives of rebellion that rubbish what is added to the basic principles that have been there for years | This theme offers a repeating construction in the narratives of the virtue of locally prescribed practice held by the participants versus the reform policy virtue of centrally prescribed practice. It constructs an immense challenge for managers: even if they could overcome the cynicism and mistrust, they believe the policies do not actually work for them and the population they serve. MacIntyre's theoretical 'mission impossible' of trying to resolve virtue clashes between different moral traditions is constructed as a socially reality in this example. |

Continued

Table   Continued

	Meanings	Argument
6	**Financial and 'must do' pressure increasing:** feeling unable to use their skills to create a more efficient service – the construction is change does not seem possible in the present confines of the finances.	Here in these narratives we see an exhibited effect of stemmed desire and ability to improve practice. The money is not an external good that is about profit but nevertheless the claim is that it forces an emphasis on costs in a similar way that a drive to make money would do. The expectation in the reform agenda placed on the service is for fast change however finances are being squeezed at the same time and changes to practices seem 'closed' rather than corrupted.
7	**Two 'currents' or 'atmospheres' with a widening gap in understanding:** The difference between the currents reported here appears to be a disjuncture in the narrative unity and therefore different understandings of what it means to be implementing change. It constructs a chasm in terms of understanding.	Further evidence of the fragmentation in narrative and therefore morality in a vertical hierarchical sense. What is interesting is that at whatever level I interviewed the construction of the gap in understanding was similar apart from where locality managers existed. The narrative was then much more coherent. This is where the narrative methodology I have employed shows its usefulness to this enquiry. Other studies have identified the multiplicity of stories and narratives or polyphony that emerges. They tend to see this as unproblematic, that it is just how organisations reveal themselves when using narrative methodology. However, this study shows that when implementing change these differences in construction of social reality are highly problematic. (I also think they offer a microcosm of society's fragmented morality). Boje termed the storytelling organisation as 'Tamara-like', which means it has different story lines running on different levels with sometimes the same, sometimes different actors. When we try to implement change into Tamara-land each grouping of actors has a different interpretation and creates a further fragmentation of morality.

Peter Hyman, the former senior government adviser, was shocked to find the policies that he was part of implementing were unworkable in practice and wrote a book about his experiences (Hyman 2005) which some claim has influenced a softening and relinquishing of power by government back to the practitioners. In this study, I found consistently that managers at all levels complained about lack of understanding from the managers above them of their day-to-day (social) reality. Whether policies are in practice workable is an issue but what is interesting for me is that it seems that the social construction of what it means to be in the midst of change appears not to transmit through hierarchical interfaces indicating narrative disjuncture. However, each level has a similar social construction of being misunderstood by the layer above. Czarniawska (1997) suggests that themes such as this are likely to be found in all large organisations undergoing change. I would agree and add that many large organisations that take on change do so using a managerialist approach that assumes a structural-functionalist model of change and therefore often miss the importance of the socially constructed nature of change and the role that ethics play in that construction.

In Chapter 9 I tell the story of what happened when I progressively fed the stories, serial and themes back to managers across Omega and further afield.

9
Feedback and Focus Groups

The purpose of this chapter is threefold: first to report on what happened when the narratives in their three forms were fed back to focus groups of managers, second to answer the question 'What do managers say they need to support them in leading the implementation of reform?' and third to ask 'Do the needs expressed by the managers bear any relationship to what MacIntyre's virtues-goods-practices-institution schema suggests is needed for a healthy institution?'

Chapters 6–8 demonstrate narrative as a way of knowing that lies in the temporal ordering of events and an 'indifference to extra linguistic reality' (Bruner 1991: 44). Bruner states that 'In narrative the perceived coherence of the sequence (temporal order) of events rather than the truth or falsity of story elements determines the plot and thus the power of the narrative as a story' (ibid.). For Bruner, there are no structural differences between fictional or factual narrative. The book does partly hold narrative in this way, but recognising that the primary research questions emphasises 'meaning to the managers', I think some social negotiation between the stories, themes and serial presented here needs to have taken place to make a claim that they represent meaning to the managers, even if we take the meaning to be represented by the structural ordering or poetic mode of their narratives. As Czarniawska (1998) asserts, contingency or the situational nature of the narrative plays as much a part in the process as aesthetics or politics. I agree with Czarniawska, and when drawing on Bruner (1991), she says 'stories are especially viable instruments for social negotiation' (1998: 6).

It should be noted that at no time during the following series of feedback sessions did I discuss or converse with theoretical models such as MacIntyre's. I just presented the findings as stories, serial and themes as presented in Chapters 6–8. Although he was there in the background as a source, the detailed conversations with MacIntyre's work came much later as I was writing up the book.

The feedback process had five distinct steps:

1. Director of mental health meeting
2. Mental health managers meeting
3. Third round of interviews with a wider group of managers
4. Focus group with all Omega managers
5. Focus group with regional managers

Each one of these steps and the outcomes are described in the five sections which follow.

9.1   Director of mental health meeting

The first stage of meaning testing was a meeting with the director of mental health. He accepted most of what I found as a richer under-standing of what he had heard snippets about in his day-to-day work. One story mode that did evoke surprise and concern in him was the kind of comic story where it was apparent that the construction was one of disengagement from the reform process. He talked about those examples in terms of *'theatrical disengagement'* from the service realities and whilst accepting that people may need this release, he also saw it as a *'profound fracturing'* of people's connection to the change pro-gramme and was keen to understand what might be going on for his staff. He wondered if they were reflecting the problems faced by users of the service – for instance, the housing estate with social problems and the people there with mental health problems who distance themselves from bureaucracy because there is no reconciliation for them – or if this style of disconnection from the organisation is simply a coping strategy they have developed within the user group to make the difficulties less real, less sharp for them. He speculated further on what might be done to make it *'theatre in the round'* or to *'unsanitise'* it to make it more con-nected to the *'real feelings and issues'*.

As highlighted earlier many of the narratives do convey a lack of reconciliation in the stories with the outcome of tragedy, comedy or a sacrifice in order to care for staff. Also for many of the managers, the virtues they try to bring together – their own personal virtues, what they value, or the virtues of their community of practice – are often at odds with the change programme.

The comic theme was the main surprise for this senior manager in my early findings, suggesting that it was an 'antenarrative' and an uncharted seam of folklore of the type exposed by Propp (1928) and more recently by Boje (1991) at Walt Disney.

Prior to the fieldwork, the director and I had agreed that we would present the findings back to the mental health managers' meeting (MHMM). Although the director was happy that what I had uncovered did represent the social reality of his managers he was now reluctant to present the findings to his managers. Ironically he felt that they had enough change to deal with and that presenting this material might just push them over the edge. Eventually after some discussion that centred around how a patient would be treated in this situation, he concluded that it might actually help managers to see that 'the organisation' was accepting their reality, that they are not alone, convey understanding and empathy of their situation and allow them to see that the organisation is listening and wants to support them in the best possible way.

So the decision was taken to present the findings back to the MHMM. Rather than tagging this presentation onto an existing agenda, a separate meeting was convened to present the findings and decide what action, if any, should be taken in the light of the findings.

9.2   Mental health managers' meeting

About half of the 12 attendees at the meeting had been interviewed and so to them the findings were not completely new. For the others it was the first time they had heard the findings. They were all, however, unanimous in their view that the findings as presented in the stories, themes and serial did offer a sample of day-to-day reality of life on the front line of mental health management in reform at Omega. This meeting took place in December 2004.

Some were concerned that the findings presented a very negative picture of the services they were managing but did accept that these were typical of the narratives circulating the service and on the whole constructing a negative picture of reform. They admitting to hearing similar stories and suspected that what they were hearing was the tip of the iceberg. My presentation had confirmed this suspicion. Furthermore they were very unhappy about most of what they heard and wanted to do something about it. But what could they do? They felt pressurised by a whole set of targets and measures to deliver on the reform programme and had little if any capacity to respond to what they saw as forces beyond their control. Some felt that I might be describing the (social) reality in any healthcare trust right now under present government pressure to modernise and therefore that I was flagging up a much wider issue that they had little power to affect.

Again, I did not include any of my analysis in the presentation; instead I asked the managers what kind of narratives they would like to be hearing in their organisation. They said they would like to hear stories that convey something along the lines of:

> We are coping with the implementation of reforms, it is difficult but we feel we can call on support when we need it to overcome the difficulties we face.

Their preferred story was of them handling the reform as a peer group but being able to call on support when they stuck. The meeting then moved to suggestions for actions. Three main actions emerged: first, to disseminate the findings across mental health services through the staff magazine; second, to inform the unions of the findings and give them a chance to comment; third, to present the findings to the chair of the Omega board, chief executive, HR director and staff side chair (chair of the joint union committee).

The latter meeting was quickly convened and about a week later I was sitting with the four people mentioned. They were already concerned about staff feedback across all service areas, not just mental health, through various channels including the staff opinion survey. For them my findings enriched their understanding of the underlying issues behind the quantitative findings they had received through the staff survey. The outcome was that I was asked to interview staff from all other service areas in the trust to find out if the social reality I was describing for mental health managers was reflected across the trust. They also wanted me to ask participants what they needed in terms of support from the organisation to help them cope with the current level of change in the organisation. A third round of interviews was therefore convened with another 21 managers representing all service areas of the wider trust.

9.3   Third-round interviews

Having fed back the findings within mental health this section reports on the interviews with managers from public health, young people, clinical governance, commissioning and performance, primary care, sexual health, HR, IT, finance and estates directorates.

This final round of interviews with managers from other service areas ran from January 2005 to March 2005. In the interviews, the findings were fed back and managers were asked if they felt the stories, themes and serials convey what it means to them to be implementing reform and if not what would they add or subtract. Most of the managers did resonate strongly with the findings with comments such as the following:

> *Exactly right. That is just how it is for us. It is nice to know that others feel the same. I can identify with the stories. That's it that's how it is for us. I think you have captured it very well. I think you have got the breadth of experiences just right.*

With regard to managers from IT and finance and estates their response was milder emotional resonance with the narratives. In general they did not feel they were on the front line of implementing service reform, more that they were in support roles responding to calls for their services. However, they did acknowledge that their colleagues in other directorates were under more direct pressure and theorised about them having pressures that were both top-down (to reform) and bottom-up (to meet user needs). Some of these pressures had filtered through to them, particularly the feeling of being under a *'barrage of must dos'*. They recognised this feeling in that they were continually being asked to change the infrastructure. One of the senior finance managers said:

> *One change such as combining budgets for mental health CMHTs would have been enough for us to handle in any one year but we are dealing with five or six major changes at the same time and that has had a resource impact. This means that we are stretched to the limit with implementing change and have insufficient capacity to meet the day-to-day operational workload which can suffer as a consequence. I suspect this happens in all service areas.*

Expressed needs, as narratives, were also collected from the managers and classified under six headings. These 'direct' narratives of need were combined with sections of narratives 'indirectly' conveying need from the narratives in the previous series of interviews. What this amounts to is narratives defining what it means to be supported in their work of implementing reform and a way of addressing the fourth research question. It also in a way brings us back to the original gap in the literature which is described by Dawson (1999) as:

> We need to understand the practitioners' world, to see it through their eyes. Only then can we hope to be able to develop a dialogue in which the findings of the research can enlighten practice.

I felt that I had reached the first stage of understanding what it means to practitioners, 'the practitioners' world', and the dialogue was beginning to develop, first to the point of understanding what managers were constructing in terms of needs and therefore opening the possibility of enlightening practice.

The narratives from their expressed needs collected from the third round interviews were categorised under six themes:

- Supporting people in change
- Leadership of change
- Communication and Understanding
- Respect for people, culture and their communities of practice
- Appropriate training and knowledge
- Working together across boundaries

The table on the next page shows narrative excerpts collated under each of the themes to show how they define the expressed needs with their narratives and their specific suggestions for how they might be met.

A second meeting with the chair, HR director, CE and staff side chair was then convened to report back on the latest findings and decide what to do next. Completely separate to my research the chair had initiated a 'board values' working group. The aim of this group was to produce the values that as a board they wanted to be demonstrating in their roles and to be encouraging throughout the organisation. The reason for this work was a belief that having and promoting a set of values would help with the problems of low morale and motivation they were experiencing at this time of significant change and reorganisation. Interestingly there were some similarities between the board values they had produced and the expressed needs from the managers even though they had been derived completely independently of each other. The table below shows both side by side.

If we were to consider the expressed needs as what managers value in the way the organisation treats them in the midst of change then we can see that the bottom-up values from the managers and the top-down values of the board have some similarities. Of interest to the analysis

Theme	Expressed needs	Specific suggestions from the interviewees
Supporting people in change	*'We can't ask people to carry on like this: overwhelmed, stressed and many off sick.'* *'I've been managing a depressed group of staff for the past two years.'* *'How do we own and manage the stress at all levels?'* *'If it were not for my staff relying on me I would have gone off sick – definitely.'*	• Facilitated peer forums to share emotional and practical burdens, good practice and create viable action plans. • Counselling and or mentoring. • Support of senior managers who can affect many people when suffering stress. • Celebrating our successes. • Making time to listen at team meetings. • A period of consolidation to recover.
Leadership of change	*'I am happy to do this 'must do' but tell me what you don't want me to do.'* *'The leadership needs to make hard decisions.'* *'Nobody has a whole overview – a feeling that there is no clear authority.'* *'We have got to have all the teams rowing in the same direction – at present they are doing their own thing.'*	• 'Care pathway' for managers. • A 'clear and public' change strategy – an organisation that knows where it is going. • Support to prioritise the current 'must dos', the previous 'must dos' and the day-to-day 'must dos'. • Skills at board level to handle the clash of cultures (for example, political vs. care, LA vs. HA, local team cultures).
Communication and Understanding	*'There is a sense of dislocation wherever you go in Omega.'* *'...two currents and atmospheres with a widening gap in understanding between senior managers and middle managers and staff.'* *'...none of us believe in the "must dos".'* *'Change is being thrust upon people.'*	• More face-to-face contact and empathy; – reconsider how we use email. • Clarity of role, vision and priorities. • Being clear about why the changes are important and how they fit with local, regional and national priorities. • Common interpretation of the 'must dos'.

Respect for people, culture and their communities of practice	*'We need to be valued as experienced, creative people.'* *'The workforce is fantastic!'* *'I don't expect people to tell me what to do but I do expect opportunities to negotiate priorities.'* *'…there is nobody to get angry with for breaking up a service that worked.'* *'The NHS can only function by bullying…'*	• Involve people early in the process. • Listen and respond to concerns. • 'Pilot and test out' change with those affected. • Build on the existing good practice and knowledge rather than replacing services. • Opportunities to negotiate priorities both internally and externally.
Appropriate training and knowledge	*'I made sure that every one went on the training programme so that we all had a common understanding.'* *'When you've tried all the management models and theories, what then?'* *'We want management development that helps us deal in a practical way with the complexity.'* *'People just get absorbed into the culture'.* *'What is a business case?'*	• Business case production skills for local needs. • Focussed skills development to cope with complex issues (for example, cultural clashes, professional identity and 'professional tribalism'). • One-to-one and/or group coaching to follow up and embed learning. • Training to ensure equity of care.
Working together across boundaries	*'I help people in other areas where I can.'* *'We forget we are all part of a PCT – we forget to work together.'* *'People get too hung up on where people are and what people do.'* *'a silo mentality'* *'I just get on and do it (work across boundaries).'*	• Form subgroups to work on the issues and make the change happen. • Share resources when others are strapped. • Improvise and innovate to find the resources rather than spending time fighting bureaucracy. • Partnering/ collaboration inside and outside.

Expressed Needs	Suggested Board Values
Supporting people in change	Dignity and respect
Leadership of change	Commitment to empower
Communication and understanding	Openness and honesty supported by clear, two-way communication
Respect for people, culture and their communities of practice	Fairness (promoting equity) + Dignity and respect
Appropriate training and knowledge	Commitment to learn
Working together across boundaries	Commitment to working in partnership

is what both the board and the managers interviewed seem to be constructing in terms of needs in the midst of change. Viewed in this light is a set of values or virtues from the organisation. Again the correlation with MacIntyre's virtues-goods-practices-institution schema is striking in that MacIntyre proposes the virtues as the ends rather than the means to the ends. A community in good order according to MacIntyre has at its heart a set of virtues that guide the way it practises its craft and that lead to excellence in the craft, internal goods of fulfilment for its people and wellbeing for all. Excellence in practice is what the government claims as an interest for healthcare. The typical ends of a corporate organisation and of the individuals in the organisation of money, status and power do not feature as needs in the accounts of our managers. What their needs could be seen to be collectively constructing is a call for moral unity, something constant in the midst of 'a barrage of must dos' changes. The examples given of their practical suggestions construct meaning and a picture of what it might be like if the needs were being met and the virtues they need were being lived out in their day-to-day working. Supporting each other and the senior managers is clearly a theme in the needs. There is much about collective practice in their language, for example, 'partnering', 'collaboration', 'peer forums', 'common interpretation', offering an indication that this is presently missing in the way they work. There is also direct mention of the 'clash of cultures' and the need to acquire the skills to deal with that clash.

When placing MacIntyre's virtues-goods-practices-institution schema and *virtues* (see Appendix 1) alongside the expressed needs and board values I arrived at the following table.

This leads me to argue that despite the cynicism constructed by the tragic, comic and romantic stories of change, managers in Omega are

Expressed Needs	Suggested Board Values	MacIntyre (1985)
Supporting people in change	Dignity and respect	*Prudence* (care)
Leadership of change	Commitment to empower	*Courage* to make and commit to virtues that are true to a common telos
Communication and understanding	Openness and honesty supported by clear, two-way communication	*Temperance* (restraint of action by considering the ideas and needs of others) *Truthfulness*
Respect for people, culture and their communities of practice	Fairness (promoting equity) Dignity and respect	Sustenance of practice-based communities *Justice*
Appropriate training and knowledge	Commitment to learn	Virtue education through story and narrative leading to excellence in practice; (re)-acquiring moral debating resources to handle virtue conflicts
Working together across boundaries	Commitment to working in partnership	Meshing of narrative quests (across practices) to clarify and refine the virtues of practice and a common telos for the institution

also constructing the need for cohesion and unity in their community and that unity is a moral unity that at its heart is very similar to what MacIntyre judges to be important for an institution in order for it to thrive. Further and wider that we as a society have landed on privatisation, market forces, choice, deciding the day as a solution, without adequately describing the problems of modernising public services. I believe that the majority of managers have a genuine desire and have tried, despite virtue and narrative disunity, to improve services. What emerges from this analysis is that change towards excellence in practice can be achieved but that moral unity (and, MacIntyre would argue, narrative unity) needs to be maintained (or established even) whilst the change is happening in order for the institution to thrive. Their responses construct what it means to maintain virtue unity and what it would look like in practice in the midst of change. MacIntyre argues that it is important for the community to derive and live out the virtues that will enable the institution and those it serves to thrive.

9.4   Focus groups – All Omega managers

In March 2005 the findings in the form of stories, serial and themes plus the expressed needs as categorised above were presented as feedback to a workshop and focus groups attended by the top 70 managers from Omega Trust. The purpose of the workshop was to see how closely the stories, themes and serial matched what it means to the managers as a group to be implementing government modernising reforms. Was what I had constructed faithful to what they would construct as a group?

During my presentation I tried to replicate the gestures and inton-ations when reading out excerpts from the transcripts – in other words, I tried to replicate the story performance. As I presented the material I was aware of the shifts in emotion of the managers and many people nodding with 'mmms' and other cues indicating strong accord. The accord was combined with some signs of embarrassment, as though I was revealing some truths that they would rather not hear broadcast. As they realised the presentation was completely anonymised they relaxed. They were giving me their full attention and moved from astonishment at the epic success stories of change through sadness with some watery eyes at the tragic stories and they surprised me with their laughter at the comic stories. It was as though this was very familiar territory to them and I had a strong sense of conveying empathy with their situation. I looked around the room and saw very little in the way of body lan-guage that said 'no this is not my experience'. The first comment I received when I finished was

> *This is so refreshing – for the first time someone has articulated what it is like for us to be on the front line of change in the NHS.*

The group was asked if the stories, serial and themes did convey what it means to them to be leading the implementation of govern-ment reform. They had opportunity to answer this question not just in plenary session but in six smaller focus groups. Some managers did reinforce some of the themes with further stories and narrative but mostly they were in agreement with what I had presented. They were then offered the opportunity to add to the needs presented and put for-ward their practical suggestions for responding to the needs. This was a creative exercise where each group tackled one category of expressed need grouped around a flip chart. All groups then rotated round the room visiting each expressed need flip chart adding their ideas. What emerged was a whole set of ideas and practical suggestions against the expressed needs that built up a further set of statements about what they would like to see happen in order to meet each expressed need.

The next stage of the workshop was suggested by the CE and HR Director. It was to create a matrix of the corporate objectives for the trust versus the expressed-need themes – that is, what is important for the trust to achieve versus what is important for the managers in terms of support to be able to implement change. In directorate groupings the managers were then asked to prioritise the top three (or less) objectives and expressed needs for their directorate, creating a three-by-three matrix. They were then asked to fill in the boxes with specific activities that would meet both the corporate objectives and the expressed needs. Most groups found this difficult, if not impossible, to achieve despite strenuous attempts to facilitate the process by a group of experienced HR people. Looking back now and drawing on the insights offered by MacIntyre, I can see that we had created a microcosm of the virtue clash and disjuncture that they describe on a typical day-to-day basis. We had asked them to reconcile two sets of virtues: what they consider to be of worth in the change process with what the organisation was being asked to do, driven by the managerialist principles embedded in reform policy. Some people aired concerns about not being able to represent the whole of their directorate and that they would like to work on the matrix back in the organisation. Some groups made valiant attempts at producing actions but the overall feeling was not as energised as it had been earlier in the session. One of the managers, I think, put it very well:

> *I was in an emotional flow when you were presenting and I did not want to move on to the more heady work of deciding what we do about it, I wanted to stay with what it meant now for us given that we are all in this together.*

For this manager moving on, as the meeting did, to thinking about what could be done to meet the needs of managers in the supplied context of the corporate objectives was an inappropriate shift. For this person it was more important to stay with the feelings evoked by the presentation and linger on that to see what emerged in terms of meaning now. The focus group had drifted back to a structural, forced approach to organisational change, trying to move people from one place to another and this outcome indicates a lack of sophistication in the approach.

Again, conversing with MacIntyre's thesis, I am struck by the fundamental difference in telos: purpose for MacIntyre is to focus on the way the community of practitioners develop virtuous practice not on the external goals of the organisation. Weaver (2006: 344) says '"What is my telos?" arises in concrete social systems of inherited conditions, categories, expectations and roles formed by and in conjunction with other people'. This is very different from having a purpose imposed on a group of people from on high. MacIntyre's analysis is that system dimensions of organisations can and do constrain and inhibit moral agency.

The exercise failed but some agreement was reached to continue the work when they returned to their directorates. Some groups arranged away days to try to solve the matrix. They did not feel they were in a position to reconcile the different values contained in each of the boxes. Ironically, before this activity could be completed another government restructuring initiative, Commissioning a Patient-led (CPL) NHS (Crisp 2005), put an end to the life of the Omega PCT. The CPL restructuring proposed that the PCT should be split into four parts which would then join other existing healthcare trusts or form their own trusts. The announcement left everyone consumed with anxiety about their jobs and where they would be posted. Any further research was curtailed by the CE, mental health director and HR manager, the original sponsors of the project. A period of uncertainty, characterised by one manager as 'law of the jungle', ensued as managers positioned and jockeyed for a reduced number of jobs. Looking back, the parallels with reality TV and the *Big Brother* household were strong. Nobody really knew who was deciding their fate: it seemed to be worked through and between people who were all at risk of losing their jobs.

9.5   Regional workshop and focus groups

The final stage of the feedback process was to run a workshop and focus groups with managers from across a geographic region of England. Again I presented the three forms of narrative as stories, serial and themes and then asked for feedback. The data further supports the argument that the current approach to change in healthcare is not well understood and as one manager puts it 'Gaps in change process lead to low morale, disillusionment, frustration and disenfranchisement'. To re-iterate my argument, I now believe one of the gaps in understanding change to be a lack of appreciation of the ethical dimension in change and the impact of the enacted virtue conflicts experienced by health professionals in their practice. This for me further explains the power of consultants and GPs who through their training and professional bodies are able to maintain a strong ethos of practice, a 'practice-based community', which as a peer group, whatever their shortcomings, stands like an oak tree next to the scattered sapling-like government change initiatives in all their varieties. Attempting to build a solid, reliable mental health service out of saplings has angered the GPs in their 'oak built' practices especially when some of 'their' resources (for example, CPNs) have been requisitioned.

I asked the focus group to prioritise their needs and the strength of feeling was overwhelming *'What is the rank order of priorities?'* For me this gave further indication that when it comes to managing organisational change, managers at all levels in healthcare are not in a position and are ill-equipped to enter a morale debate to arrive at a telos for the service. One manager said 'everything is presented as top priority which means we just end up spinning plates' which interestingly takes us back to the very first story from our manager who said that this is what it means to him to have successfully managed change in the current context.

Again, no interpretation of the data was made at the focus group and the door is left open to continue the dialogue with these managers at further forums. After the session they said they were very keen to continue the session and find out what happens next. The evaluation comments from the session were very positive and the following was fed back from the workshop organiser:

> Over 50 delegates attended this workshop and the presenter's style and workshop content was clearly appreciated. Various comments included 'Nice to know everyone feels the same', 'Good timing', 'Helps us communicate', 'Stimulating' several requested the next set of findings be made available.

Chapter 10, Discussions and Conclusions, discusses the different elements of the argument I make in this chapter and the preceding chapters to bring together my contributions and complete the story of this book.

10
Discussion and Conclusions

The purpose of this last chapter is threefold: first, to discuss the main findings from each of the preceding chapters; second, to draw out the conclusions in the form of methodological, empirical and theoretical contributions; and third, to suggest an ethical approach to leading organisational change through research, policy and management education. It begins with a recap of the aims of the study in the first section and then the major points of focus in each chapter are discussed in the next section. Following this, the third section presents the central contributions and the fourth section makes recommendations for future research. Finally implications for reform policy and management education are discussed in the last section.

10.1   Aim of the book

A first aim of the book was to illuminate what it means to managers to be leading the implementation of healthcare provision modernising reforms through their narratives and what support their narratives signal. It has been argued that given the scale and scope of change in the public sector and the significance placed on the importance of key people leading organisational change, their accounts have not been given the research attention they deserve. The last two decades have seen an increase in the literature focussing on change in the healthcare sector but that literature commonly focuses on the organisation and its effective management of change with less emphasis on the complex social realities of people, managers in this case, trying to translate a plethora of government reform policies into practice.

A second key aim was to demonstrate the strength of a synthesis of narrative approaches to deepen understanding of what it means to managers to be on the front line of leading healthcare reform. In health-care reform studies, the narrative approach has to date been under-utilised, due in part to the emphasis on structural functional theorised research which has tended to include multiple case studies and to look for common themes. In this study a single case study provided a rich seam of empirical material. It formed the basis of a detailed investigation of the social realities constructed by managers in the midst of implementing reforms and resonated strongly with healthcare managers across a region of the UK.

10.2   Narratives of the institution

This section summarises the major discussion points within each of the preceding chapters starting with the Introduction and the research questions. Much of the discussion on the findings has been woven through Chapters 6–9 and contributed to the gradual development of the arguments. Here I summarise those discussion pieces before bringing them together in the conclusion as a set of contributions.

The initial aims of this research were focussed on understanding what it means to a group of senior and middle managers from one UK primary care trust (PCT) and partnering local authority (LA) social services to be leading the implementation of mental health service 'modernisation' in one region in the UK. This was in response to calls to understand what managing change means in practice for healthcare managers in the midst of reform. For example, in an award-winning literature review on organisational change specifically aimed at healthcare managers Cameron (2001: 5) states:

> Substantial numbers of managers and clinical professionals argue that much of the evidence about effective change management is located in the heads of practitioners and has yet to find its way into the scholarly journals.

Further to the above was a call to understand how best to support managers who are in the midst of implementing change (Blackler et al. 1999; Blackler 2006). In order to respond to these calls the research commenced with the specific aims of increasing understanding of:

- What it means to managers (individually and collectively) to be implementing organisational change aimed at improving the quality of health care

- Whether they view reform as improving services or not
- The support they need

These aims were refined as the study progressed and significant themes emerged. Early analysis of the data and my exposure to writers such as MacIntyre (1985) resulted in the emergence of a number of key themes that were incorporated into the initial research aims. MacIntyre has very recently called for research stories to be told about

> ... human flourishing and failure to flourish, about virtues and vices, about the practices and institutions, about communal tradition and its erosion, about the destructive effects of the world market. And only if the story deals with all of these in their interrelationship will it tell us what we need to know. (Coe & Beadle 2007: 2)

I realised that collectively managers were telling a story of this nature, an important story, that no-one else was telling. Some writers have identified the growing cynicism towards reform within health-care management (Hunter 2000; Greener & Powell 2003) and a creeping privatisation (Pollock 2004; MacIntyre (1990b)). By employing narrative devices I add to this finding with a detailed examination of managers' stories of organisational change and the inter-subjective reality that the participants construct. At the heart of many of their narratives I argue that there is a moral conflict or dilemma and that MacIntyre's narrative-based virtue ethics schema offered a powerful way of conversing with the enacted narratives. Narrative-based studies of organisational change have revealed some insight into the constructing effects of change narratives (for example, Downing 1997; Pedersen 2006) but not from a moral perspective and not in a way that considers the purpose and virtues of the institution. Consequently, three further interests were added:

- To explore the power of a narrative approach in organisational change research and in maintaining a dialogue with participants
- To understand the nature of the ethical conflicts and dilemmas enacted in the narratives and what kind of social reality they construct
- To examine the narratives using the lens of MacIntyre's virtues-goods-practices-institution schema theory (Moore and Beadle 2006) in order to enrich organisational change theory particularly in the areas of ethics and resistance to change

It is argued that an understanding of organisational change based on MacIntyre's virtue ethics and the concept of a narrative unity adds deeper understanding of the moral dimension to public-sector change. It is further argued that a synthesis of narrative approaches offers a more rigorous exposition of the social reality than has been attempted to date.

The context for the managers and mental health organisational change under study is framed in Chapter 2. It explains the recent history behind the current NHS mental health policy initiatives that the managers in this study were attempting to implement in practice. The chapter highlights the flow from the 'modernising government' agenda (HMG 1999a) to the *NHS Plan* (DoH 2000a) and on to the *National Service Framework for Mental Health* (DoH 1999) and *Policy Implementation Guidelines* (2001a) that form the main reference points for the redesign of mental health services. This is a common policy flow for many of the service redesigns in healthcare. Key to this study is the sheer range of change initiatives that managers in healthcare are currently being asked to implement and the underlying structural functional assumptions about how they can be implemented. This chapter argues that public-sector change studies to date, in addition to neglecting the narrative accounts of managers and in particular their poetic form and constructing effects, have also underplayed the importance of considering individual and collective construction of the ethics of practice in the reform process. The findings demonstrate that these issues are crucial to the understanding of what it means to managers to be implementing organisational change, important to consider when creating reform policy and a vital part of public-sector management education, especially for those who are expected to take a lead in change implementation.

The review of healthcare organisational change literature in Chapter 3 highlights two main strands of theorising: structural functional and social constructionist. Behind much of the structural functional approaches is the belief that resistance to change can be managed either educationally or politically depending on how the resistance is defined (Kotter & Schlesinger 1979). The review finds that empirical studies of organisational change are rare and those that do exist tend towards producing a set of prescriptions or success factors. It is noted that flowing through much of this literature is the common theme of the importance of key people leading change. Managers' narrative, translation, interpretation and storytelling arise in these studies as significant but are not studied in any depth. One of the strongest calls for the kind of research produced in this book is articulated by Sandra Dawson: 'We need to understand the practitioners' world, to see it through their eyes. Only then can we hope to be able to develop a dialogue in which the findings of the research can enlighten practice' (Dawson 1999: 3).

Social constructionist (for example, Berger & Luckmann 1967; Weick 1979) studies of organisations have been sensitive to narrative and stories (White 1981; Wilkins 1983; Boje 1995; Czarniawska 1997; Gabriel 2000). A subset of that genre contends that narrative approaches are an appropriate means to study organisational change (Skoldberg 1994; Czarniawska 1997; O'Connor 2000; Currie and Brown 2003). The review argues that healthcare organisational change studies with a managerial focus are rare and this is surprising given the amount of change that managers are being asked to field. 'Tensions', 'paradoxes', 'frictions' are just some of the ways writers characterise what reform means to managers. Blackler et al. 1999 and Blackler 2006 has focussed on the healthcare managerial tensions and paradoxes and called for further understanding of what change means to practitioners, concluding that it is only through informed debate on what the changes means to practitioners that services can move forward. This study responds to that call and the previous call by Dawson by asking what it means to managers to be implementing change and what they construct in terms of needs to support them in the process of making improvements to the quality of patient care and to the access of that care.

Chapter 4 constructs a story of the narrative turn in social sciences tracing back to Propp (1928) and oppression under Stalin expressed in the folklore of the ordinary people. Disturbing echoes of oppression in the folklore of our public-sector managers are revealed in the findings and supported by Blackler's recent study of chief executives (2006). The chapter emphasises the work of one seminal writer on narrative and moral philosophy, MacIntyre, who believes that humans are storytelling animals and the primary purpose of narrative is moral education. The chapter points to a recent revival and application of his concepts to organisational studies (Moore & Beadle 2006) and highlights the lack and value of empirical research that features his concepts of 'narrative unity' and 'virtues-practices-goods' in the context of an institution. His theorising is based on the notion that our ability to maintain a collective moral debate about institutional virtues of practice has been corrupted by liberal individualistic ideology. It is argued that MacIntyre's concepts offer a powerful lens through which to view managers' narratives and reveal more about the nature of the tensions and paradoxes highlighted by Blackler et al. This is especially relevant to the public sector in change because it is trying to reconcile the interests of many different cultures and traditions. MacIntyre's schema affords a unique perspective and contributes an ethical understanding of the notion of 'resistance' in theories of organisational change.

Chapter 5 presents the narrative methodology and research design as an appropriate approach to answering the research questions. The main research question informing the study is concerned with what it means to healthcare managers to be implementing reform policy and what they construct in terms of support needs. This called for an approach that offers a way to describe a wide variety of meanings and tacit understandings in a way that would allow managers to review and approve but then be able to draw out key themes and converse with the work of MacIntyre and others. Notably, the narrative technologies of Czarniawska (1997), Gabriel (2000) and Boje (2001) provided significant contributions to the approach. Czarniawska's stories, themes and serial approach practised in her study of Swedish public-sector reform allowed the study to identify stories of organisational change but not ignore themes and a serial of change embedded in the data. Further, Czarniawska's notion of semantic and semiotic readings enabled us to ask not just what the stories mean but what the stories are signalling and constructing as a shared social reality for our managers. Classification of the stories using Gabriel's 'poetic story modes' allowed us to classify the options chosen by managers to enact the narratives and further elaborate their social construction. Boje's concept of antenarrative was helpful in looking at what was behind fragments of stories and piecing together some of what comes before the neat ordering of a narrative into a story, the 'real story' as Boje describes it. In this way, participants who may not be skilled narrators still have a voice in the findings.

The second part of the chapter translates the methodology into a practical design for the study. The longitudinal study incorporating a series of in-depth interviews for each participant offered a temporal exposition rather than just a single frame viewing. The chosen enquiry method of social poetics (Cunliffe 2002) revealed more of what might otherwise have been left in the tacit domain: metaphors, gestures and other important, but often taken for granted, semiotic aspects of a research interview. It also opened an early acknowledgement of the co-constructing effect of the one-to-one interview that was then rebalanced with further interviews and focus groups to feed back the stories, themes and serial to ensure that their social reality, rather than the researcher's, had been fairly represented.

Chapter 6 provides a stage for the localised stories of reform and their classification into epic, tragic, comic and romantic poetic story modes. Managers' narratives are interpreted through MacIntyre's lens as conveying a multitude of virtue conflicts and disjuncture. Under extreme pressure to implement myriad policies, frameworks and targets, managers enact a variety of options in their narratives in response to their ethical conundrums. Their narratives convey a sample of the social reality in situations where there is apparently no solution, where their personal values, patient needs, government policy and public interests are at odds with each other. Gabriel's 'poetic story modes' (2000) are employed to show the variety of options they choose to narrate their handling of the virtue dilemmas they face. These include epic stories of 'finding the flow' and 'being subversive', tragic stories of 'wasted talent' and 'nobody to get angry with', comic stories of 'shredding it' and 'going shopping' and romantic stories of 'my staff needing me' and 'buffering staff'. Notably the epic stories present the narrators as heroes holding onto their virtues, what they believed to be of worth, in the way they practised the leadership of organisational change. Epic stories were like islands of narrative unity in a sea of narrative disunity constructing some inspiration and courage. However, it is argued that these inspire the notion of individualism and change based on personal values rather than a set of communal virtues of practice. It is argued that anger and cynicism towards change are constructed and carried in the tragic and comic stories. The romantic stories construct the notion that despite cynicism, many managers strive for the best for their staff and patients. They also construct the idea of managers 'getting on with the job' even though they don't always agree with the direction of travel or the virtues being used to get there. This echoes the notion of 'working at a cynical distance' (Fleming & Spicer 2003: 157). They suggest that what counts as 'disruptive resistance' must be re-evaluated as radically external rather than an internal subjectivity. I argue that MacIntyre's lens provides a way of extending this idea with the notion that virtue conflict signals 'ethical resistance'[1] to the corruption of practice and needs to be listened to.

Chapter 7 brings a serial of change, embedded in the accounts, to the foreground. The shared social reality of a group of managers evolving over time with people who regularly work with each other is depicted through different episodes. The managers concerned are under a great deal of pressure to implement team structures as defined by the mental health NSF. The virtues noted as being in conflict in the stories chapter develops in the serial and as Czarniawska (1997) notes:

> Public Sector change could especially be seen to follow the serial mode, with apparently unsolvable and paradoxical problems providing endless material for fresh episodes!

In this quote we see the 'paradoxical' and 'unsolvable' nature of the problems of public-sector change that are further characterised in the serial as virtue conflicts with multiple ethical standpoints. According to MacIntyre these conflicts are irresolvable if they are based on different premises. Virtue conflicts across professional groupings are also highlighted such as those between GPs and managers and social services and healthcare services, where different sets of arguments, based on very different premises, lead to protracted disputes, assertions, shrillness and bad feeling much as MacIntyre predicts. This has been constructed elsewhere as 'tribal' warfare and consultants in particular have been singled out as 'good at protecting their interests' (Greener 2005: 97). Here we see the GPs singled out and constructed as the villains blocking change. I argue that this is in part the outcome of a reform construction and solutions which bypass a moral debate that includes looking at how the change might affect virtues of practice and the purpose of the institution as it sits within the wider society. Further, that given MacIntyre's radical analysis of society as a whole – that is, we are living in a time 'after virtue' – then it is an inevitable outcome. In support of this argument I propose an evolution of Czarniawska's serial metaphor into 'reality TV' to illustrate meaning to participants and move the debate beyond criticisms of government-led change approaches. I will explore this evolved metaphor in the theoretical contributions section.

Chapter 8 draws out narrative themes threading through the accounts of our managers. This serves the purpose of supporting the arguments that were developing from the analysis of the stories and serial and highlighting other aspects that resonate with MacIntyre's thesis. In particular we see constructions of lack of shared common purpose or telos in the accounts and the construction of 'invisible leadership', in effect open season for the narrative mode of the institution, leaving a green space for narratives that construct demotivation, cynicism and fear rather than inspiration towards a common telos and a set of virtues that work for the good of the organisation and their service users. This chapter also reveals the strong undercurrent of felt oppression through fragments of stories that led to the discovery of the production of a pantomime, Cinderella, by some of the managers. It is argued that this constructs the notion that their virtues of excellence in practice, tolerating with patience the ugly side of managerialism and its interest in money, status and power, will eventually bring them their reward, a prince who values them for who they are. I argue that this signals their interest and belief in internal goods of practice exceeding the rewards of the external goods of money, status and power. Further examples of themes which interlace with MacIntyre's narrative are highlighted in this section. Briefly, they are excellence in practice, a single set of principles corrupted by policies of efficiency and effectiveness, and the demonising of the SHA (middleman) as the corrupting influence. Finally, in naming 'narrative disjuncture and clashes' the chapter develops further understanding of what have been called 'frictions' and 'paradoxes' (Czarniawska 1997) in the context of public-sector organisational change.

Chapter 9 illustrates the power of the narrative exposition chosen, that of stories, serial and themes, in maintaining a continued dialogue with the research participants, a wider focus group of managers from Omega and a regional focus group of healthcare managers. The key finding in this chapter is that all these groups resonated with and could relate to the narratives in all their variety and forms as a fair representation of what it means to them to be leading the implementation of change. The chapter shows how the dialogue with these groups continued to the point of expressing their collective support needs in the midst of change. I argue that their collective construction of need is close to what MacIntyre's lens would highlight as missing for the well-being of the corpus of people who make up the institution and their patients.

Having discussed in brief how each chapter responds to the aims of the study, in the next section I draw out the central contributions in three main areas: methodological, empirical and theoretical and then suggest implications.

10.3   Central contributions

The central contributions of the book are elaborated in this section under three headings. Discrete methodological and empirical contributions are outlined as a precursor to the primary theoretical contributions.

10.3.1   Methodological contributions

Czarniawska (1997) demonstrated how appropriate the narrative methodology is to the study of public-sector reform processes. This study built on her approach by focussing on managers and illuminating their narrative enactments of change by drawing inspiration from Gabriel (2000) and including antenarratives (Boje 2001) to form a synthesis that offers a vivid picture of the inter-subjective social reality of the healthcare manager in the midst of change. Brown and Humphreys (2003) suggest that 'change occurs with alterations in the stories that people tell, and it is these stories that demand increased attention from scholars'. Pedersen (2006) suggests that explanation lies in the research seeking multiple meanings, stories and perspective instead of focussing on one or two dominating discursive voices in society. Rather than use narrative to manage or manipulate change this study has sought to better understand the nature of the conflict within the change stories and what those change stories do rather than solve conflicts enacted in the change stories (Downing 1997).

The methodology supported continuous dialogue and engagement with managers to the point of them constructing their support needs in the midst of change. According to Rhodes and Brown (2005) by being explicit about narrative in this way the localities of practice can be examined in terms of their complexity, contradictions and multi-vocality, and it is in these ways that narrative offers the possibility of retreating from abstraction in a way that engages with the experiences of work, management and organizing.

Czarniawska's (1997) conclusion is to draw out paradoxes from narratives of change through literary and screenplay metaphors and suggests that by confronting such paradoxes a crisis ensues that enables institutions to change. Despite drawing heavily on MacIntyre to build a case for narrative Czarniawska does not surface the ethical or virtue conflicts constructed within the narratives to understand more about those paradoxes or look at what the stories might unfold into the social reality and morality of an organisation in change. This study contributes methodologically by showing the ability of narrative to be used in this way and I now continue with the empirical contribution it has offered.

10.3.2 Empirical contributions

The empirical contributions are twofold: first, the application of MacIntyre's ideas to understanding the ethical dimension of management of public-sector organisational change; second, the themed construction of managers' needs for support in the midst of change.

MacIntyre and public-sector change

Empirically the study offers a view on the social reality of public-sector reform according to a group of managers responsible for implementing modernising reform through the lens of MacIntyre's virtue ethics. Following Ford (1999) and the interpretation of organisational change as shifting stories and conversations, what is revealed is that for many, far from engaging managers in improving services the 'change' happening in their social reality is growing cynicism, anger and mistrust of reform. This supports the conclusions drawn from other studies for example, Hunter 2000, Greener & Powell 2003 and Chapman 2004). The participants, in the main, construct reform as not working for them, their staff and their patients. What studies to date have not offered, however, is an ethical dimension to the understanding of the increasing levels of dissatisfaction. One of the issues for the managers interviewed is that they construct the virtues now expected of them and valorised by government as not leading to the public goods they and the public want. This study has shown ethical clashes to be a significant feature of the participants' narrative enactments. Suffering arising from these 'virtue clashes' are redolent in their narrative and overall construct a reform tragedy that unfolds further cynicism and fear into the narrative milieu. For MacIntyre, the resolution of those ethical clashes approximates to 'mission impossible' given the differences in moral standpoints and the loss of our moral debating resources. The data collected contained no narratives of the resolution of opposing virtues and so has affinity with MacIntyre's thesis in this area. This finding has significant implications for organisational change theory that is predicated on the shifting narrative view of change. Those implications will be discussed in the next section. Recent and strong calls for empirical research based on MacIntyre's concepts are made by Coe and Beadle (2007) and Moore and Beadle (2006). According to Beadle (2007) there have been no published studies to date that have conversed with MacIntyre's thesis in the context of public-sector organisational studies. This study claims to carry the first empirical material and analysis that mediates conversation with MacIntyre's theoretical insights and the public sector in change. It highlights a potential challenge to MacIntyre's thesis and his generalised view of managers as agents of the enlightenment and the resulting moral disarray in institutions (and society) which will be elaborated in the theoretical contributions section below.

Constructed needs in the midst of reform

Turning now to the question of what participants' narratives construct with regard to support needs. These begin with a very clear need to acknowledge that they 'can't go on like this' with people off sick and suffering depression. In addition to counselling and mentoring, many suggested facilitated peer forums to share emotional and practical burdens, good practice and create viable action plans. Alongside this was a plea for leadership input on priorities as they become inundated with a range of legislative, political, financial, social and technological 'must dos' . Well communicated understanding of what managers and their teams experience at the coalface was also marked by many as a priority in order for them to feel inspired to take on the change overhead in their roles. Some of the managers say they understand and are committed to the purpose, others just don't believe in the 'must dos' and so need a greater purpose, a wider vision, to hold on to. Respect for their communities of practice, appropriate training and development and more working together across boundaries all featured as important needs. The need for leadership skills was mentioned in the context of having a set of common models to help resolve problems together as team and giving them the ability to talk the same language. The need for coaching was also mentioned but the preference seemed to be for groups rather than one-to-one. What was being conveyed in the stories was that these latter two support needs would need to form part of an integrated whole rather than stand alones.

10.3.3 Theoretical contributions

This section outlines one primary theoretical contribution and two more theoretical contributions that could be developed further. The primary contribution is to narrative-based organisational change conceptions of resistance and also offers a challenge to organisational change management theory in general. The second contribution is to challenge MacIntyre's generalised view of all managers as agents of the market. Third, by evolving the cultural metaphor of the serial (Czarniawska 1997) I propose an updated metaphor of reality TV to convey the fragmented morality of their institutions and what it means to managers to be implementing government-led reform.

Primary contribution: A virtue ethics dimension to
organisational change management

In this section I first position the contribution in narrative-based understandings of organisational change then suggest a contribution to generic theories of organisational change management.

Virtue conflict (antagonism derived from opposing social and moral traditions) narrative enactments are very common in my study of managers in the midst of implementing healthcare reform. Soundings with other managers across the healthcare sector and the wider public sector suggest that these types of narratives are rife. I argue that the social construction of many of their tragic, comic and romantic reform narratives further exacerbates cynicism, anger, fear and mistrust (Greener & Powell 2003) of reform amongst their peers and their staff. The epic enactments of change tend to be individualistic and based on what the hero felt was right rather than meshing with a communal narrative about a telos-driven quest for the good of the service, its patients and society as a whole. It was if the heroes knew that to engage in that kind of debate was pointless given the distance between the moral standpoints. In this atmosphere of cynicism, anger, fear and mistrust some managers, in their romantic enactments, show loyalty and genuine care for their staff to the point of self-sacrifice or overprotection bordering on non-malicious abuse. MacIntyre suggests that the morally deleterious effect of managerial morality has many victims, not the least of whom are the managers themselves. I think we see this in some of the accounts of the participants, however, what we also see is their narrative enactments of resistance to an 'after virtue' morality that is embedded within policies and the government's managerialist approach to change management that is predicated on the market and a mechanised understanding of change. MacIntyre's research for his 1981 *After Virtue* thesis seems to have conducted in the private sector and his main critical thrust is an appeal to a virtue ethics within institutional orders dominated by power and with the pursuit of goods of excellence as its justification. His appeal to resistance against capitalism is to argue that one cannot lead a virtuous practice-based life within an institutional order dominated by power and with the pursuit of external goods.

The concept of common telos as both a binding, lightly held aim and something that is modified along the way in a communal, evolving narrative forms a key notion of MacIntyre's narrative unity for the individual and the institution's wellbeing. In this study we see many of the enacted change narratives corrupting the virtue, telos and practice narrative unity. Rather than the evolving communal narrative of a healthy workforce we see narratives that construct anger and cynicism towards what managers at all levels often see as externally imposed change and they demonise those bodies such as the SHA that monitor their practice. Even when they say they feel part of the change the enacted clash with their internally held virtues, what they believe to be the right way to practice, cannot, for some, be maintained. An exception is the epic stories. They were like islands of narrative unity in a sea of narrative disunity. That unity, however, was not a communal unity, it was invariably the individual holding on to what they believed was the right way to be practising the implementation of organisational change to redesign services. Nevertheless these stories were inspiring to hear even when they enacted subversion or authoritarian approaches. They construct the notion that the only way to survive and thrive in the midst of a barrage of externally imposed changes is to pursue your own personally held strategies for change. I argue that this perpetuates the construction of individual narrative quest above a communal quest for the greater good. This is similar to autopoesis (Maturana & Varella 1980) where an individual replicates the beliefs of himself or herself rather than what the communal narrative might construct. However, what Pedersen (2006) found in her study of change in a hospital is that mythic stories of heroic adventures do not generate new stories of heroes but rather tragic stories. MacIntyre simply argues that individualism leads to corruption of practice. I argue that without a communal narrative in the midst of change, carrying a set of shared virtues, then what fills the gap are a range of virtue conflict narrative enactments and other narrative fragments that construct confusion, anger, cynicism, fear and low morale. In very broad terms this leads me to argue that good or virtuous organisational change begins with and is predicated on strong socially constructed ethics of practice that provide the standards for improvement to practice and that bad or vicious change is characterised by weak or conflicting virtue ethics and the subsequent enactment of virtue conflict narratives. Sadly, much of what the participants constructed falls into the latter and, as will be highlighted in the third contribution, is not just an issue for the DoH and the Government but for our society. To re-iterate my argument, I now believe that one of the gaps in understanding change is a lack of appreciation of the ethical dimension in change and the impact of the enacted virtue conflicts narratives shared by health professionals in their practice. This for me further explains the power of consultants and GPs who through their training and professional bodies are able to maintain a strong ethos of practice, a 'practice-based community', which as a group, whatever their shortcomings, offer a degree of narrative and ethical unity.

Greener and Powell (2003), based on their survey of healthcare managers, argued that cynicism towards reform pervades this group. This book strengthens that argument and enhances understanding of the narrative-based social constructions of reform that can generate cynicism, demotivate and reduce morale. It points to unresolved moral debate to offer deeper understanding of reform initiatives that fall by the wayside only to be covered over with another initiative – a little like putting layers of new carpet over a damp floor. The moral issues, just like the moisture, keep seeping through.

Implications for organisational change theory in general

Having explained my contribution to narrative-based understandings of organisational change I now explore the contribution to the organisational change literature in general. The prominent social construction of cynicism and mistrust towards change in the narratives provides the starting point. Resistance as cynicism interpreted from a mechanistic perspective (Lewin 1952) is a force pressing against change, something to be weakened using analytical, educational/ learning, political process, sacking or the introduction of new staff (Tushman et al. 1986). Sturdy and Grey (2003: 653) believe that 'mechanistic understandings of change are (still) ubiquitous in organisational change' management. However, they do acknowledge that other 'voices' are becoming heard but 'much of importance is left unsaid'. I will briefly play back other voices in the carnival (Bakhtin and Medvedev 1928/1978) of organisational change theorising and then add my voice to the procession in a way that I hope will add to and assist that of others' in being heard.

From a humanist perspective Casey (1999) suggests that 'cynicism protects against both commitment to the company and its encroachment into the private realm of (relative) individual choice'. Resistance as cynicism from a post-structuralist perspective is interpreted as a conservative force in contemporary workplaces because individuals express cynicism (just as we see here) but they still practice the corporate rituals. Willmott (1993) has described this as an unplanned ideological phenomenon and drawing on Kunda (1992) suggests that workers actually collude with the relations of power they seek to escape because the very possibility of them being able to express their cynicism and resistance is evidence of the institution's commitment to openness and freedom. There is also the notion that resistance reinforces the structures of domination that were the object of resistance in the first place (Piccone 1978) and provides an element of vitality termed 'middle-class radicalism' without seriously threatening the domination (Fleming & Spicer 2003). The latter pair develop this theme by drawing on Žižek (1989) who suggests in a similar vein to MacIntyre that the enlightenment has collapsed into a pervasive cynicism because of the devastation modernity has visited upon humans, animals and the environment during the 20th century. They suggest that in emphasising the external nature of subjectivity the 'stressed worker' becomes the 'stressful workplace', the 'tired employee' becomes the 'exploitative organisation'. Attention is then focussed on these negative HRM categories and we lose interest in the 'realistic' response of individuals in the midst of external circumstances. They conclude with this quote from Braverman:

> Beneath this apparent habituation, the hostility of workers to degenerated forms of work which are forced upon them continues as a subterranean stream that makes its way to the surface when employment conditions permit... it renews itself in new generations, expresses itself in the unbounded cynicism and revulsion which large numbers of workers feel about their work, and comes to the fore as a social issue demanding solution. (Braverman 1974: 151 quoted in Fleming & Spicer 2003: 175)

I build on Fleming and Spicer's conclusion to offer an ethical dimension to the theme of resistance and 'degenerated forms of work' which further challenges the theory that organisational change can be managed, measured and manipulated. Sturdy and Grey (2003) raise concerns about the dominance of the view that organisational change is inevitable, desirable and or manageable and they argue a case for research that provides 'alternative (additional) voices and therefore choices' (ibid.: 659). They suggest that MacIntyre, amongst others, challenges theories that underpin organisational change management.

> ... MacIntyre's (1981) contention (is) that the social sciences have completely failed to develop predictive generalities, and moreover, that they will never do so. OCM has no such inhibitions. For example, in Pettigrew et al., although there is a familiar recognition of a 'complex, dynamic and internationally conscious world', a 'search for general patterns of change' remains (2001: 697). If OCM is, as we have suggested, both managerialist and universalist, what might be done to articulate a different kind of understanding of change? (Sturdy & Grey 2003: 657)

They go on to suggest that understanding the socially constructed nature of OCM 'corrodes the assumptions upon which OCM is built' and say

> This is crucial because, if change is not inevitable and desirable but contingent and contested, then the organizational and political consequences are potentially profound. (ibid.)

From a social constructionist perspective, Blackler et al. (1999) interpret resistance in healthcare change programmes as 'tensions' and suggest we need to understand how to support those who have to translate policy into practice. From a narrative perspective Czarniawska (1997) identifies 'frictions' and 'paradoxes' as an inevitable aspect of change in the public sector and suggests that by confronting such paradoxes we bring crisis to institutions which enable them to change. However, in this literature there is tacit support for change as 'inevitable and desirable'. This is not the case in Humphreys and Brown's (2002) notion of change complicating and for me *challenging* people's sense of what they stand for. Currie and Brown's narrative study of change in a UK hospital (2003) follows a similar line to Humphreys and Brown's and claims that workers authored a range of counter narratives that placed limits on governments' attempts at hegemonic control. One of their participants says 'A lot of people in the health service as a whole have felt that many of the changes are based on impractical ideology' (2003: 582). Currie and Brown do not follow the 'ideology' cue. However, for MacIntyre, as I have discussed earlier, ideology plays a key role in understanding resistance and conflict. In conversing with MacIntyre's narrative-based virtue ethics thesis I offer an alternative voice in the form of what it means to those who are under the influence of change as 'inevitable and desirable' from the 'epochal' framing of the need for transformation of public services (du Gay 2003). My interpretation of resistance follows Fleming and Spicer's (2003) view of a 'healthy' contestation of this influence on their working lives. I argue that this is a form of 'ethical resistance' and is a socially constructed outcome from enacted virtue conflict narratives that seek to protect healthcare practices from being corrupted. I argue that 'ethical resistance' is intended to resist vicious change – that is change that has a weak ethical status, inherently conflicting ethics or that has ethics purely in service of the attainment of external goods of money, status or power. As we see in the accounts of the participants and as suggested by MacIntyre these are ethics that have a corrupting influence on practice and foster narrative disunity and moral disarray. The managers narrate their virtue-to-virtue combat with ethics that in some cases are reflections of wider ideological battles (for example, market vs. communitarianism) and that are only reconcilable with the violence of assertion. War metaphors abound in the data, such as 'under siege', 'trench warfare' and 'fighting a losing battle'. Using MacIntyre's lens I suggest they are fighting for the ethics of what they believe to be virtuous practice in health care, a public service ethos and for their way of improving services. This notion has resonance with the context and tactics of Svejk, the fictional soldier created by Hasek (1973), who resists the discipline of the Austro-Hungarian Army through subtle forms of subversion that were invariably invisible to his superiors. Fleming and Sewell (2002) suggest Svejkian tactics in the workplace might help to 'undermine or dissolve power relationships in practical ways that also help to 'unmask' the ideological absurdities that shore up them up'. I argue with Sewell that far from being just an 'ideology of resistance' the collective construction of 'ethical resistance' has the potential to undermine modernisation approaches that to managers do not appear to engage with their concern to protect their practices from corruption.

If the modernisation process did engage with this concern then I argue that it would be highly challenging to the notion that the kind of organisational change that brings service improvements and excellence can be managed. Informed by MacIntyre, it suggests the kind of change that improves practice in any sustainable way needs to come from the centre of that practice, from the practitioners and be grown in a meshing of their personal narrative unities. Not only should it come from the centre but it should also be situated in a continuum of social history and of the society in which the practice has evolved along with other practices that together seek wellbeing for society as a whole, not money, status or power. This is backed up in the empirical data that contains an expression of what participants need to improve services. Their needs include: peer forums to share emotional and practical burdens and create viable change; respect for their culture and communities of practice; building on existing good practice and knowledge rather than replacing services and change fitting with local, regional and national priorities. Their evolving narratives seeking a telos that brings excellence in virtuous practice cannot be modelled as function or structure. In this version of organisational change resistance theory, the notion that we can set targets, decide on a set of interventions strategies, prescribe practice in policies and guidelines and manage those interventions is inappropriate. Structural functional conceptualisations have been turned into public-sector change imperatives, created perverse effects (Pidd 2005) and arguably, in some case, led to a tragic waste of public funds, emotional effort and physical energy.

This book is not against change but it does add to the chorus of voices that speak out against a purely mechanistic theorised approach taken to manage change in the public healthcare sector and the wider public sector. It is for bringing new knowledge to communities of practitioners, knowledge that helps them to emancipate themselves from the dominating discourse that says organisational change is 'inevitable, desirable and manageable' (Sturdy & Grey 2003: 659) and to seek ethical and sustainable improvements to practice. Hunter's conclusion is that the public healthcare sector can 'manage on its own' resonates to a point but to leave the sector in a time warp is unacceptable. An option for achieving a better balance between forcing change and undermining change is to inform communities of healthcare practitioners and policy makers about the antecedents of their ethical clashes and allow them to engage with the moral debate of what kind of health service (and world) they wish to build and fight for together. This option has been piloted with practitioners and is discussed in the last section of the thesis as a postscript.

In the next section I focus on MacIntyre's generalisation of all managers being agents of the market and challenge this view with findings from the study.

Second theoretical contribution: MacIntyre and the manager

In MacIntyre's view, when narrative carries a set of virtues and a communally agreed morality for the institution, then high morale is the outcome. In this case of public-sector change we note that low moral cohesion seems to construct low morale. Although many structural theorists have pointed to the importance of key people leading reform, the moral dimension of their leadership has received little attention. For all the government rhetoric on the importance of leadership and maintaining values, for example, the virtues of healthcare practice, this aspect seems to be missing when policies are implemented. In its absence we see the kind of moral fragmentation and disarray that MacIntyre's thesis suggests is a fall-out of the growing liberal individualistic way of life: we are living and working in institutions that are 'after virtue'. For policy makers this points to consideration of morality in the midst of reform as a vital component for the wellbeing of staff and their ability to take on and implement change.

Additionally, by viewing stories of virtues in conflict as reflections of different ideological horizons and their dramas as hot spots of movements in history, this book attempts to build on other Western European public-sector reform studies which describe, for example, 'tensions', 'disempowerment' (Blackler et al. 1999; Blackler 2006 respectively), 'friction', 'paradoxes' (Czarniawska 1997) and 'identity fragmentation' (Humphreys & Brown 2002) to offer deeper understanding of the challenge of reconciling at a practice level virtues that have well rooted, historical antecedents in different ideological discourses.

In this study, participants expressed their needs in the form of narratives. The match between their needs and MacIntyre's appeal for a virtuous practice-based life working towards 'common good' is striking and demonstrates in this case a public service ethos that is still very strong. What we find here are managers trying to defend their public service ethos, an ethos very similar to MacIntyre's practice-based community ethos, and clashing with imposed virtues that do not fit with what they believe to be virtuous practice. Managers show remarkable loyalty to their staff, who respond by following them. However, this study finds many managers, in the midst of a reform 'battle' for the morality of healthcare practice, losing their way. This finding suggests that MacIntyre's generalised thesis of the market-formed, plastic and fragmented morality of all managers does not seem to apply in this particular public sector context. However, the enacted narratives of their virtue battles do contribute to the fragmentation and confusion of morality in the institution. This is subtly different from what MacIntyre is suggesting but we could argue that it has the same outcome. MacIntyre suggests that management education should 'unfit them (managers) for the contemporary world' (Beadle 2002 quoting Knight 1998: 267). I suggest that management education has a role in (re) constructing their courage to reclaim the moral (high) ground necessary for them to continue managing the provision of equitable high quality healthcare.

In the next section I again take a springboard from Fleming and Spicer's Braverman quote (2003: 175) and the assertion that cynicism 'comes to the fore as a social issue demanding solution' by way of modern cultural metaphor, reality TV, that I hope will convey my understanding, informed by MacIntyre, of the nature of that social issue.

Third contribution: 'Reality TV' of reform

In this section the literary genre of the serial (Czarniawska 1997) is developed into the new metaphor and genre of reality TV to convey the overall sense of meaning (or lack of) to managers in the reform process. In this respect, the study demonstrates the reciprocal relationship between 'art' and the institution in society.

The Community mental health teams 'serial' in seven episodes in Chapter 7 constructs a developing theme of tragedy at the gradual destruction of a community of practice and a reduction in level of service offered to patients. The stage in the serial is grieving the loss and picking up the pieces of a 'broken' service. One coping mechanism is disengagement, seeing the whole thing as theatre in which they have no control over the action, meaning that when things go wrong it is not their fault – it is just the playwright following a whim such as another fashionable initiative or meaningless target, a virtual object (Blackler et al. 1999). Searching for a more modern cultural metaphor, I ask if this is more like a reality TV show where the group are given different tasks, then we all watch to see how they cope. Am I, the researcher, like the video diary they speak to in a private room? I go away and produce the show, this book, which you the audience see as episodes in the life of the 'National Health Service Reality TV' show. In this way I explicitly recognise that this book is an example of 'textual collusion' in which the 'producer' and 'audience' are deeply implicated in relations of power (Fuller & Lee 1997), like the 'power effects' (Foucault 1984) described by (Rose 1999) that could be said to be analogous to the *Big Brother* scenario. The suggestion by Czarniawska (1997) that we are all part of the reciprocal process between media, art, organisational field fashions and organisational life would mean that an updating of the serial metaphor was inevitable.

On reflection, my sense of the whole experience to date is of a *Big Brother*-type reality TV show. As researcher I felt like the video diary for these managers. They all came into the role because it is something that they really wanted to do. Now they are in it, the full range of emotions are present as they feel supported on the one hand and yet on the other they are all part of a conspiracy to select each other for the axe to meet financial targets. The frustration and despair is of only having a faceless 'big brother' to answer for the losses they feel. Some just tolerate the experience as they work through a number of imposed and apparently silly tasks. Managers who now want to leave work alongside others who are clear that it will bring them and the audience of service users something worthwhile.

Some of the features which parallel reality TV are:

- Researcher as the 'video diary'
- Participants volunteered to join the healthcare sector
- Feeling supported by colleagues on one level
- Part of an invisible conspiracy that is gradually reducing their number
- The frustration and despair of only having a faceless 'big brother' to answer for the losses
- Others just tolerate the experience as they work through a number of imposed tasks that seem farcical
- A proportion of managers are very clear that they are able to handle the challenge and thrive

- Managers who now want to leave work alongside others who are clear that it will bring them and the audience of service users something worthwhile
- Some managers have a game plan
- The minutiae of daily life are examined by a panel of 'experts'

Below I have taken the genres of serials and conventional drama as contrasted by Czarniawska (1997: 120) and put my development of reality TV alongside it in the third column to show the different techniques at play. I have also added a moral dimension to the list.

The third round interviews revealed an increasing number of what they considered to be farcical and shifting 'must dos' given to the members of the 'National Health Service Reality TV' household. Another parallel is that the NHS is a highly visible organisation in the media as we regularly see news reports covering stories such as hospitals unable to keep infections down, foundation hospitals, rebellion by GPs, closure of wards and failure to meet waiting list targets.

The overall sense is of the participants being involved with something that they are unhappy about, aware that they are angry about it but apparently unable to voice their complaint or anger at the way they are being treated in any kind of satisfactory way.

Conventional drama technique	Variations of the technique in serials	Further variations in Reality TV
Personification	Confused	People play themselves.
Identification	Many possible (static, fragmentary personalities)	Set of identified people (spiced up with well known celebrities).
Suspense	Open structure of events	Whole series of mini-suspenses as people are selected for removal.
Unmasking	Repetitions	Series of tasks that test individuals and the group.
Climax	No resolution	Predictable form of climax of one individual left.
Catharsis	Interruption	Intense emotions are analysed by 'experts.'
Single moral message	Moral themes	No moral compass: fragmented and confused ethics.

10.4   Future research

This study began the process of testing the findings and analysis with wider groups of healthcare managers and considerable resonance was found. Through conference papers exposure of the findings to senior managers in other public-sector services has been initiated. They too resonate strongly with the findings. In this vein, further research could be carried out with groups of managers from other public services undergoing reform to understand what it means to them to implement reform through a similar synthesised narrative methodology.

10.4.1   Extending this study

Further substantive engagement and challenge to the dominant managerialist notions embedded within theories of organisational change management needs to be made in order to offer alternatives. One option is to extend the type of narrative-ethics-change based theorising used here. Questions such as 'What do managers need to support them in developing the resources for moral debate in the midst of change?', 'What narrative enactment would managers use to describe moral resolution?' and 'How would genuine engagement with the moral issues alter the social reality of reform?' would be a start point for further challenge and alternatives.

Another option would be to take one specific redesign to healthcare services and involving not just managers but other stakeholders for example practitioners, health professionals, users and carers to extend the narratives of leading change to add further meanings and constructions from these different perspectives on modernising reform.

Another avenue would be to follow the dialogue through with managers and continue to sample their narratives as their needs are met in the way they describe to see what constructions emerge. This was option was explored in pilot project with a group of regional managers and the final section and postscript describes that activity.

10.4.2   New research agendas

New organisational change related research which could spawn from this study is in the area of further exploration of MacIntyre's concepts related to the leadership of organisational change programmes in the private sector as well as the public sector to examine how they serve organisational change theory building.

Methodological research avenues might ask what other aspects of organisational studies might benefit from the synthesised narrative approach as described in this book. Studies which aim to understand the meaning that organisational actors attach to managerialist institutional activities that impact on them would be suitable, for example, appraisals, reward and recognition, performance management, leadership development and project management. In particular studies that maintain a dialogue of meaning to the point of establishing what actors say they need to support them would enable theorisation in a similar way.

10.5 Implications for reform policy, theory and management education

MacIntyre asserts that managers are the agents of the enlightenment project and the 'principal social characters' (Beadle 2002) responsible for the domination of goods of effectiveness over those of excellence and joint authors of institutional moral breakdown alongside therapists and aesthetes. Thomas and Anthony (1996) argues that if managers, especially in the public sector, have to rely on central 'imperative co-ordination', targets, performance measures and the like then 'those communities have already broken down'. Anthony, however, lays the blame squarely at the management educators' door with 'the false and morally bankrupt perversion of management practice that it has so assiduously peddled'. I argue alongside one of the comments from the manager who says 'I can't name one individual, we are all a part of it'. Czarniawska's insightful art replicating life and vice versa in her *Dramas of Institutional Identity* (1997) is another way of saying this.

So what are the implications given the conclusion that we as a society are colluding in the construction of a tragedy in our public services? My ideal call is to work on a broad front (art, media, education, practitioners, policy, theorists) and my specific and realistic call falls into three areas: reform policy, organisational change theory and management education. I now discuss implications for those three areas in more detail, the latter in the form of a research application and as a postscript to the book.

10.5.1 Implications for reform policy

This study suggests uncomfortable lessons for current UK and perhaps international public reform policy, its implementation and management. For healthcare policy makers the question might be, 'If reform in its present approaches means cynicism, anger, mistrust and alienation for many of the people it expects to be leading organisation change then what are the alternatives?' This then leads to more fundamental questions such as:

- What is the purpose of reform?
- Is reform the appropriate story/theory/solution – construction?
- If it is then what approaches to reform would engender optimism, inspiration, trust and engagement for health service staff?
- If reform is not an appropriate construction then what is?

Grint (2005) suggests that a persuasive rendition of the context dictates the preferred engagement approach to take. He cites the pre-war Iraq situation, constructed as a crisis by the Bush and Blair administrations and therefore needing emergency action and military force to resolve. That construction has since proved to be unsustainable. The aftermath of insurgency and suicide bombings has also revealed missing complexities in that construction. Similarly I argue that modernising the healthcare sector has been constructed by the government and policy makers as a mechanical problem (Morgan 1986) in the main to be measured and performance managed. This is not surprising given the dominance in the field of functional structural models of change (Sturdy & Grey 2003). We see here in these findings the narrative enacted aftermath of missing the complexity of the situation and particularly of missing the ethical complexities involved.

To explore the above questions further I return to the argument made at the end of Chapter 7. We are experiencing the outcome of a narrative flow of reform missing a moral debate that includes looking at how the change might affect virtues of practice and the purpose of the institution as it sits within wider society. Further, that given MacIntyre's radical analysis of society as a whole – that is, that we are living in a time 'after virtue' – then we might view this as an inevitable outcome. Serial policy initiatives that fail and are resurrected with different names (Jessop 2000), it could be argued, are symptomatic of unresolved moral debates. We see swings from assertion of one initiative to counter assertion of another the next wins on the basis of the previous failure. The newly asserted initiative then fails and all the while the moral debate is being avoided and not surprisingly, since it would be like asking Truman in the 1998 film about a reality TV show *The Truman Show* to break out of his artificial village life. Eventually he finds courage and a ladder, climbs up and knocks on the fake ceiling, realisation dawns, and we, the audience all cheer inside.

I argue that reform in its present construction of restructuring, targets and measuring performance against those targets is inappropriate. We need a different construction.

As one alternative, MacIntyre offers a neo-Aristotelian virtues-goods-practices-institution schema as described earlier (and summarised in Appendix 1) which sounds attractive but which I would argue is unrealistic to achieve for the healthcare sector as a whole as opposed to in localised communities of practice. What is more possible, in my opinion, is to develop understanding with managers of the ideological horizons reflected in their narratives of organisational change and to support them in developing their collective narrative and construction of the issues in a way that is faithful to their public service ethos and the principles of practice improvement that both they and the government desire for healthcare. The participants expressed a strong need for 'facilitated peer forums' of this nature and the outcomes of a pilot programme that met this need are discussed in the last section of the book as a postscript.

At a reform policy formulation level, in addition to reviewing the theoretical base for reform approaches, the recommendation would be to pay more attention to the ethical genealogy and matching of peer reform policies and with those intended to dovetail with existing practices on the ground.

10.5.2   Implications for theory

The call is to further understand through narrative the virtue dilemmas faced by managers in the midst of reform and to take this enquiry to other areas of the public sector. Findings in this study suggest that organisational change theory in general and public-sector organisational change theory in particular needs to pay more attention to narrative understandings of organisational change. Using this understanding this book has challenged existing notions of resistance to change by reframing through a virtue ethics lens as narrative opposition to constructed virtues that, to the participants, mean corruption of their practice and their ability to achieve excellence in practice. It has highlighted the lack of attention paid to the 'virtue conflict' narrative and the cynicism constructing effects of enactment forms such as epic, tragic, comic and romantic.

The difficulty of resolving conflicts has been constructed as 'old versus new' and 'frictions' by Czarniawska, who makes this observation of her stories from the Swedish public sector in change:

> The encounters between the old and the new and the resulting friction are, in fact, a recurring topic in the stories that follow. (Czarniawska 1997: 79)

Moral concerns are raised in her stories by the participants but the link with MacIntyre is not explored in this context. Nor is the notion of wider ethical battle constructions in which the participants are part of a scene. Theorising in these areas has the potential to inform practitioners with a wider understanding of their situation so that as a peer group they can decide if they are engaged in a worthy battle for them to commit so much physical and emotional energy to and if not what battle, if any, they want to be in. This requires moral debate. Sometimes, as we have seen in this case study, that choice is completely taken away (temporarily) and it becomes pure survival. That, as Czarniawska (1997) points out, is what power is about.

What this study conveys is a tragedy and misuse of power, constructed by the participants: so much money, energy and emotion are spent on so much that uses so little of their input and that has so little impact on the quality of services. A recent consultative report (DoH 2007) on the reform programme has strong concurrence with this construction.

> Patients … sometimes feel like a number rather than a person. They do not know how to access the services they need to help them stay well and independent. They cannot always see a GP or practice nurse when they need to … The public say they are sometimes confused about which NHS service they should use. They hear a lot about changes but do not know why they are being made.
>
> Some staff tell me that they haven't been listened to and trusted. They do not feel that their values – including wanting to improve the quality of care – have been fully recognised. Nor do they feel that they have always been given the credit for the improvements that have been made. (DoH 2007: 2)

Wider implications for reform theory, drawing on MacIntyre, would be to ask if the public healthcare sector (like many other public sector institutions) has lost the resources to identify what is important through moral debate and therefore where to focus spending. Questions such as 'Is restructuring implemented as an alternative to moral debate?' and 'Do the debates emerge untouched at the other side of restructuring?' might offer further challenges to public-sector reform theory based on structural understanding of change.

This study is not without hope and in the next and final section of the book I discuss a management education pilot programme that was based on the research and the theorising discussed here.

10.5.3 Implications for management education – a postscript

Following the empirical data on expressed needs I felt Omega Trust and the DoH were under a moral (if not a legal, duty of care) obligation to respond to the participants' calls. The HR and mental health directors agreed and a proposal to support the managers in mental health initially with a series of themed learning sets was produced. However, due to severe financial constraints, the organisation decided it could not fund such a proposal. A further application was made for 'no strings' external funding from a pharmaceutical company but although they were initially very enthusiastic their offer eventually came to nothing. Shortly after this let-down the news came through that Omega would be cut in four and its parts grafted onto other trusts so as to make health trust provision co-terminous with county boundaries and county councils. This was known as the commissioning a patient-led (CPL) restructure (Crisp 2005) and was one of Sir Nigel Crisp's (former NHS chief executive) last initiatives before he resigned in early 2005. After this announcement managers at all levels became consumed with concern for their jobs as 13 separate trusts were to become 6 and simple maths regarding the number of directors and managers required evoked fight-or-flight responses. All discussions around learning sets or support to managers of the kind they had described fell off the priority list at this point. The law of the jungle seemed to prevail as the institution which contained their narratives was suddenly looking at the end of its narrative. This was 'reality TV' situated in the jungle of the healthcare sector. All was not lost, however, and after the findings were presented at a regional health care conference, the deputy director of a government healthcare support agency and I formed a pilot regional programme called Leading Change in the Public Sectors (Conroy 2007) as a collaborative venture with an Higher Education (HE) partner.

Needs expressed by managers in this research provided strong pointers to the kind of management education they would like to support them with service improvements. Their needs were combined with MacIntyre's notion that it is through conflict and sometimes only through conflict that we learn what our ends and purposes (telos) are and with the question 'Of what (wider) conflicts is (my conflict) the scene?' (adapted from MacIntyre 1985). This combination produced a programme (Conroy 2007) that was designed to open awareness of the wider ideological battles and allow them to debate what that awareness means for their practice decisions. By raising awareness of the wider social and ethical debates through researchers' commentary we attempted to meet management education needs in a 'self-forming' rather than a 'self-enslaving' (Thomas and Anthony 1995: 292) management education programme. Downing (1997) suggests that it is the manager's job to resolve the conflicting change stories. By drawing on MacIntyre's *After Virtue* I argue that the challenge of resolving virtue conflict is like asking managers to take on 'mission impossible' given the well-rooted antecedents of the virtues at stake.

MacIntyre's theoretical underpinning, managers' expressed needs and a considerable amount of consensus across other trusts grounded the programme in a solid theoretical and empirical base. Six sessions were designed, each in response to the constructed needs of participants and the wider groupings of managers. By opening the discussion with managers about the antecedents of their virtue clashes the programme was designed to allow them to discover options that, in the midst of reform, still offer them 'internal goods' (a feeling of excellence, wellbeing and satisfaction) in their management of health and social care practice. Further that the programme be faithful to a collective purpose of improving the quality of health care offered by the services they manage.

The cohort of 24 delegates was made up from people in executive, management team and direct report positions in health and social care organisations. They were people who are accountable for leading the translation and implementation of reform policies, guidelines, frameworks and measures into healthcare practice improvements. Each of the six meetings offered an incisive commentary and an opportunity for delegates to explore personal thinking on the application of ideas to real-time issues within their organisational setting. The debates were facilitated in small groups of around six people and each person was given an opportunity to discuss their work issues. After the small groups, the plenary session reconvened and delegates had a further chance to raise issues and questions with the commentators. Three months after the programme was completed participants were interviewed and asked what the programme had meant for them at a personal and service level. Some of their comments are given below.

Personal outcome narratives:

- *'Increased my appetite for reading and keeping up with developments'*
- *'Made me quite angry. Found it cathartic'*
- *'I came out of 'Leading Change' a changed person'*
- *'Kaboom: it clarified the difference between leadership and management'*
- *'Leadership is about breaking the rules'*

Organisational/ service outcome narrative:

- *'I am more courageous now in my assertion of doing the right thing in the organisation rather than meeting targets'*
- *'I am encouraging more networking – something that I never made time for in the past'*
- *'There is no way we would have taken on this new work without understanding the values at stake'*
- *'Now I feel it is not about who we commission more about what patients need'*

Unexpected outcomes for some were that the programme seemed to (re-) construct courage; rekindle their 'narrative quest'; and develop a clearer purpose for them and their organisation. Was this mission possible?

Final comment from a delegate:

> *I made every single one – it was a pleasure to go to – I enjoyed it personally and professionally.*

The enthusiasm with which this pilot programme was received adds further support to the argument that public-sector organisational change theory and the policy on which it is based need to pay more attention to narrative constructions of change, virtue conflict and engaging managers in line with their constructed needs in the face of those conflicts. This work also supports the view offered by Moore and Beadle (2006) that MacIntyre's thesis offers rich concepts for the furtherance of managerial and organisation studies by demonstrating an application to the development of organisation change theory in particular.

One way of applying this research and supporting managers has been successfully piloted and the field is open for other applications of MacIntyre's ideas and support programmes to be designed based on the type of theorising contained here.

Appendix 1: MacIntyre's Virtues-Goods-Practices-Institution Schema

These definitions are drawn, in the main, from Moore and Beadle (2006).

- **Virtues:** disposition to act and feel in a certain way that enables us to achieve internal goods of wellbeing. Without justice, courage, truthfulness, temperance and prudence practices could not resist the corrupting power of the external goods that of are concern to institutions.
- **Internal goods** *of excellence:* both the excellence of products and the perfection of the individual in the process. For MacIntyre these are the proper ends derived from an exercise of the virtues in practice.
- **External goods** *of effectiveness:* money, status, power – can be corrupting of practice. When achieved these are always some individual's property and possession.
- **Practice:** any coherent and complex form of social activity where internal goods of excellence can be extended, such as medicine, fishing, nursing, football, chess, architecture, construction and painting.

The aim internal to such productive crafts, when they are in good order, is never only to catch fish, or to produce beef or milk, or to build houses. It is to do so in a manner consonant with the excellences of the craft, so that there is not only a good product, but the craftsperson is perfected through and in her or his activity. (MacIntyre 1994: 284)

The ideals and the creativity of practices are always vulnerable to the acquisitiveness and competitiveness of the institution.

Institutions

> Institutions are characteristically and necessarily concerned with external goods. They are involved in acquiring money and other material goods; they are structured in terms of power and status, and they distribute money, power and status as rewards. (MacIntyre 1985: 194)

No practice can survive for any length of time unsustained by institutions. The association and tension between practice and Institution and between internal and external goods.

- *Narrative quest:* search for our telos *(eudaimonia:* blessedness, happiness, prosperity, being well and doing well) – our developing story, not always characterised fully but connected to a communal narrative that becomes clearer along the way as we seek wellbeing for all.

Notes

1 Introduction

1. Virtue conflict as written in this thesis means antagonism or a clash derived from opposing social and moral traditions and standpoints.
2. Some very encouraging outcomes from a pilot management education programme based on the analysis in this thesis and the expressed needs of the participants are summarised in the last section of the conclusions as a postscript.
3. Internal goods (of excellence): both the excellence of products/ services and the perfection of the individual in the process. According to MacIntyre the achievement of both are reliant on a communally agreed set of virtues acquired through participating in practice.
4. Trust-wide through focus groups, regionally through workshops and UK-wide through conferences.

2 The Healthcare Sector and the Modernising Agenda

1. The participants sometimes refer to changes that are government imperatives as 'must dos'.
2. Pseudonym.

3 Organisational Change and Healthcare

1. Activity theory is a methodology for understanding change through activities. Activity Theory's core model is a triangular relational framework of Group, Individual and Object (that the group is working on). Engestrom argues for the unit of analysis in any organisation to be the socially distributed activity systems.
2. The issue of paradox in public sector reform is also highlighted by Czarniawska (1997) in her study of the reform of Swedish public administration. This aspect will be explored in more detail in the methodology section.
3. Ricoeur's central thesis is that the registering of human time and identity, whether it be individual or collective, is entrusted to narrative.

4 Turning to Narrative

1. The 'narrative turn' means a turn to recognising narrative as a fruitful medium for studying within the social sciences.
2. The 'linguistic turn' means a turn to recognising linguistics as a valuable medium for research in the social sciences.

3. Hermeneutics is the science of interpreting texts especially the books of the bible.
4. Values are the subjective principles of worth to an individual or an organisation.
5. An enquiry style that takes into account metaphor, gestures, body language etc. and all the taken for granted signals used in conversation to co-construct meaning.
6. Dostoevsky challenged the monological novel and 'enlightenment' thinking with a series of polyphonic type novels.
7. 'Ideology' as used in this thesis means 'norms, values and beliefs directing the political attitudes and actions of a group' and is not meant to be a critical or negative term (Noth 1995: 12).
8. There are shades of Lave and Wenger's (1991) 'communities of practice' and 'legitimate peripheral participation' concepts here but they focus on learning about practice per se rather than virtuous practice.
9. Liberal Individualism refers to a social movement that believes in freedom of choice for the individual and a market in which to make those choices.

5   Research Methodology

1. By *unfold* I mean stories and narrative that convey messages to others and in this context a moral message just as in oral communities that transmit their traditions and moral code through cascaded storytelling.
2. *Tamara* is a play by John Krizanc in which a dozen characters unfold their stories in different rooms before a walking, sometimes running, audience. The spectators are expected to choose which characters to follow from room to room and take different meanings from the performance.
3. Trust-wide through focus groups, regionally through workshops and UK wide through conferences.

6   Stories: Epic, Tragic, Comic and Romantic

1. Aristotle (*Nichomachean Ethics*) defined a particular type of societal grouping called a *polis* in which relationships were not just based on friendships but on a shared sense of telos (purpose) for the group (city state Thomson (1955)). Through the *polis* flows a narrative that carries the virtues via storytelling that contribute to conducting all practice in a way that brings wellbeing for all (*eudaimonia*) in the *polis*.
2. Ricoeur characterised mimesis 3 as the restoration of narrative to the time of action and of suffering (1984, 1:70). In other words it is the movement to action based on what the listener takes from the story.
3. MacIntyre's (1985: 273) account of the virtues proceeds through three stages: a first which concerns virtues as necessary to achieve the goods internal to practice, a second that sees them as qualities contributing to the good of a whole life, and a third which relates them to the pursuit of a good for human beings the conception of which can only be elaborated and possessed within an ongoing social tradition.

4. Refer to Chapter 4, Turning to Narrative, for an explanation of Propp's folklore of oppression.
5. Narrative unity is the notion that, like narrative, our lives have a beginning, middle and ending and they only make sense as a unity of life. MacIntyre argues that the virtues find their point and purpose not only in seeking the good of life as a whole but in sustaining those traditions which provide practices and individual lives with their necessary unity and context. Lack of the virtues is corrupting of practice and therefore, it might be argued, of a person's narrative unity.
6. Cognitive behavioural therapy.
7. *Big Brother* is a UK Channel 4 reality TV programme. A mix of celebrities and volunteers from the public are imprisoned together in a house fitted with cameras and the viewers observe selected highlights in their interactions as they work through a list of imposed tasks. An 'expert' panel analyse the participants' interactions and make comment.
8. The manager, aesthete and therapist according to MacIntyre (1981) are (or were) moral representatives of their culture in the same way as Victorian England was partially defined by the character of the public school headmaster.
9. Refers to Svejk, the fictional 'good soldier' created by Hasek (1973), who resists the discipline of the Austro-Hungarian Army through subtle forms of subversion that were invariably invisible to his superiors.
10. Fagin is a character from a Charles Dickens novel, *Oliver Twist*, who pays very close attention to the counting of his money and bullies small boys into stealing for his own ends.
11. The findings have been presented at academic and practitioner conferences around the UK which have been attended by managers from the NHS and the wider public sector.
12. In February 2000 Victoria Climbié died as the result of severe physical abuse and neglect that had spanned several months. She was in the care of her father's aunt who had brought her to the UK from the Ivory Coast because her parents had wanted a better life for her.
13. Agenda for Change is supposed to benefit staff by evaluating every post and giving everyone a job description and ultimately pay equity for people in equivalent roles so that nobody is paid less or more than they should be.
14. Antenarrative can be seen as anti-narrative, running against another story line and for Boje it is the 'real story' the messy disjunctures of real life as opposed to a crafted and emplotted narrative.

7   Serial: Community Mental Health Team Formation

1. In this film, Jim Carrey is Truman, a man whose life is a fake one. The place he lives is in fact a big studio with hidden cameras everywhere, and all his friends and people around him, are actors who play their roles in the most popular TV series in the world: The Truman Show. Truman thinks that he is an ordinary man with an ordinary life and has no idea about how he is exploited.

10   Discussion and Conclusions

1. This term is now used very freely, and retrospectively, so that abolitionists and activists such as Gandhi are referred to as 'ethical resisters' although they didn't apply the term to themselves. It now seems to be particularly involved with whistleblowing (De Maria 2006).

Bibliography

Aaltio-Marjosola, I. (1994). From a 'grand story' to multiple narratives: Studying an organizational change project. *Journal of Organizational Change Management*, 7(5), 56–67.

Alvesson, M. and Wilmott, H. (eds) (1992). *Critical Management Studies*. London: Sage.

Andersen, N. Å. (2003). Polyphonic organisations. In T. Hernes and T. Bakken (eds), *Autopoietic organization theory*. Oslo: Abstakt, Liber, Copenhagen Business School Press.

Anderson, D. (2005). 'What you'll say is...': Represented voice in organisational change discourse. *Journal of Organisational Change Management*, 18(1), 63–77.

Argyris, C. and Schon, D. (1978). *Organisational learning: A theory of action perspective*. Reading, MA: Addison Wesley.

Aristotle (1963). *Politics and poetics*. New York: The Viking Press. Castillo, GA.

Ashburner, L. (2001). *Organisational behaviour and organisation studies in health care: Reflections on the future*. Basingstoke: Palgrave.

Bakhtin, M. M. (1986). *Speech genres and other late essays*. Austin: University of Texas Press.

Bakhtin, M. M. and Medvedev, P. N. (1978). *The formal method in literary scholarship*. (A. J. Wehrle, trans.). Baltimore: Johns Hopkins University Press (Original work published 1928).

Barthes, R. (1977). Introduction to the structural analysis of narrative. In *Image, Music, Text*. Fontana: London.

Beadle, R. (2002). The misappropriation of MacIntyre. *Reason in Practice*, 2(2), 45–54.

Beadle, R. (2007). Personal email correspondence with the author confirming the lack of MacIntyre-inspired research in the UK public sector.

Benton, T. and Craib, I. (2001). *Philosophy of social science*. Basingstoke: Palgrave.

Berger, P. L. and Luckmann, T. (1967). *The social construction of reality: A treatise in the sociology of knowledge*. Allen Lane, Penguin: London.

Bhaskar, R. (1978). *A realist theory of science*. Hassocks: Harvester Press.

Bhaskar, R. (1989). *Reclaiming reality: A critical introduction to contemporary philosophy*. London: Verso.

Blackler, F. (2006). Chief executives and the modernisation of the English National Health Service. *Leadership*, 2(1), 5–30.

Blackler, F., Kennedy, A. and Reed, M. (1999). Organising for incompatible priorities. In A. L. Mark and S. Dopson (eds), *Organisational behaviour in health care: The research agenda*. London: Macmillan.

Boje, D. M. (1991). The storytelling organization: A study of story performance in an office-supply firm. *Administrative Science Quarterly*, 36(1), 106–126.

Boje, D. M. (1995). Stories of the storytelling organisation: A postmodern analysis of Disney as 'Tamara-Land'. *Academy of Management Journal*, 38(4), 997–1035.

Boje, D. M. (2001). *Narrative methods for organisational and communication research*. London: Sage.

Boje, D. M., Luhman, J. T. and Baack, D. E. (1998). Hegemonic stories and encounters between storytelling organisations. *Journal of Management Inquiry,* 8(4), 340–360.

Braverman, H. (1974). Labor and monopoly capital, the degradation of work in the twentieth century. New York: Monthly Review Press, Chapters 4–9.

Brereton, M. and Temple, M. (1999). The new public service ethos: An ethical environment for governance. *Public Administration,* 77(3), 455–74.

Brewer, K. B. (1997). Management as a practice: A response to Alasdair MacIntyre. *Journal of Business Ethics,* 16, 825–833.

Brown, A. D. and Humphreys, M. (2003). Epic and tragic tales: Making sense of change. *Journal of Applied Behavioral Science,* 39(2), 121–144.

Brown, A. D., Humphreys, M. and Gurney, P. (2005). Narrative, identity and change: A case study of Laskarina Holidays. *Journal of Organizational Change Management,* 18(6), 312326.

Brown, J. S. and Duguid, P. (1991). Organisational learning and communities of practice: Towards a unified view of working learning and innovation. *Organisation Science,* vol. 2/1, Feb. 1991, 4057.

Bruner, J. (1986). *Actual minds, possible worlds.* Cambridge: MA:Bruner, J. (1991). The narrative construction of reality. *Critical Inquiry,* 18, 1–21.

Bruss, E. (1976). *Autobiographical acts: The changing situations of a literary genre.* Baltimore: Johns Hopkins University Press.

Bryant, M. and Cox, J. W. (2004). Conversion stories as shifting narratives of organizational change. *Journal of Organizational Change Management,* 17(6), 578–92.

Bryman, A. (2006). Leadership in higher education. Keynote speech, 5th International Studying Leadership Conference, Cranfield University, Cranfield. Dec 2006.

Burgoyne, J. G., Mumford, M. J., Hindle, A. and Brown, D. H. (1997). A multi-disciplinary identification of issues associated with 'contracting' in market-orientated health service reforms' *British Journal of Management,* 8(1), 39–49.

Burrell, G. and Morgan, G. (1979). *Sociological paradigms and organisational analysis.* London: Heinemann.

Calman, K., Hunter, D. and May, A. (2002). *Make or break time? A commentary on Labour's health policy two years into the NHS Plan.* Durham: University of Durham School for Health.

Cameron, M., Cranfield, S., Iles, V. et al. (2001). *Managing change in the NHS: Making informed deci*sions on *change: Key points for health care managers and professionals,* Booklet produced by NHS NCCSDO. London: LSHTM.

Casey, C. (1999). Come, join our family: Discipline and integration in corporate organizational culture. *Human Relations,* 52(2): 155–178.

Chapman, J. (2004). *System failure: Why governments must learn to think differently* (2nd ed.). London: Demos, www.demos.co.uk.

Chia, R. and Tsoukas, H. (2002). On organizational becoming: Rethinking organizational change. *Organization Science,* 567–582.

Clark, B. R. (1972). The organizational saga in higher education. *Administrative Science Quarterly,* 17, 178–184.

Coe, S. and Beadle, R. (2007). Could we know a practice based community if we saw one? Conference Proceedings: Alasdair MacIntyre's Revolutionary Aristotelianism: Ethics, Resistance and Utopia London Metropolitan University, 29 June to 1 July.

Coffield, F. (2006). *Running ever faster down the wrong road: An alternative future for education and skills.* Inaugural lecture, Institute for Education, London, Dec. 2006.

Collins, D. and Rainwater, K. (2005). Managing change at Sears: A sideways look at a tale of corporate transformation. *Journal of Organizational Change Management,* 18(1), 16–30 (15).

Conroy, M. (2007). Leading change: Research, application and evaluation. Paper presented at MBS/Kings College ESRC Public Sector Seminar, Manchester April 2007. http://www.mbs.ac.uk/research/documents/ESRCMervConroy.pdf

Conroy, M. (2005). NHS Leadership and change: Identity narratives and organisational change. In *4th International Studying Leadership Conference Proceedings,* Lancaster University Management School, December 2005.

Crisp, N. (2005). Commissioning a patient–led NHS. Memo to all CEs of NHS organisations, local authorities, directors of social services, DoH gateway reference 5312 dated 28 July 2005.

Cunliffe, A. L. (2002). Social poetics as management inquiry: A dialogical approach. *Journal of Management Inquiry,* 1(2), 128–146.

Currie, G. and Brown, A. D. (2003). A narratological approach to understanding processes of organizing in a UK hospital. *Human Relations,* 56(5), 563–586.

Czarniawska, B. and Gagliardi, P. (2003). *Narratives we organize by.* Amsterdam: John Benjamins.

Czarniawska, B. (1997). *Narrating the organisation: Dramas of institutional identity.* Chicago: University of Chicago Press.

Czarniawska, B. (1998). *A narrative approach to organisation studies.* London: Sage.

Czarniawska, B. (2004). *Narratives in social science research.* London: Sage.

Daft, R. L. and Weick, K. (1984). Towards a model of organisations as interpretation systems. *Academy of Management Review,* 9(2): 284–95.

Davies, B. and Harre, R. (1991). Positioning: The discursive production of selves. *Journal for the Theory of Social Behaviour,* 20(1): 44–63.

Dawson, S. (1999). Managing, organising and performing in health care: What do we know and how can we learn. In A. L. Mark and S. Dopson (eds), *Organisational behaviour in health care: The research agenda.* London: Macmillan, 724.

Dawson, S., Sutherland, K., Dopson, S. and Miller, R. (1998). *The relationship between R and D and clinical practice in primary and secondary care: Cases in adult asthma and glue ear in children.* London, North Thames NHSE, R & D Committee.

Department of Health (1989). *Working for patients.* London: HMSO.

Department of Health (1997). *The new NHS: Modern, dependable.* London: HMSO.

Department of Health (1998a). *A first class service: Quality in the new NHS.* London: HMSO.

Department of Health (1998b). *Modernising social services promoting independence, improving protection, raising standards.* London: HMSO.

Department of Health (1999). *National service framework for mental health: Modern standards and service models.* London: HMSO.

Department of Health (2000a). *The NHS plan: A plan for investment, a plan for reform.* London: HMSO.

Department of Health (2000b). *The NHS cancer plan.* London: HMSO.

Department of Health (2000c). *Coronary heart disease: National service framework for coronary heart disease – modern standards and service models.* London: HMSO.

Department of Health (2001a). *The mental health policy implementation guide.* London: HMSO.

Department of Health (2005a). *Commissioning a patient-led NHS.* London: HMSO.

Department of Health (2007). *Our NHS, our future.* Summary of the October 2007 nationwide consultation key findings emailed to all NHS employees on 1/11/07. London: DoH.

De Maria, W. (2006). Brother secret, sister silence: Sibling conspiracies against managerial integrity. *Journal of Business Ethics,* 65: 219–234.

Downing, S. J. (1997). Learning the plot: Emotional momentum in search of dramatic logic. *Management Learning,* 28(1), 27–44.

du Gay, P. (1998). Alasdair MacIntyre and the Christian genealogy of management critique. *Cultural Values,* 2(4): 1362–5179,421444.

du Gay, P. (2003). The tyranny of the epochal: Change, epochalism and organizational reform. *Organization,* 10(4) 663–684.

Dundes, A. (1980). *Interpreting folklore.* Indiana University Press, Bloomington.

Dyck, B. and Weber, M. J. (2006). Conventional versus radical moral agents: An exploratory empirical look at Weber's moral-points-of-view and virtues. *Organisazation Studies,*Sage, 27(3), 429450.

Engestrom, Y., Miettinen, R. and Punamaki, R-L. (eds). (1987). *Perspectives on activity theory.* Cambridge: Cambridge University Press.

Fleming, P. and Sewell, G. (2002). Looking for the good soldier, Svejk: Alternative modalities of resistance in the contemporary workplace. *Sociology,* 36(4): 857–873.

Fleming, P. and Spicer, A. (2003). Working at a cynical distance: Implications for power, subjectivity and resistance. *Organisation,* 10(1), 157–79.

Ford, J. D. (1999). Organisational change as shifting conversations. *Journal of Organisational Change Management,* 12: 480–500.

Foucault, M. (1984). What is an author? In P. Rabinow (ed.), *A Foucault reader* (2nd ed.). New York: Pantheon.

Fuller, G. and Lee, A. (1997). Textual collusions. *Discourse: Studies in the Cultural Politics of Education,* 18(3): 409–415.

Gabriel, Y. (1995). The unmanaged organisation: Stories, fantasies, subjectivity. *Organisation Studies,* 16(3), 477–501.

Gabriel, Y. (2000). *Storytelling in organisations: Facts, fictions and fantasies.* London: Oxford University Press.

Gadamer, H-G. (1993). *Truth and method.* London: Sheed and Ward (Originally published in German, 1960).

Greener, I. (2005). Health management as strategic behaviour: Managing medics and performance in the NHS. *Public Management Review,* 7(1), 95–110.

Greener, I. and Powell, J. (2003). Health authorities, priority-setting and resource allocation: A study in decision-making in New Labour's NHS. *Social Policy and Administration,* 37(1), 35–48.

Griffiths, R. (1983). *Enquiry into NHS management* (The Griffiths report). London: HMSO.

Grint, K. (2005). Problems, problems, problems: The social construction of 'leadership'. *Human Relations,* 58(11), 1467–1494.

Habermas, J. (1992). *Postmetaphysical thinking.* Cambridge, MA: MIT Press.

Harrison, S. (1988). *Managing the NHS.* London: Chapman and Hall.

Hasek, J. (1973). *The good soldier, Svejk.* (Cecil Parrot, trans.). London: Heinman.

Hazen, M. A. (1993). Towards polyphonic organization. *Journal of Organizational Change Management,* 6, 15–26.

Hearn, J. and Parkin, H. (1995). 'Sex' at 'Work': The Power and Paradox of Organisational Sexuality. London: Prentice Hall.

HMG (1990). NHS and Community Care Act. London: TSO.

HMG (1999a). *Modernising Government.* London: TSO.

HMG (1999b). Modernising Government Summary http://archive.cabinetoffice.gov.uk/roleofcentre/modagenda.htm#mg.

HMG (1999c). *Saving lives: Our healthier nation.* London TSO.

HMG (2000). *Reforming the Mental Health Act.* London: TSO.

HMG (2001). Health and Social Care Act. London: TSO.

HMG (2002). National Health Service Reform and Health Care Professions Act. London: TSO.

HMG (2003). Health and Social Care (Community Standards) Act. London: TSO.

Hood, C. (1991). A public management for all seasons? *Public Administration*, 69, 3–19.

Humphreys, M. and Brown, A. D. (2002). Narratives of organisational identity and identification: A case study of hegemony and resistance. *Organisation Studies*, 23(3), 421–47.

Hunter, D. (1996). The changing roles of personnel in health and health care management. *Social Science and Medicine,* 53(5), 799–808.

Hunter, D. (2000). NHS can manage on its own. *Health Service Journal*, vol. 110, May 25th 2000, 18–19.

Hutchins, E. (1993). Learning to navigate. In S. Chaiklin and J. Lave (eds), *Understanding practice: Perspectives on activity and context* (pp. 35–63). New York: Cambridge University Press.

Hyman, P. (2005). *1 out of 10: From Downing Street vision to classroom reality.* London: Vintage.

Iles, J. and Sutherland, K. (2001). *Managing change in the NHS: Organisational change – A review for health care managers, professionals and researchers.* Literature review produced by Cambridge University Judge Institute for the NHS SDO. London: LSHTM.

Jabri, M. (2004). Change as shifting identities: A dialogic perspective. *Journal of Organisational Change Management*, 17(6), 566–577.

Jessop, R. (2000). The dynamics of partnership and governance failure. In G. Stoker (ed.), *The new politics of local governance in Britain* (pp. 11–32). Basingstoke: Macmillan.

Kallinikos, J. (2006). Representing organization: knowledge, management, and the information age. *Information technology and people*, 19(4), 390–393. ISSN 0959-3845.

Kaye, M. (1995). Organisational myths as storytelling as communication management: A conceptual framework for learning as organisation's culture. *Journal of the Australian and New Zealand Academy of Management*, 1, 1–13.

Kermode, F. (1967). *The sense of an ending: Studies in the theory of fiction.* New York: Oxford University Press.

Kotter, J. P. and Schlesinger, L. A. (1979). Choosing strategies for change. *Harvard Business Review*, March–April, 106–114.

Kunda, G. (1992). *Engineering culture: Control and commitment in a high-tech corporation*. Philadelphia: Temple University Press.

Lapsley, I. (1994). Market mechanisms and the management of health care: The UK model and experience. *International Journal of Public Sector Management*, 7(6), 15–25.

Lave, J. and Wenger, E. (1991). *Situated learning: Legitimate peripheral participation*. Cambridge: Cambridge University Press.

Learmonth, M. (2003). Making health services management research critical: A review and a suggestion. *Sociology of Health & Illness*, 25(1), 93–119.

Lewin, K. (1948). *Resolving social conflicts: Selected papers on group dynamics* (G. W. Lewin, ed.). New York: Harper and Row.

Lewin, K. (1952). *Field theory in social science*. London: Tavistock Publications.

Lieblich, A., Tuval-Mashiach, R. and Zilber, T. (1998). *Narrative research: Reading, analysis and interpretation*. London: Sage.

Lyotard, J-F. (1979). *The postmodern condition: A report on knowledge*. Manchester: Manchester University Press.

MacIntyre, A. (1985). *After virtue: A study in moral theory*. London: Duckworth.

MacIntyre, A. (1988). *Whose justice? Which rationality?* London: Duckworth.

MacIntyre, A. (1990b). The privatization of good: An inaugural lecture. *The Review of Politics*, 52(2), 344–361.

MacIntyre, A. (1994). A partial response to my critics. In J. Horton and S. Mendus (eds), *After MacIntyre: Critical perspectives on the work of Alasdair MacIntyre* (pp. 283–304).

MacIntyre, A. (1995). *Marxism and Christianity*. (2nd ed.). London: Duckworth.

MacIntyre, A. (1999b). Social structures and their threats to moral agency. *Philosophy*, 74: 311–329.

Mangham, I. L. (1995). MacIntyre and the manager. *Organization* 2(2): 181–204.

Martin, J., Feldman, M., Hatch, M.-J. and Sitkin, S. (1983). The uniqueness paradox in organizational stories. *Administrative Science Quarterly*, 38, 438–453.

Maturana, H. and Varela, F. (1980). *Autopoiesis and cognition: The realization of the living*. Boston: D. Reidel.

McAdams, D. P. (1996). Personality, modernity, and the storied self: A contemporary framework for studying persons. *Psychological Inquiry*, 7, 295–321.

McCann, D. P. and Brownsberger, M. L. (1990). Management as a social practice: Rethinking business ethics after MacIntyre. In D. M. Yeager (ed.), *The annual of the Society of Christian Ethics* (pp. 223–45). Washington, D.C.: Georgetown University Press.

McConkie, K. L. and Boss, R. W. (1994). Using stories as an aid to consultation. *Public Administration Quarterly*, 18, 377–395.

McConkie, M. L. and Wayne, R. B. (1986). Organizational stories: One means of moving the informal organization during change efforts. *Public Administration Quarterly*, 10, 189–205.

McNulty, T. and Ferlie, E. (2004). Organisational transformation in health care? *Organisation Studies*, 25 (Oct), 1381–1412.

Meyer, J. C. (1995). Tell me a story: Eliciting organizational values from narratives. *Communication Quarterly*, 43, 210–224.

Mitroff, I. I. and Kilmann, R. H. (1975). Stories managers tell: A new tool for organizational problem solving. *Management Review*, July, 18–22.

Moore, G. and Beadle, R. (2006). In search of organisational virtue in business: Agents, goods, practices, institutions and environments. *Organisation Studies*, 27(3), 369–389.

Morgan, G. 1986. *Images of Organisation*. Thousand Oaks: Sage.

Neilson, R.P. (2006). Introduction to the Special Issue. In Search of Organizational Virtue: Moral Agency in Organizations. *Organization Studies*, 27(3), 317–321.

Nietzsche, F. (1968). *The Will to Power*. (W. Kaufmann, trans.; R. J. Hollingdale, ed.). New York: Vintage.

Noth, W. (1995). *Handbook of semiotics*. Bloomington and Indianapolis: Indiana University Press.

O'Neill, O. (2002). *A question of trust*. Cambridge: Cambridge University Press.

O'Connor, E. (2000). Plotting the organization: The embedded narrative as a construct for studying change. *Journal of Applied Behavioral Science*, 36(2), 174(19).

Omega (2003). *Building a new kind of service*. Omega Local Implementation Plan for Adult Mental Health.

OPM (2003). Learning from the NHS in change: A study on the management of major structural change in the NHS. OPM: Office for Health Management.

Oswick, C., Grant, D., Michelson, G. and Wailes, N. (2005). Looking forwards: Discursive directions in organizational change. *Journal of Organizational Change Management*, 18(4), 383–390.

O'Toole, L. M. and Shukman, A. (1978). *Russian poetics in translation*. Oxford: Holdan Books.

Passmore, J. (1962). *John Anderson: Studies in empirical philosophy, John Anderson and twentieth-century philosophy* Sydney: Angus and Robertson.

Peck, E. (1997). The challenge of managing community health teams. *Health and Social Care in the Community*, 5(1): 40–47.

Pedersen, A. R. (2006). The story of a good idea: Employee's tales of organizational change in a Danish hospital ward. Paper given at 1st Conference on Rhetoric and Narrative in Management Research, RNMR-06 Barcelona, May 11–13, 2006.

Perls, F. S. (1972). *Gestalt therapy: Excitement and growth in the human personality*. London: Souvenir Press.

Perrow, C. (1991). A society of organizations. *Theory and Society*, 20(6), 725–62.

Peters, T. and Waterman, R. H. (1982). *In search of excellence*. New York: Harper and Row.

Pettigrew, A. M. (1987). Context and action in the transformation of the firm. *Journal of Management Studies*, 24(6), 649–670.

Pettigrew, A. M., Ferlie, E., Mckee, L. (1992). *Shaping strategic change-Managing change in large organizations: The case of the National Health Service*. London: Sage.

Pettigrew, A. M. et al. (2001). Studying organisational change and development: Challenges for future research. *Academy of Management Journal*, 44(4), p697, 17p.

Pidd, M. (2005). Perversity in public service performance measurement. *International Journal of Productivity and Performance Measurement,* 54(5/6): 482–493.

Polkinghorne, D. (1988). *Narrative knowing and the human sciences.* Albany: University of New York Press.

Pollock, A. M. (2004). *NHS plc: The privatisation of our health care.* London: Verso.

Polyani, M. (1966). *The tacit dimension.* London: Routledge and Paul.

Propp, V. (1928). *Morphology of the folktale.* Austin: University of Texas Press.

Rhodes, C. (2000). Reading and writing organizational lives. *Organization,* 7, 7–29.

Rhodes, C. (2001). *Writing organization: (Re) presentation and control in narratives at work. Advances in Organization Studies 7.* Amsterdam/Philadelphia: John Benjamins.

Rhodes, C. and Brown, A. D. (2005). Narrative, organisations and research. *International Journal of Management Reviews,* 7(3).

Ricoeur, P. (1983–1985). *Time and narrative (Temps et récit)* (3 vols.) (Kathleen McLaughlin and David Pellauer, trans.). Chicago: University of Chicago Press.

Ricoeur, P. (1991). Narrative identity. *Philosophy Today,* 35(1), 73–81.

Rivett, G. (1998). *From cradle to grave: 50 years of the NHS.* Trowbridge: Cromwell Press. With updates up to 2007 from http://www.sochealth.co.uk/news/NHSreform.htm

Rose, N. S. (1999). *Governing the soul: The shaping of the private self.* London: Free Association Books.

Rousseau, J. J. (1762). The Social Contract or Principles of Political Right.

Schein, E. H. (1985). *Organisational culture and leadership.* London: Jossey-Bass.

Seddon, J. (2003). *Freedom from command and control: A better way to make the work work.* New York: Productivity Press.

Senge, P. M. (1990). The leader's new work: Building learning organisations. *Sloan Management Review,* 32, 7–23.

Senge, P. M. (1992). *The fifth discipline: The art and practice of the learning organisation.* Century Pubs.

Severn, M. (2006). *A passenger-led jumbo jet? Morecambe Bay Medical Journal.* Kendal: Dixon Printing.

Shotter, J. and Cunliffe, A. L. (2002). Managers as practical authors. In D. Holman and R. Thorpe (eds), *Management and language: Managers as practical authors.* London: Sage.

Skoldberg, K. (1994). Tales of change: Public administration reform and narrative mode. *Organisational Science,* 5(2), 219–238.

Smith, A. (1776). An inquiry into the nature and causes of the wealth of nations, in four volumes, Edinburgh.

Smith, J., Walshe, K. and Hunter, D. J. (2001). The 'redisorganisation' of the NHS. *British Medical Journal,* 323: 1263–4.

Stake, R. E. (1995). *The art of case study research.* Thousand Oaks, CA: Sage Publications.

Stocking, B. (1985). *Initiative and inertia in the NHS.* London: Nuffield Private Hospitals Trust.

Stocking, B. (1992). Promoting change in clinical care. *Quality in Health Care*, 1:56–60.

Sturdy, A. and Grey, C. (2003). Beneath and beyond organizational change management: Exploring alternatives. *Organization*, 10(4): 651–662.

Thomas, A. B. and Anthony, P. D. (1996). Can management education be educational? In R. French and C. Grey (eds), *Rethinking management education*. London: Sage.

Thomson, J. A. K. (1955). *The Ethics of Aristotle: The Nicomachean Ethics*. Penguin Classics. Re-issued 1976, revised by Hugh Tredennick.

Traynor, M. (1999). *Managerialism and Nursing: Beyond Oppression and Profession*. London: Routledge.

Tsoukas, H. (2005). Afterword: Why language matters in the analysis of organizational change. *Journal of Organizational Change Management*, 18(1), 96–104.

Turnbull, S. (2000). Corporate ideology and its influences on middle management: A study of middle managers' responses to an organisational values programme. Ph.D. thesis, Lancaster University.

Turner, V. (1957). *Schism and continuity in an African society*. Manchester: Manchester University Press.

Tushman, M. L., Newman, W. H. and Romanelli, E. (1986). Convergence and upheaval: Managing the unsteady pace of organisational evolution. *Californian Management Review*, 29, 29–44.

Vaara, E. (2002). On the discursive construction of success/failure in narrative of post-merger integration. *Organization Studies*, 23(2), 211–248.

Van Maanen, J. (1979). The fact and fiction in organisational ethnography. *Administrative Science Quarterly*, 24, 539–549.

Van Maanen, J. (1988). *Tales from the field*. Chicago: University of Chicago Press.

Wanless, D. (2001). Securing good health for the whole population: Preliminary report. London: Department of Health.

Wanless, D. (2004). Securing good health for the whole population: Final report. London: Department of Health.

Watson, T. J. (1982). Group Ideologies and Organisational Change. *Journal of Management Studies*, 19(3), 259–275.

Watson, T. J. (1994a). *In search of management: Culture, chaos and control in managerial work*. London: Routledge.

Watson, T. J. (1994b). Managing, crafting and researching: Words, skill and imagination in shaping management research. *British Journal of Management*, 5, special issue, S77–S87.

Watson, T. J. (2003). Ethical choice in managerial work: The scope for managerial choices in an ethically irrational world. *Human Relations*, 56(2), 167–185.

Weaver, G. R. (2006). Virtue in organizations: Moral identity as a foundation for moral agency. *Organization Studies*, 27(3): 341–368.

Weber, M. (1958). *The Protestant ethic and the spirit of capitalism* (T. Parsons, trans.). New York: Scribners.

Weick, K. E. (1979). *The social psychology of organizing* (2nd ed.). Reading, MA: Addison-Wesley.

Weick, K. E. (1995). *Sensemaking in organisations*. Thousand Oaks, CA: Sage.

White, H. (1981). The value of narrativity in the representation of reality. In W. J. T. Mitchell (ed.), *On narrative*. Chicago: Chicago University Press.

Wilkins, A. (1983). Organizational stories as symbols which control the organization. In L. Pondy, G. Morgan, P. Frost, and T. Dandridge (eds.), *Organizational symbolism* (pp. 81–92). Greenwich, CT: JAI Press.

Willmott, H. (1993). Strength is ignorance; slavery is freedom: Managing cultures in modern organizations. *Journal of Management Studies,* 30(4), 515–552.

Willmott, H. (1998). Towards a new ethics? The contributions of poststructuralism and posthumanism. In M. Parker, *Ethics and Organizations* (pp. 76–121). Sage: London.

Žižek, S. (1989). *Sublime Object of Ideology.* London: Verso.

Index